The NAACP's Legal Strategy against Segregated Education, 1925 – 1950

BY MARK V.

The NAACP's Legal Strategy

The University of North Carolina

TUSHNET

against Segregated Education,

1925–1950

Press, Chapel Hill and London

93 92 91 90 89   6 5 4 3 2

Library of Congress Cataloging-in-Publication Data

Tushnet, Mark V., 1945–
    The NAACP's legal strategy against segregated education, 1925–1950.
    Bibliography: p.
    Includes index.
    1. Segregation in education—Law and legislation—
United States—History. 2. National Association for
the Advancement of Colored People—History. I. Title.
KF4155.T87 1987   344.73'0978   86-24971
ISBN 0-8078-1723-6   347.304798
ISBN 0-8078-4173-0 (pbk.)

To Thurgood Marshall

Acknowledgments

Research for this project was supported by grants from the Rockefeller Foundation's program of Fellowships in the Humanities, the American Bar Foundation's Program in Legal History, the Research Committee of the Graduate School of the University of Wisconsin–Madison, and the Georgetown University Law Center. It had its genesis in conversations with Herbert Hill. I would like to thank Elizabeth Alexander, Derrick Bell, Herbert Hill, Dennis Hutchinson, James Jones, Willard Hurst, Kathryn Powers, Deborah Rhode, and Stephen Wasby for their comments. Jennifer Jaff, James Rosenfeld, and Steven Halpert provided helpful research assistance in the project's later stages. Rebecca and Laura will have to wait again; there is only one person to whom this could be dedicated.

Introduction

In 1896 the United States Supreme Court decided *Plessy* v. *Ferguson*.[1] That case endorsed the idea that it was constitutionally permissible to maintain a regime of racial segregation if the services a state provided were equal. From the beginning black activists knew that "separate but equal" was a slogan that only thinly disguised the reality of the subordination of black to white. The National Association for the Advancement of Colored People, founded in 1909, took undermining the system of racial subordination as its goal from the outset.[2] Because subordination was linked to segregation, and segregation to the legal doctrine of "separate but equal," it was natural for the NAACP to try to destroy the constitutional doctrine that *Plessy* established.

What follows is the story of the campaign conducted by the NAACP against segregated schools, from the inception of the campaign in the mid-1920s to its culmination in the early 1950s, when the organization decided to pursue the litigation that goes under the name of *Brown* v. *Board of Education*.[3] Some parts of the story have been told before, most notably by Richard Kluger.[4] My narrative has a narrower scope than his, in regard to both the period of time covered and the subject matter discussed. It is informed by a concern for the constraints placed on the litigation strategy by organizational needs, and for the significance of the NAACP campaign as it applies to the theory and practice of public interest law in general. It is therefore an interpretation as well as a narrative of the events.[5]

An introductory summary of the interpretation may assist in understanding what follows. The interpretation relies on the conception of litigation as a social process. By doing so, it helps bring into focus a number of otherwise disconnected aspects of the narrative, and allows one to understand how public interest litigation actually works. Understanding litigation as a social process requires that close attention be paid to what might be called internal aspects of the litigation campaign, that is, to the details of organizational politics and the imperatives of practical litigation.

The conception of litigation as a social process draws on analytic models from several disciplines. The people involved in these events are seen as attempting rationally to pursue their goals under circumstances of uncertainty and limited resources; this part of the conception relies on economic analyses of political action and on what has been called the "resource mobilization" interpretation of social movements.[6] Economics and sociology also emphasize that the outcomes of social processes need not be those intended by the actors: economists argue that the invisible hand of the market produces aggregate outcomes that no one intends, and sociologists examine the unintended consequences of intentional actions. The social process of litigation is in this regard no different from other social processes, and my interpretation attempts to identify the role played by aggregate processes and unintended consequences.

A further limitation on the "resource mobilization" perspective is that it is most useful in identifying the circumstances under which some form of social movement activity can be expected to occur, but does little to explain more precisely why that activity occurs when it does and in the form that it takes.[7] Sensitivity to the actual events requires attention to the roles of chance—unexpected events or decisions by individuals outside of the movement—and choice—decisions by insiders to pursue one path rather than another that in retrospect seems almost equally sensible.[8] This sensitivity is particularly important where, as in this narrative, the number of decision makers is quite small;[9] personal preferences and personalities are likely to be more important here than in the economists' or sociologists' efforts to understand larger-scale outcomes.

I also rely on recent work by legal scholars examining what they have called "institutional reform litigation,"[10] of which the NAACP's campaign against segregated schools was a precursor. These studies have illuminated the problems lawyers and judges have in managing this sort of litigation. The conception of litigation as a social process, which is shaped by the contributions of economists, sociologists, and legal scholars, provides the structure for the narrative, but in general I have withheld explicit discussion of that conception until the concluding chapter.

The conception of litigation as a social process indicates the prominent role that internal elements play in the interpretation. External elements had, of course, some influence on the shape of the litigation campaign, and these are discussed at appropriate points. For example, the development of a force of talented black lawyers affected some aspects of the campaign, as did broader discussions in the black community about appropriate strategies to combat segregation. In the concluding chapter, I argue that these external elements had two kinds of effects. First, they set the initial conditions for the litigation effort, but as the campaign developed its own dynamic, the effects of the initial conditions diminished. Second, they produced an atmosphere that made one decision seem more sensible than another. But the external elements were loose enough to allow the small number of people involved in the litigation effort to draw whatever conclusions they desired. Thus it seems sufficient to indicate in rather broad outlines what those external elements were. To develop them in detail would suggest that there was a closer connection between the details of the external elements and the details of the litigation campaign than the evidence justifies. The external elements had an atmospheric effect that had no dramatic direct consequences, and the interpretation I offer of the overall shape of the litigation effort subordinates the external to the internal elements.

Chapter 1 examines the initial planning, which was shaped by interactions between NAACP officials and their source of funding, whose primary interests affected the plans the NAACP proposed. In chapter 2 the initial stages of the planning specifically for litigation are described. Here the main influence on the plans was the view different planners took of the place litigation should have in a general attack by the black community on race discrimination. Competition between the NAACP and the Communist party for leadership of the black community gave further shape to the litigation campaign, as is discussed in chapter 3. Although the NAACP's limited resources constrained the litigation throughout the campaign until the late 1940s, resource limitations had a particularly dramatic impact, examined in chapter 4, in leading the NAACP to make its first sustained effort in Maryland under the direction of Charles Hamilton Houston and his protégé Thurgood Marshall. Chapter 5 describes the two early cases that provided the foundation for later efforts.

Chapter 6 returns to the theme of unanticipated constraints with a discussion of the ways in which defendants' strategies retarded the progress of the litigation campaign. Chapter 7 examines the impact that segments of the NAACP's membership and an impatient legal staff had on litigation decisions. The concluding chapter then focuses on the implications of the preceding material for the theory and practice of public interest law.

The conception of litigation as a social process explains why I have defined the subject as I have.[11] As indicated above, the narrative essentially ends with the decision to pursue the *Brown* cases. The place *Brown* holds in conventional understandings of desegregation may lead readers to think that the narrative ends before the real story does. But litigation as a social process begins when people start to see that they might understand what has happened to them as something for which the legal system may provide a remedy.[12] It continues through interactions between clients and lawyers, in which grievances are molded into a form that the legal system might understand.[13] The social process does not end when a court decides a case. It extends through the implementation or evasion of the court's decisions, and includes the search for legislative alternatives to the outcome the court reached.[14] Thus the process that is *Brown* v. *Board of Education* began in 1950 and ended two decades later when the courts and federal executive agencies began a serious effort to implement the 1954 decision. Because the *Brown* litigation was a social process, I have devoted a few pages in the conclusion to show that the beginnings of this new chapter in the politics of race in the United States contained some incidents analytically similar to those discussed in earlier chapters. But ending this story in 1954 would impose a false closure on a process that continued for many years thereafter.[15]

A final theme of the interpretation deserves mention at the start. The NAACP and its lawyers were developing a new form of litigation, and it is hardly surprising that they did not anticipate all the hurdles they would face. It takes a special talent to determine the proper response to unexpected developments. Where those developments require coordination of competing interests and desires, as they did through much of the litigation campaign, that talent is best called a flair for politics. The NAACP was favored in having on its staff a number of people with enormous political skills. Their skills varied somewhat, and not everything that each staff member did was exactly what was needed in the circumstances. But Walter White, Charles Hamilton Houston, and especially Thurgood Marshall repeatedly came up with responses to unanticipated constraints that kept the litigation effort going. They and their clients are the central figures in what follows.

The NAACP's Legal Strategy against Segregated Education, 1925–1950

1. Setting the Course:
The Grant
from the Garland Fund

The NAACP was founded in 1909 by a biracial group desiring to counter an increase in white violence against blacks throughout the country. Its founders believed that existing tactics for black advancement neglected issues of civil and political rights and reflected too moderate a position on economic issues. In addition to conducting lobbying efforts and publicity campaigns, the NAACP soon established a legal redress committee. Its legal activities included responses to white violence, such as legal defense and resistance to the extradition of blacks accused of interracial violence. Several cases supported by the NAACP reached the Supreme Court, where they were presented by the association's president, Moorfield Storey, a former president of the American Bar Association. The NAACP's cases included *Buchanan* v. *Warley,* which held unconstitutional municipal ordinances requiring residential segregation, and *Moore* v. *Dempsey,* which overturned a conviction of a black obtained in a mob-dominated proceeding. These cases, and other activities associated with the courts, strengthened the NAACP's commitment to obtaining and solidifying the political and civil rights of blacks, and the cases attracted new supporters with similar commitments.[1]

Reflecting both an accurate view of the organization's prior activity and its aspirations for the future, the Annual Report for 1926 gave "legal victories" pride of place in the foreword. "[F]or the present," the report said, the courts, especially the federal courts, "where the atmosphere of sectional prejudice is notably absent," would provide the best avenue to protect the rights of blacks. Legal victories in the cause of civil rights had the advantage of being "definite" and "clear-cut" and could be "built upon." The report treated "increasing attention to law" as "a new development" for the NAACP. No longer simply sources of propaganda, legal cases "represent[ed] advances as concrete as any." The report emphasized that these gains were achieved at an "exceedingly low price," because "the foremost lawyers" contributed their services free or at extremely low rates. "The legal work of the Association, therefore, constitutes a definite benefit at a cost almost negligible, whose value the Negro and the friends of justice may easily determine for themselves."[2] From 1925 to 1930 the NAACP gradually began to develop a plan for coordinating litigation, as its leaders saw the opportunity to obtain a substantial grant from a left-wing foundation, the American Fund for Public Service, founded by Charles Garland.

While he was an undergraduate at Harvard College in 1919, Garland inherited over one million dollars from his father. Garland had become convinced of the need for radical change in the United States. Initially he wanted to refuse the inheritance as unearned and tainted money. The executors of the estate objected, arguing that doing so would cause legal difficulties. Roger Baldwin suggested to Garland that he accept the bequest and turn it to good purposes.[3] After settling approximately $200,000 on his wife,[4] Garland created the American Fund for Public Service in 1922, giving it $800,000 then and later transferring to it a $500,000 bequest he received from his grandfather.

The Garland Fund, as it was generally known, was designed to disburse its entire capital for the support of "new or experimental agencies." Its focus was left-wing but not rigidly sectarian. Among its incorporators were Norman Thomas; Robert Morss Lovett, a liberal professor of English at the University of Chicago;[5] and Roger Baldwin. Its board of directors included Scott Nearing, an antimilitarist who had been a socialist candidate for Congress; Rabbi Judah Magnes, a prominent Jewish liberal; William Z. Foster, a labor organizer who had joined the Communist Party of the United States shortly after it was founded in 1921; and James Weldon Johnson, then the secretary, or executive director, of the NAACP. Elizabeth Gurley Flynn, a prominent labor organizer who later joined the Communist party, served as an important staff member. The fund's first donation went to provide food for striking miners, and in response to an attack by the American Federation of Labor in 1923, the fund issued a statement of its policy, indicating that it gave its money for "producers' movements" and "the protection of minorities," with priority given to research, publication, workers' education, and experimental enterprises.[6]

Baldwin became the chief administrator of the fund. It is therefore important to sketch the development of his general political views, because they affected his actions at the Garland Fund. He had started his career as a social worker in St. Louis in 1906, and had quickly become deeply involved in civic reform activities. He met Emma Goldman, the noted anarchist, in 1908, and, as his friendship with her deepened, his political views moved leftward. By the time the United States entered World War I, Baldwin had become a staunch adherent of left-wing causes. In 1917 Baldwin moved from St. Louis to New York to work with the American Union Against Militarism, intending to support its efforts to secure a negotiated peace. Just after he began to work with the union, though, the United States declared war on Germany. Baldwin found that he had to devote most of his time to defending the rights of antiwar activists and those of conscientious objectors to the recently instituted draft. He created a Bureau for Conscientious Objectors, later renamed the Civil Liberties Bureau, as a department of the Union Against Militarism. The bureau's activities were in some tension with the aims of the union; its defense of opponents of the war made it difficult for the union to lobby effectively for a negotiated peace. Within a few months the tension had become so great that the union and the bureau formally separated. Baldwin became the director of the National Civil Liberties Bureau in October 1917. The bureau supported conscientious objectors and radical opponents of the war, such as members of the Industrial Workers of the World who were being prosecuted for obstructing the war effort.[7]

Baldwin's opinions on how people on the left could use the law were thus shaped by his increasingly radical views and by his experience with law as a method of defense. He brought those views with him to the Garland Fund, and held them throughout the period of his involvement with it. In 1918 Baldwin explained that he could not support the Socialist party because it sought to use political methods to overthrow capitalism; he favored economic methods and noted with approval that the more radical Socialist Labor party "resorted to political means only to prevent the other side from using the power of the state against them." The Civil Liberties Bureau was reorganized in late 1919 and 1920. Baldwin, who had just finished a prison term for his refusal to be inducted, was willing to join the newly named American Civil Liberties Union as its director. But he insisted that the ACLU board agree that "[t]he cause we now serve is labor." The ACLU would seek "1) those directly engaged in the labor struggle . . . , 2) those who by their writing and speaking are close to labor problems, and 3) those who stand on general principles for freedom of expression." Writing in 1934 as a strong supporter of the Soviet

Union, Baldwin explained, "I champion civil liberty as the best of the nonviolent means of building the power on which worker's rule must be based. If I aid the reactionaries to get free speech now and then, if I go outside the class struggle to fight against censorship, it is only because those liberties help to create a more hospitable atmosphere for working-class liberties."[8]

For Baldwin, then, the law was to be used instrumentally and defensively. One final aspect of Baldwin's views can be found in his opposition to the adoption of the Wagner Act, which put the force of national law behind labor's effort to unionize industrial workers. He appears to have regarded the entire New Deal as designed to "protect . . . the propertied classes as against other classes."[9] By making the capacity of the working class to organize dependent on the power of a state ultimately controlled by the capitalist class, the Wagner Act would deprive the working class of power it might achieve by self-mobilization. A movement that relied on exercises of state power on its behalf could not achieve real power; instead of replacing the existing structures of power with new ones and redistributing power from the state to the people, it would only ratify the power of the state as a whole. Baldwin's attraction to the instrumental and defensive use of law, and his concern about the disempowering consequences of affirmative uses of law, affected the Garland Fund's responses to requests from the NAACP for financial assistance.

The NAACP received several early grants from the Garland Fund, including $3,365 in 1925 to pay for advertisements that were part of the NAACP's antilynching campaign. During 1924 and 1925, the NAACP negotiated for a more substantial grant. Writing at the suggestion of Johnson, Moorfield Storey, the president of the NAACP, requested a grant to defray legal expenses incurred in the defense of Ossian Sweet, who had been charged with murder when a member of a white crowd was killed during a mob attack on Dr. Sweet's new home in a white neighborhood of Detroit.[10] Storey, referring to "the nation-wide fight against segregation," noted that membership fees were insufficient to support the four pending cases that the NAACP thought were most important: the defense of Dr. Sweet, two challenges to racially restrictive zoning and covenants, and the ongoing attack on the white primary in Texas. The fund agreed to give the NAACP $5,000 and pledged up to $15,000 to match other donations to a legal defense fund. Within seven weeks, the NAACP raised $15,000, and it received over $20,000 from the Garland Fund shortly thereafter.[11] In fact, from 1925 to 1929, the NAACP received over $31,500 from the fund, making it the fund's third largest recipient of grants. Although the first and second on the list were labor-oriented groups, the NAACP received slightly more for defense work than the fund gave for labor defense.[12]

In addition to its grants for legal defense, the NAACP received $5,000 from the Garland Fund to support investigations of the financing of black schools in the South. The money was used to pay for studies of Georgia, Mississippi, North and South Carolina, and Oklahoma, and to subsidize the publication of the results in *The Crisis*, the NAACP's magazine. These articles marked the first explicit connections among the Garland Fund, the NAACP, and the fight against discrimination in education. The available records do not indicate that the grant represented the conscious initiation of a long-term program. Rather, it seems likely that it was conceived of in the first instance as a subsidy to *The Crisis*, a journal always in need of financial assistance, and secondarily as an important contribution to a campaign to publicize the connection between the educational and economic positions of blacks. As the NAACP came to focus on education litigation, the articles served as an important background for and resource in discussions that eventually were concerned with long-range plans. The articles appeared between September 1926 and July 1928. They were serious academic reports, unlike an earlier, more journalistic article on black schools in Florida. The article on North Carolina in May 1927 stated that the subsidy for publication had been exhausted and that future articles would be "in curtailed form without an exhaustive presentation of facts and figures," which would make them "perhaps more readable."[13]

The reports included statistics on the disparities in per capita expenditures for white and black students, information on the differences in salaries paid to white and black teachers, and pictures of schools for white and black children. The report on Georgia, for example, showed an average per pupil expenditure of $36.29 for whites and $4.59 for blacks, and average teachers' salaries of $97.88 per month for whites and $49.41 for blacks. Comparable figures for Hinds County, Mississippi, were $24.37 and $4.77 in per capita student expenditures; in Coahoma County, Mississippi, the average white teacher received $133.76 per month, and the average black teacher received $40.75. The disparities in North Carolina were smaller, which according to an editorial note made the article "much more pleasant reading than the earlier ones." North Carolina, it said, was "without doubt the best" of the southern states, because of changes in attitude brought about through "missionary work . . . [by] a series of far-sighted and public spirited men." Unlike the ratios of 8 and 5 to 1 reported for Georgia and Mississippi, the ratio of expenditures for white pupils to those for black pupils was less than 2 to 1. Similarly, teachers' salaries in North Carolina averaged $98.20 for whites and $66.53 for blacks. Still, the salary structure reported at one level set the minimum for blacks at $100 per month and the minimum for whites at $133 per month. The report concluded that discrimination was probably increasing in North Carolina even as the absolute quality of black education was also improving. The report on South Carolina had none of these even slightly hopeful notes. Discrimination was marked and had increased in past decades. Unlike the situation in North Carolina, where the average class size in black schools was 30.5 pupils and that in white schools 26.3, in South Carolina black classes were on average slightly more than twice the size of white classes. The per capita expenditures on whites were $36.10 and on blacks $4.17, and in 1925 the average annual salary for white teachers was $885 and that for blacks $261.

W. E. B. Du Bois, the editor of *The Crisis*, used information on disparities in expenditures on education in his editorials throughout the 1920s. For example, in opposing a bill to provide federal aid to education on the ground that such aid would inevitably be distributed so as to enhance existing disparities in expenditures on black and white education, Du Bois printed a column of statistics on disparities to support his conclusion that the aid, administered by local authorities, would only make whites more effective racists. After the Garland Fund series ended, Du Bois's editorial "Education" stated: "The next step before the National Association for the Advancement of Colored People is a forward movement all along the line to secure justice for Negro children in the schools of the nation. . . . In open defiance of the constitution . . . and of their own state laws, the funds dedicated to education . . . are systematically spent so as to discriminate against colored children and keep them in ignorance. . . . There must be a way to bring their cases before both state and federal courts."[14]

These concerns, coupled with the successful relationship that had been established with the Garland Fund—a relationship of course solidified by Johnson's presence on the board of directors of the fund—led to a more ambitious program. The course of interaction is unclear, but beginning in August 1929 and continuing through May 1930, the fund's Committee on Negro Work—consisting of Johnson; Morris Ernst, a member of the

NAACP's Legal Committee; and Lewis Gannett, a literary critic active in the American Civil Liberties Union—developed a proposal to give the NAACP, with which the Committee on Negro Work had consulted, a sizable grant.[15]

In its earliest form, the committee's proposal responded to the fund's relatively traditional leftist concerns about working people by noting that blacks were the largest and "most ineffective bloc of the producing class." The committee thought it would "waste time and money" to "conduct isolated test cases and isolated fights," as the NAACP had been doing. Instead, it proposed "to finance a large-scale, widespread, dramatic campaign to give the Southern Negro his constitutional rights, his civil and political equality, and therewith a self-consciousness and self-respect, which would inevitably tend to effect a revolution in the economic life of this country." Mentioning explicitly "equal rights in the public schools, in the voting booths, on the railroads, and on juries," the draft proposal argued that "these rights must precede any real economic independence and unionization will be accelerated by such a campaign." The draft suggested that between $214,000 and $229,000 be allocated to forty-five coordinated lawsuits, including eleven to be filed simultaneously—one in each southern state—challenging unequal spending on black and white schools. The lawsuits and the attendant publicity would, the committee said, "create the psychological conditions" for unionization.[16]

As the committee's proposal worked its way through the Garland Fund, the subsequent drafts continued to stress the connection between litigation and the fund's concern for unionization of workers. As submitted to the Garland Fund's board, the proposal said that the rights it identified were "the necessary basis of any real economic independence; their significance to later campaigns for unionization is obvious." But it did not include Walter White's suggestion that some money be allocated to the NAACP's challenges to seats held by southern senators or to research on racial discrimination in the prosecution of crime.[17] The final proposal increased the request to approximately $300,000, and, apparently in response to concerns about the proper recipient of fund money, said that only the NAACP "could effectively carry the brunt" of a legal campaign.[18]

But it was precisely the legal focus that concerned some of the fund's directors. In October 1929, Roger Baldwin sent a draft of the NAACP proposal to L. Hollingsworth Wood, a friend and member of the original board of directors of the American Civil Liberties Union. Baldwin wrote, "Would you take the time to look over the enclosed report which is made by a committee of this Fund. It amazes me. My own view is that such a legalistic approach will fail of its object because the forces that keep the Negro under subjection will find some way of accomplishing their purposes, law or no law. My personal view is that the whole problem should be approached from the economic standpoint and primarily that of the union of white and black workers against their common exploiters." Wood was president of the National Urban League, an organization primarily concerned with advancing the economic interests of the black community by securing employment for blacks who migrated to urban centers and by providing social services to them.[19] The Urban League and the NAACP had identified different tasks for themselves, and it was natural for Baldwin to emphasize to Wood these differences.

Yet Baldwin also expressed a common view on the left in the 1920s and 1930s. Clearly it affected the way in which the fund approached the NAACP's proposal. Later, under the pressure of the Depression, elements in the NAACP came to share the concern that economic issues had to be addressed. Though the course of the litigation campaign was not altered by division within the NAACP over its merit, it is useful to examine later developments in order to understand the ideological framework within which the litigation proposal was formed. This examination shows that litigation was a choice made by the NAACP in the face of arguments that other ways of using its resources would be more productive.

The NAACP's choice to pursue litigation was brought into question in a celebrated controversy provoked by W. E. B. Du Bois in 1934, after the NAACP had received some money from the Garland Fund but before much had been done to begin litigation. Because the Depression had made more apparent than ever the relationship between the state of the economy and the status of blacks, Du Bois formulated a position that put him at odds with the overwhelming majority of the NAACP's leadership during those years. He began by asserting that the black community had "unrealized strength," which led him to advocate the exercise of collective power by a community united from within. Thus, in April 1933 he suggested that blacks develop "consumers and producers cooperation," which he believed would support black autarchy in the United States and multiracial cooperation by the oppressed internationally.[20]

Du Bois's editorial "Segregation," in *The Crisis* for January 1934, pushed the argument further. He wanted to distinguish segregation from racial discrimination, and argued that "there is no objection to colored people living beside colored people if the surroundings and treatment involve no discrimination." Black people, he said, should organize themselves and insist that public policy be nondiscriminatory; but that did not entail the eradication of the color line for blacks and their community:

Doubtless, and in the long run, the greatest human development is going to take place under experiences of widest individual contact. Nevertheless, today such individual contact is made difficult and almost impossible by petty prejudice, deliberate and almost criminal propaganda and various survivals from prehistoric heathenism. It is impossible, therefore, to wait for the millennium of free and normal intercourse before we unite, to cooperate among themselves in groups of like-minded people. . . . It is the race-conscious black man cooperating together in his own institutions and movements who will eventually emancipate the colored race, and the great step ahead today is for the American Negro to accomplish his economic emancipation through voluntary determined cooperative action.[21]

The editorial elicited substantial disagreement from other leaders in the NAACP. They defended their version of NAACP principles, which, Du Bois's adversaries said, equated opposition to segregation and racial discrimination with support for the irrelevance of race to public policy and, more important, to political action.[22] In the face of this disagreement, Du Bois elaborated his position in the succeeding months. His February editorial recounted NAACP opposition to instances of racial discrimination, but argued that it was time to face up to tensions between the NAACP's practice and the cry of "No segregation." The NAACP "has never officially opposed separate Negro organizations—such as churches. . . . It has never denied the recurrent necessity of united separate action on the part of Negroes for self-defense and self-development; but it has insisted and continually pointed out that such action is in any case a necessary evil involving often a recognition from within of the very color line which we are fighting without. That race pride and race loyalty, Negro ideals and Negro unity, have a place and function today, the N.A.A.C.P. never has denied and never can deny." Du Bois urged that the question of separate development be faced directly. Segregation was a fact of life, and racial organization had to be considered not a necessary evil, but a positive force for black development.[23]

His next editorial framed the dilemma as "complete": "compulsory separation of human beings by essentially arbitrary criteria . . . is the cause of human hate," and yet, "where separation of mankind into races, groups and classes is compulsory, . . . the only effective defense that the segregated and despised group has . . . is internal self-organization." The implications were clear. Abolition of legal discrimination might well be meaningless, and efforts to that end might be the wrong way to rectify the position of blacks in the United States. "A black man born in Boston has a right to oppose any separation of schools by color. . . . But this black man in Boston has no right, after he has made this academic pronouncement to send his own helpless immature child into school where white children kick, cuff or abuse him, or where teachers openly and persistently neglect or hurt or dwarf its soul."[24]

The controversy continued until June, with Du Bois insisting that one could not say "No segregation" and "Race pride and Race initiative" at the same time. The NAACP Board of Directors attempted to finesse the issue by rejecting Du Bois's position and by adopting instead a resolution that opposed "enforced segregation." Du Bois quite rightly noted that the resolution did not address the real questions: what was the proper position to take on such things as the improvement of black colleges and schools or the construction of segregated housing projects? In June, Du Bois resigned from the NAACP, citing the segregation controversy as an important cause. He said that the NAACP ought to be open about what its position would inevitably be anyway—opposition to segregation coupled with vigorous support for the improvement of segregated institutions as long as discrimination remained in force.[25]

As Du Bois's editorials indicated, the debate over segregation was associated with another debate, about the degree to which the NAACP should focus on economic issues. From its inception, the organization had been primarily concerned with vindicating the legal rights of blacks; although it repeatedly devoted some effort to economic issues, the NAACP always gave them an auxiliary place in its activities.[26] Even as Du Bois moved closer to a break with the NAACP, its board was debating changes in the organization's emphasis. In September 1934 the board received a report from a study committee that explicitly argued for reversing the traditional priorities given civil liberties and economic issues. The committee argued that the program must emphasize the common disadvantages shared by black and white workers, and should utilize direct action techniques as a means of building the political power of black and white workers. In the end the committee's proposed program was rejected; the NAACP leadership was concerned about the new program's costs, its ideological assumptions, and, most important for the purposes of this discussion, the difficulties of "adapting an existing organization" to a new program.[27]

The debate over economics and civil liberties had obvious implications for decisions about how to challenge segregation. Charles Thompson, dean of the School of Education at Howard University, devoted the annual yearbook issue of the *Journal of Negro Education* in July 1935 to "The Courts and the Negro Separate School," a topic that had become important as the NAACP began to develop a focused litigation strategy. The essays included one by Du Bois, reiterating his position, and several addressed to the utility of litigation as a strategy for eliminating segregated schools. Two opposed positions were stated; not surprisingly, they paralleled positions articulated in the broader debates over economics and segregation. One might be called "economic instrumentalism," and the other "autonomous legalism." Those who held the former view regarded legal rules as among the instruments wielded by the economically powerful in their own interests; they concluded that litigation was likely to be futile unless it was preceded by alterations in the distribution of power and, ultimately, of wealth. In contrast, the "autonomous legalists" thought that the expressed norms of fairness embodied in American law could, at least occasionally, be employed with significant effect to remedy racial segregation, even if segregation was in some sense the product of economic forces and interests. The center of gravity of NAACP leaders lay with the legalists, whose contributions to the *Journal* yearbook presented that position in a reasonably developed form. We should not, however, exaggerate the ideological coherence of the positions taken by mainstream NAACP leaders. The NAACP leadership tended to be nonideological in the sense that its members accepted the premises and results of American democracy on every issue other than race and did not attempt to link the race issue in a systematic way to anything else. Walter White, for example, is said to have believed that "liberal reform . . . offered the surest guarantee for the ultimate creation of a racially just society."[28]

Ralph Bunche's contribution to the yearbook presented the economic instrumentalist position in a broad essay on the tactics of minority groups. Civil libertarianism, including resort to the courts, rested on the "inherent fallacy . . . in the failure to appreciate the fact that the instruments of the state are merely the reflections of the political and economic ideology of the dominant group." According to Bunche, the NAACP had "conducted a militant fight under this illusory banner." The difficulty was that "the Constitution is a very flexible instrument and that, in the nature of things, it cannot be anything more than the controlling elements in the American society wish it to be." Bunche then telescoped ruling-class wishes into "public opinion," which was "seldom enlightened, sympathetic, tolerant or humanitarian." Even if occasional victories might be won from the courts, essentially at random, they would prove to be hollow. "[T]he status of the Negro . . . is fundamentally fixed by the functioning and demands of [the economic] order," which the courts could not affect. Law suits, "while winning a minor and too often illusory victory now and then, are essentially inefficacious in the long run. They lead up blind alleys and are chiefly programs of escape." Bunche thought that black progress depended on the betterment of, and alliances with, the white working class.[29]

There were two difficulties with economic instrumentalism. First, it identified the needs of the ruling class with public opinion. Even if one accepted the proposition that contemporary public opinion was shaped by the immediate needs of the ruling class, one could plausibly distinguish between immediate and long-term needs. Second, economic instrumentalism treated the ruling class as a single entity. It did not imagine, for example, that the dominant elites in the South, even if they controlled public opinion there, might be only a fragment of the national ruling class, and that the interests of the ruling class as a whole might differ from those of its southern fragment.

These problems provided the opening for the autonomous legalists to exploit. Dean Thompson's essay in the 1935 yearbook was titled "Court Action the Only Reasonable Alternative to Remedy Immediate Abuses of the Negro Separate School."[30] It displayed the fundamentally nonideological character of this strand of NAACP thought. He relied on the legal analysis summarized in another chapter of the yearbook[31] for his assertion that blacks "*can* resort to the courts with a reasonable certainty of favorable decisions." Thompson first argued that no alternatives to litigation were reasonable. Migration was inconceivable, revolt suicidal, and appeals to the sense of fairness of whites likely to be useless. Thus blacks "*must* resort to the courts. They have no other reasonable, legitimate alternative." The objections to litigation rested on the judgment that public opinion was not in the blacks' favor and that litigation too would be futile. Thompson replied that court decisions could both test and shape public opinion; blacks should not assume, for example, that courts would interpret ambiguous statutes against them or that whites would resist the reasonable resolution of ambiguity in their favor. Litigation, then, might succeed, and favorable results need not be nullified by resistance. "Circumvention is not a universal practice; and, even where it is attempted, it is not always successful; and, even where it is successful, the very subtlety necessitated by circumvention, either makes administration of the practice so difficult as to defeat itself in the long run, or furnishes another opening for attack."

The differences between the legalists and the instrumentalists had not yet crystallized in 1930, when the NAACP proposal for a litigation campaign was submitted to the Garland Fund's board of directors. Yet the differences, even though not as open as they later became, clearly shaped the Garland Fund's response to the NAACP proposal. The directors initially approved a tentative allocation of $100,000, one-third of the NAACP's request, and did so by a vote of five in favor and four against. The opponents included Roger Baldwin. At the same time that it approved the $100,000 grant, the board of directors also appointed Scott Nearing, a labor-oriented opponent of the grant, to the Committee on Negro Work. He was later replaced by Clarina Michelson, a member of the Communist party who shared his views on the relative importance of economic and legal work. During the next several months, Walter White, acting secretary of the NAACP while Johnson was on leave, attempted to allay the concerns expressed by opponents of the grant. He assured the Committee on Negro Work that blacks cared about self-assertion, as the size of the NAACP's membership showed, and defended an emphasis on law as stimulating blacks to vigilance and aggressive actions. He also enumerated for Johnson, for transmittal to the Garland Fund's board, the NAACP's activities regarding black labor. By March 1930, after learning that the Garland Fund, when it actually appropriated money for the NAACP proposal, would grant no more than $100,000, if that, White expressed some irritation over the negotiations, writing Johnson that he was "handicapped" until he knew what the Committee on Negro Work wanted from him.[32]

Finally, when Ernst told White that the committee needed much more detail on what the NAACP would do with the grant, White presented the committee with an extensive memorandum that for the first time combined proposals with a specific idea of implementation. The program contained the same elements as before—for example, the NAACP's branches would be encouraged to send to the national office cases of discriminatory exclusion of blacks from grand juries and the NAACP would pursue suits against residential segregation—but the school campaign now took shape. The money would be used to support suits by taxpayers in seven states in the Deep South, seeking to equalize expenditures on black and white schools. "Such taxpayer suits . . . will (a) make the cost

of a dual school system so prohibitive as to speed the abolishment of segregated schools; (b) serve as examples and will give courage to Negroes to
bring similar actions; (3) cases will likely be appealed by city authorities,
thus causing higher court decision[s] to cover wider territory; (4) focus as
nothing else will public attention north and south on the vicious discrimination in the apportionment of public school funds." The campaign,
White said, would be "mapp[ed] out" at first by "a very able lawyer" who
would be hired for at least a year to study the law, supervise the drafting
of complaints and briefs, and coordinate the litigation. The litigation
campaign now had an organizational component, the creation of a staff
position for litigation, and a substantive one, the use of litigation to secure judgments that would directly increase the costs of segregation,
create favorable precedents to increase those costs indirectly, and mobilize the black community.[33]

White's memorandum had the effect of bringing into the open the conflict between the Garland Fund's interest in labor organizing and the
NAACP's focus that had been submerged at earlier stages. In late May 1930
the Committee on Negro Work reported to the fund's board that it could
not devise a compromise, and endorsed the NAACP's plan. It noted the
lack of success that had attended direct expenditures on organizing black
workers, and it agreed with the NAACP that the civil liberties strategy
could have a "really revolutionary" effect by giving the black community
"the courage and opportunity to fight its own way." The Garland Fund's
aims, the committee said, could be "partly" realized through the NAACP,
at a relatively low cost. A majority of the fund's board was persuaded. In a
series of votes, the proposal's supporters defeated attempts to divert some
funds from the NAACP to the International Labor Defense (ILD) and the
American Negro Labor Congress, both of which were more left-wing
than the NAACP. The final vote on the grant was six to five in favor. Again
Baldwin was in the minority, which consisted of the more radically ori-
ented directors; the majority consisted of people closer to traditional liberalism. Later Charles Garland noted his discomfort with criticism of the
fund for radicalism when it had given money to the NAACP: if the fund
was to be criticized, it was for "assisting right wing movements at the
expense of the more radical." He preferred the ILD to the NAACP, "whose
conduct in the Scottsboro case has been anything but advanced or radical." Walter White commented that the members of the Communist party
on the fund's board of directors "fought bitterly to the very end to get the
money appropriated to the I.L.D. instead of to the NAACP."[34]

The board established a joint committee, three persons from the fund and two from the NAACP, to administer the $100,000 it released "for an intensive campaign against specific handicaps facing the Negro, which include: Unequal Apportionment of School Funds, Barring of Negroes from Juries, Jim Crow Cars, Residential Segregation by Property Holders' Covenants, Disfranchisement, and Civil Liberties Defense." The lawyer hired to coordinate the campaign would develop "personal and frequent contacts" in supervising the cases. Seven suits in the Deep South were now suggested, commensurate with the scaling down of the grant. "[T]he psychological effect upon Negroes themselves will be that of stirring the spirit of revolt among them; upon whites, it will increase their fear of and respect for the Negro and hasten the efforts to end these injustices."[35]

White sent a letter announcing the program to over 100 people, including teachers and heads of organizations that might assist it, and the NAACP immediately began searching for the lawyer to plan and coordinate the campaign. By early September, two main candidates appeared: William Hastie, a recent black graduate from Harvard Law School who White thought "has not yet had enough experience," and Nathan Margold, a protégé of Felix Frankfurter, as were also Hastie and Charles Hamilton Houston. Houston, deeply involved at that time in upgrading the Howard University Law School to provide talented black lawyers to serve the race, wrote White that Margold, with whom he had talked, was a "remarkable chap. . . . He is indefatigable, [and] has an unusual mind." Houston also assured White that Hastie was guaranteed a job at Howard.[36]

Houston's letter apparently satisfied White, and Margold was hired on October 4, 1930. Margold had followed the Frankfurter path into public service—the Law Review at Harvard, service as an assistant in the Office of the United States Attorney for the Southern District of New York, teaching at Harvard for a year, and a private practice with a heavy component of public interest work. The NAACP agreed to pay him $3,000 in October, $3,000 more in three months, and another $4,000 over the following years for an additional two months' work. White emphasized that "this is a NAACP project," and that Margold was responsible to the NAACP, not to Roger Baldwin or the Garland Fund. Margold was committed to full-time work on the plan for only three months; he also extracted an agreement that he would be allowed to argue the NAACP's cases before the Supreme Court unless the NAACP decided that it was advisable to have an attorney "of great eminence and reputation"—presumably a prominent white lawyer in the tradition of Moorfield Storey or Louis Marshall, who had argued all five of the NAACP's Supreme Court cases between 1913 and 1927—to do so.[37]

The financial arrangements with Margold did not work out well, largely because of tensions between Roger Baldwin and the NAACP over the proper use of the grant. These tensions arose immediately after the NAACP began to use the money. A. Philip Randolph requested assistance from the joint committee to support a lawsuit against the Pullman Company's captive union. According to White, everyone on the committee except Baldwin thought that it would be a waste of money to help Randolph, and as the first item of business at a meeting on October 2, 1930, the committee denied the request. Baldwin, who had been late for the meeting and had missed the vote, was upset, and told Randolph that "part of the $100,000 . . . was designated for use for Trade Union work among Negroes." White replied that Baldwin must have had in mind earlier proposals, and quoted the section on "Labor" from the report adopted by the Garland Fund, which said that Negroes as such "suffer . . . disabilities which the white laborer does not face," and that the "problem of organizing the Negroes . . . belongs to the sphere" of a different subcommittee of the fund. Baldwin then urged the joint committee to give "very careful consideration" to the matter. "Whatever the technical situation is," he wrote White, "this is distinctly a job where the interests of Negroes are challenged at a critical point involving their whole relation to the white labor movement and a considerable relation to the white public." White thought that "yielding in this instance would simply open the door for the Fund, and more particularly for Roger, to dump onto us every application, wise or otherwise, which may come for work among Negroes." The issue was not revived.[38]

Similar tensions affected the NAACP's financial arrangements with the fund. The fund had two commitments to the NAACP: in addition to the $100,000 pledged for the legal campaign, it had an outstanding loan of $2,500. In August 1930 the NAACP notified the fund that it could not repay the loan because of reduced membership and donations during the Depression. In May 1931, just before the Margold Report was delivered, the fund refused to cancel the note and suggested that it be set off against further installments to the legal fund. The NAACP was able to pay Margold his first $3,000, but in June 1931 the Garland Fund delayed a second installment for several weeks.[39]

However, the Garland Fund was not simply trying to use leverage on a debtor. On May 18, 1931, the *New York Herald-Tribune* reported that the capital of the Garland Fund had been exhausted. Much of that capital had been paid out by the fund in the form of loans, and apparently the fund's directors expected to be able to recirculate the money when the loans were repaid. But, as the experience with the NAACP illustrated, the Garland Fund's ideological commitments tied it to financially marginal organizations such as socialist newspapers and labor-organizing schools, which of course found repayment difficult. Furthermore, the collapse of the stock market had reduced the value of the fund's holdings. White reported to the NAACP board in November 1931 that the Garland Fund had requested "that a revised program should be worked out to fit as nearly as possible the reduced funds which would be available . . . for the legal campaign." By June 1932, when the next installment of Margold's fee was due, the Garland Fund said that it had no money for that purpose, and Lewis Gannett wrote White, "Frankly, I don't feel the N.A.A.C.P. has behaved as it should about that 1929 loan." White called the letters requesting payment of the loan "sheer gall" and noted that the letters, signed by Anna Marnitz, a staff worker for the fund, were "the hand of Esau but the voice of Jacob—Roger Baldwin." Ultimately the fund paid Margold's expenses but not his salary installment, and over the next year the NAACP dribbled money out to Margold from its general funds. On May 24, 1933, Margold was appointed solicitor of the Department of the Interior; accounts were settled with the NAACP agreeing to pay Margold $7,500.[40] Finally, in July 1933, the Garland Fund gave the NAACP $10,000 for use in attacking segregated schools and Jim Crow railroad cars. Roger Baldwin wrote White that it was doubtful that more would be given later, and White informed the NAACP board that the fund was "divided almost equally" on even the $10,000 grant.[41] Thus, the NAACP ultimately received slightly more than $20,000 of the original $100,000 commitment.

In an effort to obtain more funds, White and Houston, who succeeded Margold on the NAACP staff, reported to the joint committee three times in 1935 on the litigation campaign. The details of that campaign will occupy much of the next chapters. For now it is enough to note that the first report, in March, mentioned difficulties in starting a salary equalization suit in South Carolina, and informed the committee of plans to sue the University of Maryland. The second, in July, noted that "interest on the part of Negroes was not keen" at the trial of the Maryland lawsuit. The November report, by Houston, culminated with a request for an additional $10,000 to support the litigation effort and from $3,000 to $5,000 for publicity and promotion, which seems to have been the aim of the series of reports from the beginning. Houston mentioned divisions in the black press over the wisdom of suing the University of Virginia, and pressures on applicants to withdraw or lose their jobs. He insisted that "if this program is to be anything more than a gesture, it will have to be extended beyond 1936." He had to move cautiously and avoid "unnecessary losses," which required him to be extremely careful in selecting potential plaintiffs. This, and the fact that "it takes a long time to get a mass of people to move," plus "vested interests" among blacks, meant that the "program must not move forward any faster than it can carry with it substantial support among the Negro groups." Not surprisingly, nothing came of this request.[42]

The NAACP's last contacts with the Garland Fund occurred in 1937 and 1938. Walter White had heard from Morris Ernst that the fund had obtained $10,000 from repayment of loans. After learning from Roger Baldwin that the fund's much lower budget was committed to Garland's current favorite project, organizing farm workers, Houston called Garland in an effort to persuade him that the NAACP's litigation was "tied in with agricultural organization." In a long letter to Baldwin, Houston described the arguments he had made to Garland: "[W]e used the courts as dissecting laboratories to extract from hostile officials the true machinations of their prejudices; and . . . the resulting exposures were often enough in themselves to produce reforms. Likewise we use the courts as a medium of public discussion, since it is the one place where we can force America to listen. I explained [to Garland] how we attempted to activate the public into organized forms of protest and support behind the cases, under the theory that a court demonstration unrelated to supporting popular action is usually futile and a mere show." Baldwin was unconvinced.[43]

Houston then sent a memorandum to a still-existing joint committee to administer the Garland Fund grant to the NAACP, in which he described the litigation on behalf of black teachers, a matter that will be taken up in detail in later chapters. Houston noted that the teachers were "cowed and so afraid of incurring official displeasure that they have not dared contribute to the support of the program as they should." A budget Houston sent showed that the Garland Fund's money had been spent in roughly equal $8,000 portions on Margold's salary, the salaries of NAACP staff counsel who replaced Margold, and litigation expenses. He concluded:

[N]o attempt has been made to discuss the general relation of the educational program to the whole struggle of labor to organize and obtain greater security and higher living conditions. But three things may be indicated in closing: 1. The withholding of education from the Southern Negro is deliberate and based on a program of exploitation. Ignorance makes this exploitation easier both on the plantation and in the city industries. It affects both Negro and white workers. 2. The drive for equalization of teachers' salaries is a fundamental drive against wage differentials, which is one of the curses of Southern industrial life. 3. Improving education for the Negroes in the South will inevitably spur Southern officials on to improve education for the poor whites.

In the end, the only result was a grant of $700, conditioned on the NAACP's raising a matching amount.[44]

The NAACP's Annual Report for 1934 put the best face on the arrangements with the Garland Fund in saying that "shrinkage in the assets of the . . . Fund, due to the depression, resulted in drastic reduction of the funds available."[45] But what had also happened was the sort of mutual disenchantment that can occur when two parties interact and gradually discover that what had seemed to be congruent interests were actually divergent. The NAACP had never been fully committed to using the Garland Fund's money in ways that would assist labor organizing in any direct way. It saw the fund as a source that could be tapped for the NAACP's own purposes. Some maneuvering and subtlety in the phrasing of the funding proposals had to occur to get the money, and obtaining the money was what the NAACP cared about. The directors of the fund were both more ideological and more radical than the NAACP's leaders. It is not surprising that the relationship proved hard to sustain. Financial exigency played a role in the breakdown, of course, but it would make the situation seem more subject to simple economic constraints than it actually was to give financial problems first place. At least as important was the process of repeated negotiation between the NAACP and the fund. In the process the NAACP made statements about its intentions that unsympathetic readers could later complain were not completely accurate; the Garland Fund resisted further commitments when it failed to be persuaded that the ways in which the NAACP actually used the grant promoted the fund's interests despite the apparent inconsistencies between the initial statements and the results.

The narrowness of the votes by which the Garland Fund decided to support the project proposed by the NAACP should make one cautious about developing large-scale explanations of these events. The interests of the fund and the NAACP overlapped but also conflicted. For ideological reasons the directors of the fund thought it important to support activities in the black community, and the presence of strong supporters of the NAACP among the directors made the choice of the NAACP's program seem almost a necessity. Yet the radical cast of the fund was different from the liberal one of the NAACP, which meant that the relationship was always subject to strain. I have already noted that political skill ultimately played a large part in the NAACP's campaign. The aspect of political skill that should be emphasized here is the ability to persuade people whose views conflict that their mutual interests will be better served by accommodating, suppressing, or avoiding the conflicts than by persisting in them. With that in mind, one can see how the roles of Johnson and White were of some significance. Though they were in a position to act as political brokers, neither did so. White, in particular, was unable to frame his approaches to the fund in ways that might have been politically effective, and several times he made the political mistake of losing his temper. Later, other leaders of the litigation campaign displayed greater skill.

The Garland Fund proposal did not mandate significant changes in the surface appearance of what the NAACP had been doing. The NAACP's commitment to destroying the constitutional basis of segregation had been expressed repeatedly in grand jury, Jim Crow transportation, and housing cases, the areas other than education covered in the proposal to the Garland Fund. The terms of the proposal did little more than add school segregation to the list. Because the issue was new to the NAACP's concerns as an organization, Margold devoted half of his report to school segregation; the other half dealt with residential segregation, where previous lawsuits had brought novel and difficult issues to the fore. In the other areas the law was clear enough to make unnecessary the kind of focused attention Margold gave to school and residential segregation.[46] But the grant had less obvious and more important effects: it helped to focus the NAACP's concerns somewhat by articulating a policy of litigation dealing with several broad areas rather than a policy of response to immediate pressures, and it provided the impulse for creating a legal staff within the organization. The creation of that staff and the initial visions of Margold and Houston are the subjects of the following chapter.

2. The Legal Background: From Margold to Houston

The state of the law of racial discrimination as it stood in 1930 conditioned the ways in which the NAACP's lawyers would choose to attack educational inequities in the 1930s. Their individual perspectives on the role of litigation as part of the black community's political efforts also affected their decisions. After examining the legal background and the Margold Report, this chapter describes the role that race-consciousness played in the development of the legal staff. The next chapter examines the impact that the staff's own views had on the shape of the litigation campaign.

In 1890 the Louisiana legislature passed a statute that required all railroad companies to provide "equal but separate accommodations for the white, and colored, races." The black community in New Orleans, concerned about the legislative successes of racism in their state, organized a test case in which Homer A. Plessy, a light-skinned man who described himself as "seven-eighths Caucasian," boarded the white car of a train. When the state began to prosecute him for violating the segregation statute, Plessy sought a ruling that would prohibit the trial judge, John H. Ferguson, from proceeding with the trial, on the ground that the segregation statute violated his constitutional rights. After his arguments were rejected by the state courts, Plessy appealed to the United States Supreme Court.[1]

The Supreme Court held in 1896 that the statute was constitutional. Plessy argued that the statute violated the requirement of the Fourteenth Amendment that "no state shall deny . . . the equal protection of the laws." Justice Henry Billings Brown's opinion for the Court distinguished between political equality, which was guaranteed by the amendment, and social equality, which "in the nature of things" could not be guaranteed by law. Laws separating the races were common as exercises of the general regulatory powers of the state—its police powers. Like all exercises of the police powers, segregation statutes had to be reasonable, "and extend only to such laws as are enacted in good faith for the promotion of the public good, and not for the annoyance or oppression of a particular class." The Court held that Louisiana's railroad segregation statute satisfied the standard.

Two things stand out in the Court's opinion. First, although the case is taken to be the origin of the doctrine that states could require "separate but equal" facilities, equality of facilities was required not by the Court's analysis of the Constitution but by Louisiana's segregation statute. If equality entered the constitutional analysis, it did so through the "reasonableness" requirement: a segregation statute that did not require equal facilities might be unreasonable because it did not promote the public good. This left room for defenders of segregation to argue that inequalities in facilities were reasonable and rested on acceptable judgments about what would indeed promote the public good. Second, *Plessy* did not involve schools. Yet Justice Brown drew his primary historical support for the distinction between political and social rights from the widespread acceptance, "even by courts of states where the political rights of the colored race have been longest and most earnestly enforced," of segregated schools. Here he relied on a 1849 decision of the Massachusetts Supreme Judicial Court upholding segregation in the Boston schools. In addition, the "[un]questioned" acceptance of segregated schools showed that Louisiana's decision to segregate railroad cars was reasonable.[2]

A case decided three years later demonstrated that the "separate but equal" doctrine had indeed become accepted in education. The Augusta, Georgia, school board maintained segregated elementary and high schools. As the black population grew, the board found that it needed more space to accommodate the younger black students. It decided to convert the black high school into a black elementary school, and did not open another black high school. Black parents and taxpayers challenged the board's actions, but they did not question the operation of a "separate but equal" school system. Instead they sought to enforce equality. Unfortunately for their case, they sought relief in the form of an injunction against collection of taxes from them. The Supreme Court said that this remedy would be inappropriate. An injunction "would either impair the efficiency of the high school for white children or compel the Board to close it. But if that were done, the result would only be to take from white children educational privileges enjoyed by them, without giving to colored children additional opportunities for the education furnished in high schools." The Court said that "different questions might have arisen" if the plaintiffs had sought to compel the board, "out of the funds in its hands or under its control, to establish and maintain a high school for colored children." This emphasis on remedy was undercut, though, by a parallel emphasis on the board's discretion in allocating money, limited only by the rule that it could not act out of "hostility to the colored population because of their race." The Court also stressed the impropriety of "interference on the part of Federal authority with the management of [public] schools . . . except in the case of a clear and unmistakable disregard of rights secured by the supreme law of the land."[3]

Had the Court adhered to the view that school boards had broad discretion in allocating funds among black and white schools, legal challenges to unequal facilities would have been quite difficult to win. Schools have a large number of characteristics, and school boards would have been able to defend an attack on one inequality by arguing that it had acted reasonably in compensating for that inequality by providing enhanced facilities in another area. For example, a board might have said that, in light of the probable careers of black students, it was reasonable to replace academic programs with vocational ones. The premise might have been incorrect, but a lawsuit challenging the premise would certainly have been more difficult to win than one challenging unequal physical facilities. Fortunately, in their early consideration of legal action, lawyers associated with the NAACP did not have to worry about this problem, for two reasons. One was practical. They knew, and the studies undertaken with the earlier Garland Fund grant had shown, that in the Deep South black schools were inferior to white ones by any measure a school board might offer. So long as they were thinking of attacks on segregation in the Deep South, they had no reason to worry about complexities resulting from what school boards might wish to represent as reasonable exercises of school board discretion.

The second reason for unconcern was legal. In 1914 the Supreme Court decided another case involving segregated railroad facilities. Oklahoma's segregation statute required separate but equal coach facilities, but explicitly allowed railroads to haul sleeping cars and dining cars reserved for whites without hauling similar cars for blacks. The state justified the provision on economic grounds. The demand for sleeping and dining cars for blacks was too small to make it practical to require equal access to these special services. Although they rejected the blacks' claims on other grounds, five justices of the Court found this argument in defense of the statute "without merit" because "it makes the constitutional right depend upon the number of persons who may be discriminated against, whereas the essence of the constitutional right is that it is a personal one." The state might permit railroads to refrain from providing services for which overall demand was insufficient, the Court said, "but if facilities are provided, substantial equality of treatment of persons traveling under like conditions cannot be refused." This conclusion rested on the important proposition that "it is the individual who is entitled to the equal protection of the laws." Thus, if *any* black was denied a "facility or convenience" available to others, the Constitution was violated.[4]

This doctrine seems to confirm the remedial emphasis pointed to in the high school decision, and to eliminate its emphasis on discretion. Under the "separate but equal" doctrine, the state could require railroads to provide separate facilities for blacks and whites. As Oklahoma saw it, the railroads were willing to provide a package of facilities to whites, to the extent that demand and cost allowed, and a different package to blacks, to the same degree as determined by demand and cost. On this analysis, it was improper to compare differences in details within the packages, for what mattered was that the packages as a whole were equal. The economic defense of Oklahoma's law rested on the proposition that if railroads had to provide the special cars for the few blacks who demanded them, they would have to reduce their services elsewhere. That is, Oklahoma's defense was in effect one of compensating inequalities: the railroads compensated for the lack of special cars by making other services available, which would not be available if the special cars were. In saying that constitutional rights are personal, the Court had to mean that the defense of compensating inequalities was unavailable. Particular details within packages of services could be compared when any individual black claimed inequality as to that detail. In the context of education, the argument implied that a school board could not say to a black who wanted to attend an academic program that it had no such program because other blacks needed vocational programs more. In this way, the "separate but equal" doctrine finally received its constitutional grounding. *Plessy* said that exercises of the police power had to be reasonable. The Oklahoma case said that a state could not compensate for inequality along one dimension by providing other blacks with advantages along other dimensions, for that would deny the personal nature of constitutional rights. Such compensating inequalities were therefore unreasonable.

The logic of the "personal right" doctrine cannot be pushed too hard. No two facilities will be exactly the same, and the courts would inevitably recognize some defense that inequalities are reasonable. However, the doctrine does provide powerful support for adopting some simple measure of equality such as per capita expenditures. Each student is the beneficiary of the same per capita expenditure by definition, and the courts would not have to concern themselves with the distribution of that amount between gymnasiums and libraries, academic and vocational programs, plumbing and roofing, and so on through all the activities in which schools engage. In the end the NAACP never had to face the question of compensating inequalities. By the time southern school boards recognized that some moves in the direction of equal facilities were required by law and by practical politics, and so came closer to the point where the defense of compensating inequalities would have been plausible, the NAACP was well on its way toward abandoning a strategy that focused on material inequalities.

The final element in the legal picture was *Yick Wo* v. *Hopkins*.[5] San Francisco had an ordinance that required a permit to operate hand laundries in wooden buildings. The Court held that the manner in which the ordinance was administered violated the Constitution, because permits had been issued to virtually all non-Chinese applicants and to no Chinese ones. *Yick Wo* meant that inequalities between black and white schools might be unconstitutional even if no statutes explicitly required unequal expenditures or facilities.

With the law in this state, Margold had some difficulty in producing his report. A little over a week after the contract was signed, Margold gave the NAACP an able twelve-page criticism of the draft brief in the pending Texas white primary case.[6] Then, urged by White to get a preliminary report done by January 1931, he went to work on preparing the plan. But Margold found it difficult to write a report. At the end of March 1931, he apologized for the delay: "It has not been easy to achieve simplicity without superficiality, or to devise basic lines of attack which are sound in theory and feasible in practice."[7] In addition, Margold's full-time commitment had expired and his other legal jobs began to press on him. Finally, on May 13, 1931, he sent in the preliminary report on the school campaign, and three days later, the final portion dealing with residential segregation by restrictive covenant.

The report ran to 218 legal-sized pages. After a brief introduction, about one hundred pages were devoted to an analysis of legal routes by which segregation in schools could be challenged. These differed from the routes contemplated by those who presented the original proposal to the Garland Fund. To the extent that it had mentioned education litigation, the Garland Fund grant was designed for taxpayers' suits in Deep South states, aimed at equalization. Johnson, who took part in the development of that grant, explicitly distinguished between equalization and a direct attack on separate schools. Johnson would have instituted coordinated actions to equalize expenditures "in three or four sections of the country," including South Carolina, Virginia, Tennessee, and perhaps southern California or New Mexico. If separate schools were attacked, it should be done outside the South—for example, in "parts of Pennsylvania . . . and certain sections of the Southwest." He thought it "would be worst [sic] than futile" to challenge separate schools in the Deep South.[8] Margold presented a perceptive legal analysis, which rested on political judgments that differed from Johnson's. He argued that a direct attack on separate schools was both legally and politically possible. A legal technician, he mentioned publicity only in the context of white concerns. Unlike those who developed the NAACP's earlier proposals, he did not think of the lawsuits as a means of galvanizing the black community.

The report began with the observation that, as a matter of law, it was relatively easy to demonstrate that disproportionate expenditures on black schools violated the law. But developing the proper remedy for that violation would be difficult. Margold found that southern states had a wide range of statutory schemes regulating expenditures. Some states required equal expenditures; the apparent remedy, in most of these states, was an action for mandamus, an order from the state courts directing state officials to comply with clear law. Indeed, Margold argued that in these states no remedy from the federal courts was available, because, he said, noncompliance with state law does not violate the federal Constitution.[9] A second group of states left apportionment of funds to the discretion of various officials; there, unequal expenditures could not be remedied in state courts, but a federal remedy was available. The final group required a "fair and equitable division" of funds. In these states, both state and federal remedies might be available, but establishing a right to relief would be difficult because the statutes appeared to authorize a variety of defenses; for example, Margold believed that in the third group of states, a school board might prevail by showing that the costs of running black schools were lower than those of running white schools or that the cost of living for black teachers was less than that for white teachers.

Margold argued that lawsuits aiming at a remedy whose direct effect would be to equalize expenditures would be too complex. Mandamus would have to be brought against each official responsible for expenditures, and Margold anticipated difficulties with finger-pointing defenses, in which each defendant would claim that someone else was responsible for what had happened. In addition, because the suits would have to challenge an exercise of discretion after the fact, mandamus was retrospective, making it necessary to start over each year. This, Margold said, would lead to an "appalling" number of lawsuits. Finally, his analysis of state law led him to conclude that mandamus in state courts probably could not succeed. Most states required only equal apportionments among but not within counties, and it was the allocation between black and white schools in each county that was the NAACP's concern.

Margold therefore concluded that the idea of using mandamus in state courts as the vehicle for the attack on segregation was misconceived. He argued that the campaign should focus, instead, on three easily proved facts: that state law required separate schools, that expenditures were obviously unequal, and that state remedies were in practice unavailable. "We have, in a word, a case of segregation irremediably coupled with discrimination." In this light, the campaign should seek, in effect, simple declarations of unconstitutionality rather than orders directing that expenditures be equalized. Once those declarations were obtained, state officials could decide whether to equalize expenditures or to desegregate the schools. In a passage central to his argument, Margold wrote:

It would be a great mistake to fritter away our limited funds on sporadic attempts to force the making of equal divisions of school funds in the few instances where such attempts might be expected to succeed. At the most, we could do no more than to eliminate a very minor part of the discrimination during the year our suits are commenced. We should not be establishing any new principles, nor bringing any sort of pressure to bear which can reasonably be expected to retain the slightest force beyond that exerted by the specific judgment or order that we might obtain. And we should be leaving wholly untouched the very essence of the existing evils.

On the other hand, if we boldly challenge the constitutional validity of segregation if and when accompanied irremediably by discrimination, we can strike directly at the most prolific sources of discrimination. We can transform into an authoritative adjudication the principle of law, now only theoretically inferrable from *Yick Wo v. Hopkins,* that segregation coupled with discrimination resulting from administrative action permitted but not required by state statute, is just as much a denial of equal protection of the laws as is segregation coupled with discrimination required by express statutory enactment. And the threat of using adjudication as a means of destroying segregation itself, would always exert a very real and powerful force at least to compel enormous improvement in the Negro schools through voluntary official action.

Finally, to those who feared that to attack segregation risked "the danger of stirring up intense opposition, ill-will and strife," Margold argued that "a similar danger would be entailed by any sort of effective action which we can hope to take in our campaign." Inequality in expenditures occurred because it was "just as deeply entrenched as segregation." Margold thought that "a really effective campaign to force equal if separate accommodations, resulting as it necessarily would, either in a heavy increase in taxation or an appreciable decrease in the efficiency of white schools, would entail just as much intensity of feeling as will the course of action which I earnestly recommend to the committee for approval." Margold's conclusion reiterated his argument that the NAACP should "attack the practice of segregation, *as now provided for and administered.*" He claimed that the strategy he proposed would leave it open to the South to use some other form of segregation, "a form which will render equality imperative and provide Negro parents with effective, practicable means of forcing derelict educational officers to perform their duties properly." By emphasizing that the legal attack still left open the possibility of separate schools so long as they were equal, and by conducting a careful publicity campaign to allay white concerns, the NAACP could, according to Margold, reduce "the danger of inciting ill-will and alienating enlightened public opinion." [10]

All in all, the Margold Report was a powerful piece of work. It effectively undermined the approach the NAACP had presented to the Garland Fund by demonstrating how difficult it would be to bring equalization suits, and showed how equalization litigation could take a form that would be both an indirect and a direct attack on segregation. The distance from the Garland Fund's intentions was measured not only in legal terms, but also in terms of Margold's inattention to the use of publicity within the black community as a method of community organization.

Over the next year, Margold worked on a number of projects that had no connection with his report; he advised the NAACP about its challenge to Louisiana's requirement that voters demonstrate "understanding" of the Constitution, and assisted in presenting the NAACP's revision of New Jersey's civil rights act. In June 1932 Margold gave White a summary of his activities, noting that no suits had been instituted. He said that the original conception of a coordinated campaign should be implemented when sufficient money became available.[11]

As we have seen, however, the prospects for a well-funded campaign continued to diminish. Charles Hamilton Houston had been consulting extensively with the NAACP while he retained his position at Howard Law School. When the Garland Fund's final appropriation of $10,000 was approved in 1933, Walter White proposed Houston as Margold's successor. Houston was appointed to the staff of the NAACP as special counsel in May 1934. By October, Houston concluded that the available funds required that the legal effort be concentrated. It should try to "(1) . . . strengthen the will of local communities to demand and fight for their rights; [and] (2) to work out model procedures through actual tests in court."[12] Thus, with Houston's appointment, the legal campaign once again became part of a broader conception of community mobilization.

Walter White's letter to Margold informing him of Houston's appointment hinted at the reason; White said that "a colored lawyer with the dignity, ability and tact of Mr. Houston would encounter far less hostility than a white lawyer."[13] What mattered was race. In the early 1930s, the NAACP began actively to recruit black lawyers to its Legal Committee in order to stimulate membership activity in the branches, to demonstrate the advance of the race into areas previously dominated by whites, and to respond to pressure from black lawyers seeking recognition for their own achievements. August Meier and Elliott Rudwick have carefully detailed the gradual displacement of white attorneys by blacks in the NAACP's work.[14] Prominent white lawyers played the major role during the 1920s, in part because there were too few black attorneys with enough experience and standing in white courts to do the difficult job of changing the law through advocacy. As the NAACP began to take an increasingly prominent place in the organizational life of the black community, this situation became increasingly difficult to sustain politically. The leadership of the black community wanted the organizations that served the community to represent it as well, and the best representatives would themselves be black. The NAACP's leaders believed that a litigation effort directed by black lawyers would be responsive to black concerns, because there would be no need to educate the lawyers on the issues that blacks might be sensitive to, and that black lawyers would show to blacks and whites that white prejudices were unfounded.

Carter Woodson surveyed the black professional community in the early 1930s and reported his results in 1934. For information about the black bar, Woodson relied on a survey that Houston had conducted for the Laura Spelman Rockefeller Memorial as a basis for reorganizing the law school at Howard University. Woodson found few black lawyers in the South, except for small numbers in cities like Norfolk, Durham, Atlanta, Jacksonville, New Orleans, and Houston. Black lawyers were not highly regarded as leaders of the black community. Most were sole practitioners who had to devote themselves to the fee-generating aspects of the profession. Woodson did note that younger lawyers were more aggressive in their concern for the community.[15]

The emergence of a new generation of lawyers facilitated the transition within the NAACP. A small number of brilliant young black lawyers—Houston, William Hastie, Leon Ransom—became available in the late 1920s to assist the NAACP. Under the guidance of Houston, they revitalized the Howard Law School and made it perhaps the first public interest law school, with an institutional focus on the effects of the legal system on the black community. Evidence of the upgrading of Howard came in many forms. The evening program was eliminated in 1932, and entrance requirements were raised. The effect was tò reduce enrollment from over eighty in 1929 to thirty-seven in 1933. Black teachers replaced a number of white, mainly part-time teachers in 1931. An accreditation report in 1933 noted that Howard's staff then had four full-time teachers, of whom three were black, and seven part-time teachers, of whom four were black. Only two of the teachers were over forty-six years old. Further, the report said, the upgrading was likely to be sustained even if, as seemed likely, Houston left Howard. The program had strong support from the university administration, and Houston, having trained such potential successors as Ransom and Hastie, was no longer irreplaceable. Thus, the effects transcended the accomplishments of any single person. By the late 1930s, the bulletin of Howard Law School could say, "Only through an institution like Howard, devoted solely to service of its people, can we develop more and more men like these—men to whom the race and the nation must equally turn for guidance in the future." It said that all the faculty members "have been active in the struggle for equality of opportunity" and "key their courses to prepare the students to carry on that battle. No law school except Howard has a course devoted solely to ways and means of protecting and enlarging the liberties of its constituency. . . . Not only has Howard developed such a course—Civil Rights—but whenever possible it relates its regular law courses to the Negro—how can the accepted devices of the law be adapted to peculiar Negro problems?" [16]

In the early 1930s, the NAACP moved to recruit the new black elite lawyers. For example, in June 1932, Walter White suggested to James Cobb, a member of the NAACP's board of directors who had resigned from the Legal Committee after taking a judgeship, that Houston and Louis Redding be added to the committee, along with other young black lawyers "who can in this fashion be definitely interested in and made a part of the Association." The next year he suggested to Arthur Spingarn that Homer Brown, the president of the Pittsburgh branch, be appointed. According to White, Brown was not as brilliant as Houston, but "he is able, self-sacrificing and intensely loyal to the N.A.A.C.P." His appointment would generate favorable reactions in the branches and would be "a definite answer to some of the less able and more ambitious lawyers who for selfish reasons want to use the Association." Houston, Redding, and Brown joined the Legal Committee, which expanded from seven members in 1931 to sixteen in 1933.[17]

This expansion, which occurred just when the NAACP was acquiring a legal staff, transformed the Legal Committee. Headed by Arthur Spingarn since 1913, the Legal Committee in the 1920s was an important resource for the NAACP. In his capacity as assistant secretary of the NAACP, White screened requests for assistance, summarized the ones worth more attention, and sent them to Spingarn. When necessary, White and Spingarn consulted other members of the Legal Committee. In addition, Spingarn gave legal advice regarding the affairs of the NAACP; for example, he reviewed contracts for the organization and wrote letters urging executors of estates that included bequests to the NAACP to transfer the money promptly. After White became acting secretary in 1929 and then secretary in 1931, his successor as assistant secretary, Roy Wilkins, took over those coordinating efforts. However, Spingarn and the Legal Committee were consulted less frequently about NAACP litigation after Houston became special counsel. The Legal Committee became an honorific organization. Two changes thus occurred. The legal work was transferred from Spingarn and the largely white Legal Committee to the black NAACP staff, and the Legal Committee itself acquired more black members.[18]

Houston and Hastie became deeply involved in NAACP litigation, as we will see in the next chapter. But Houston's appointment as special counsel was the most important event in the displacement of white attorneys. That appointment culminated an extensive debate between White and Roger Baldwin. When the Garland Fund released its final $10,000 in 1933, White immediately proposed Houston, the "ideal person," as special counsel. White wrote, "[Houston's] very deep interest would enable us not only to secure a man who would have all the intellectual and legal background necessary but one who will have a definite personal interest which would cause him to do the job better and less expensively than would otherwise be the case." To Spingarn, White wrote that Houston's appointment would be "strategically valuable" for the NAACP because it would "tie up to the Association . . . the young colored men and women of the country as nothing else would." Baldwin was skeptical. He wanted Margold to "look [Houston] over," and doubted that Houston's academic credentials made him "the man to argue cases unless he's had a lot of court experience."[19]

White then added Hastie's name, and Baldwin suggested Noel Dowling, Karl Llewellyn, and Nathan Greene, three white lawyers with impeccable academic credentials. White now preferred Hastie. His "ability, experience and interest would outweigh the advantages of having a New York lawyer." Further, Hastie was "so tactful" that he would be able to "get along with any southern white lawyers which we may have occasion to employ." Baldwin was unconvinced, and by October Hastie had received an offer of a position as assistant to Margold at the Department of the Interior. The salary was greater than the one the NAACP could promise, but Hastie remained interested in the NAACP job. Baldwin's opposition or apathy was unchanged, though, and Hastie accepted Margold's offer. In April 1934, White and Spingarn gave in to Baldwin, and after meeting with Llewellyn, they suggested that the members of the Garland Fund's Committee on Negro Work consider Llewellyn. Morris Ernst thought that Llewellyn would be "swell," and Baldwin called him an "excellent choice." But Llewellyn turned the job down. Finally in May the committee, and Baldwin, gave in to White. Baldwin approved the appointment of Houston "with reservation." White noted with satisfaction, "Charlie is the best person for this job." Southerners would "expect a colored man to be interested in his people, and if he is a tactful person like Charlie he can overcome through his knowledge of the South and conditions there whatever difficulties may arise better than can a northern man who is unfamiliar with the southern situation." He also thought that "the choice of a colored man as highly regarded as Charlie would have a most favorable effect on our branches." He proposed, and the NAACP board of directors agreed, that Houston be hired full time, with the NAACP making up the difference between the salary Houston negotiated and the $2,000 that would be provided from the Garland Fund grant.[20]

The approach proposed to the Garland Fund emphasized publicity and equalization suits, whereas the Margold Report emphasized a direct challenge to segregation. This shift reflected the NAACP's attempt to appropriate for the organization the idea of systematic planning to accomplish social change through litigation. The replacement of Margold with Houston reflected the confluence of other organizational concerns. As White's comments make clear, race pride played a part, as did the simple availability of such men as Houston and Hastie. They were extraordinarily talented lawyers, who would have been attractive to any openminded client. Houston's appointment was one of a series of events in the black legal community in the 1930s that both expressed and symbolized the belief within that community that the interests of blacks would best be advanced by blacks. By placing a black man as talented and vigorous as Houston in the position of special counsel, the NAACP strengthened its position in the black community. In this light, the exchanges between Baldwin and White over the appointment can be seen as just another episode in the negotiations between the Garland Fund and the NAACP, with the latter especially sensitive to its own organizational needs.

A shift in personnel was symbolic, and it is perhaps not surprising that Houston soon put his own stamp on the NAACP's litigation. In effect, the Margold Report was replaced by a partial return to the initial approach in which litigation served as a tool for organizing blacks in the South. Houston now built that approach into the NAACP staff, and its successes could be treated, at least for internal purposes, as generated from within the organization. Here again a number of internal organizational needs and opportunities—the availability of black lawyers, concern over the effect on the membership of continued reliance on whites, and Houston's desire to use litigation to organize the community—affected the outcome.

3. The Influence of the Staff

When Houston became a member of the staff, the NAACP had an employee whose primary duty was the conduct of litigation. But Houston was not just another employee, and his view of his role had a major effect on the developing campaign against school segregation. Between 1933 and 1950, the NAACP's legal staff handled three types of school desegregation suits: suits seeking the desegregation of public graduate and professional schools, suits seeking to equalize the salaries of black and white teachers, and suits occasioned by inequalities in the physical facilities at black and white elementary and secondary schools.

In mid-1935 Houston set out the reasons for focusing the litigation effort on education. "Education . . . is a preparation for the competition of life," he wrote. " [A] poor education handicaps an individual in the competition." To the black National Bar Association's convention, Houston was perhaps even more forceful: "Economically inferior education makes [Negroes] less able to stand competition with whites for jobs." Further, inferior education made it difficult for "young Negro men and women [to be] courageous and aggressive in defense of their rights." Houston argued that salary cases were clear and "implicated all the questions of inequality," while graduate and professional cases were essential to the development of "the leadership of the race." He insisted that "discrimination in education is symbolic of all the more drastic discriminations," such as those in politics and employment. Blacks had to eliminate segregation, then fight for mass education to form a coalition with poor whites. But, Houston concluded, the legal program was only one part of a comprehensive and long-term social struggle, which included strikes and picketing. "We cannot depend upon the judges to fight all of our battles like the champions of old nor can the Negroes dump all of their problems in the lawyers' laps and go off to sleep."[1]

34

Three aspects of Houston's general outlook affected his approach to suits against discriminatory practices and deserve special attention: his conception of his personal role in the campaign, his desire to develop an educated leadership class in the black community, and his desire that litigation serve the goals not simply of the black community but of the NAACP as well. In a letter to his father in 1938, in which he discussed affairs at Howard University, Houston described himself as "much more of an outside man than an inside man. . . . I usually break down under too much routine. Certainly for the present, I will grow much faster and be of much more service if I keep free to hit and fight wherever circumstances call for action." Thus, although Houston was responsible for the conduct of what at some points had been thought of as a systematic and coherently organized litigation campaign, he was more comfortable with pinpoint activities, frequently responsive more to the demands of the moment than to those of the plan. It was possible, of course, for Houston to see what he did—the lightning trips to get a lawsuit moving, the intensive review of a large number of suits scattered all over the country—as effective administration. When NAACP branches expressed concern that Houston had left their area in the middle of a trial, he wrote the attorneys who remained: "This is no star performance. I am primarily the administrator of the campaign, and . . . my ideal of administration is to make the movement self-perpetuating. . . . The best administration is self-executing. . . . Our idea should be to impress the opposition and public that what we have is a real program, sweeping up from ground influence and popular demand; that it is a program which is going to go on without regard to personnel; that Negroes not only have a few lawyers but dozens who can push the program through."[2] It turned out that grassroots origins and support for specific lawsuits were conditions for the success of litigation, but even though Houston wanted that kind of support, it inevitably diminished the degree to which a coordinated campaign could be conducted. Houston himself did not find that troublesome, because after each significant point in the campaign had been passed, he could look back and construct something that he could understand and present to others as a strategic plan despite the fact that what had really happened was the accumulation of isolated responses to local demands.

If Houston's ideas about how to administer the campaign affected the general course of litigation, his ideas about black leadership affected one specific element in the campaign. As academic dean at Howard's law school, Houston had converted it into a fully accredited institution. The cost was a drastic reduction in enrollment, but the benefit, Houston thought, was more than adequate, as a better faculty produced new attorneys who, though fewer in number than had come from Howard before, were far more qualified to be lawyers for and leaders in the black community. Although Houston took particular interest in cases involving challenges to segregated law schools, much of the litigation involved other professional and graduate schools, and seems to have been motivated by a desire to develop a "talented tenth" that really was a tenth.[3]

Houston's personal interest in graduate education should not be overemphasized, though it seems to have had some influence on the new attention given to litigation involving that subject. Neither the Garland Fund proposal nor the Margold Report had singled out the graduate and professional levels for special attention; indeed, they had been so concerned with elementary and secondary education that they failed to consider graduate and professional challenges in any detail. Houston desired to improve the condition of blacks in all areas; he actively urged the NAACP to broaden its concern for economic issues during the debates of the 1930s, and he served as counsel to blacks challenging discrimination in the railroad industry and unions.[4] Elements other than Houston's personal interest influenced the emergence of graduate school litigation. Blacks were graduated from colleges each year, and a few of them were sure to be ambitious enough to want the education available in white graduate and professional programs. A survey of black colleges in 1938 found over 35,000 students enrolled. In the academic year 1937–38, almost 4,500 students were graduated from four-year programs at black colleges. Thus, the plaintiffs were more readily available in these cases than in cases involving elementary and secondary education, where becoming a plaintiff meant putting one's job or one's children at substantial risk. Further, the legal theory in graduate cases could be clarified easily. Southern states did not have many graduate and professional programs for blacks, so the problems were not of "separate but equal" but were rather problems of "separate and nonexistent." For example, in 1943 Georgia, Florida, Louisiana, Mississippi, and South Carolina had no professional schools for blacks. Even in a state that gave blacks scholarships for out-of-state graduate education, it was fairly easy to formulate the attack on "separate but equal" by emphasizing the geographical line drawn by the state itself.[5]

Houston exercised great care in screening potential plaintiffs for the university-level challenges. To some extent, the NAACP wanted to support only those candidates whose applications could be denied only if race were the sole consideration; thus it refused to support challenges by non-residents or those by graduates of unaccredited schools.[6] But, because of the obligation imposed by law on many state professional schools to accept all qualified applications, the NAACP's caution had to rest on some complex social judgments. One was the reality that, to whites, a "qualified" black applicant had to be better than a "qualified" white applicant. For example, writing in 1933 Hastie described the desirable plaintiff as a person who would be "of *outstanding* scholarship . . . neat, personable, and unmistakably a Negro." The plaintiff would be "a valuable object lesson which shows the whites in the community that there are negroes . . . who measure up in every respect to collegiate standards."[7] Discriminatory definitions of qualification and concern for appearances, then, supported the NAACP's judgment about the relevant characteristics of litigants whose cases should be brought.

Finally, the consequences of litigation for the NAACP's organizational effort affected the suits seeking to equalize the salaries of white and black teachers. As with all organizations, the NAACP had to select its activities to advance its interests. Those interests were in both the substance of its campaigns and the use of the campaigns to increase membership and other resources. Thus the NAACP's antilynching campaign in the 1920s was conducted with the express aim of not only securing a federal law against lynching, but also attracting new members.[8] Everyone involved in the process thought that equalization litigation could provide incentives to join the NAACP. For example, shortly after he joined the staff in 1937 Thurgood Marshall suggested that a suit to equalize the salaries of black and white teachers in North Carolina could be used to "build up interest in the Association," and the NAACP generally refused to handle such suits unless a joint committee composed of representatives of the local branch of the NAACP and of the teachers was established. The idea was clear enough. As Marshall put it, successful salary suits were "giving a material benefit to Negroes in general," not just teachers, as the increased salaries circulated within the black community to "physicians, dentists, lawyers and other professional and business men." According to Marshall, "this type of case has, perhaps, one of the greatest appeals to a larger N.A.A.C.P. program."[9]

The NAACP's leaders had another reason to conduct activities that would strengthen the organization in the South. By increasing the southern membership, they would be in a better position to defend the organization against internal weaknesses that could be exploited by the

Communist party and its allies. Houston and other NAACP leaders were sensitive to the economic issues urged on the NAACP from the left, and Houston was more willing than White to cooperate with Communists.[10] Nonetheless Houston wanted to maintain the NAACP's role as a strong and independent organization. The organizational environment of the early 1930s shaped Houston's understanding. At that time, the NAACP perceived a serious threat to its leadership in the black community from the Communist party. The focus of the conflict was the Scottsboro case, in which the International Labor Defense, a party-dominated group, seized control from the NAACP of a case that had received wide popular attention. The Scottsboro case involved the prosecution of a number of young black men for rape, and its story has been well told already,[11] but the pervasive impact of the challenge from the left on the NAACP and on Houston in particular bears emphasizing. During the discussions of the NAACP's economic program in 1934, which were described earlier, Roy Wilkins, then assistant secretary, expressed concern that liberals and radicals thought the NAACP weak because it had no economic program, and Houston stated that the organization was "top heavy with white-collar interests and attitudes."[12]

As the Scottsboro example suggests, often the challenges from the left arose from cases involving the defense of accused criminals. Roy Wilkins had urged Arthur Spingarn to relax the NAACP's policies regarding criminal defense, which came close to requiring that the accused be innocent. The desire to protect innocent blacks and to guard against attacks by the Communist party affected the NAACP's response in a number of cases. For example, in late 1931, the NAACP's national office received a letter from the president of the Jackson, Mississippi, branch asking for help for Tom Carraway, whose execution was scheduled for the next day. The national office was drawn into an incredibly complex and uncoordinated series of maneuvers, both legal and political. The local attorneys made repeated requests for money, strongly intimating that it would be used to bribe those who could commute Carraway's sentence. Part of the local strategy was to hire Bidwell Adam, who had recently been the state's lieutenant governor. Walter White subsequently wrote Adam: "The Communists . . . are loudly and vociferously contending throughout the North and in Europe that all southerners are vicious in their attitude towards the Negro. Concrete examples of distinguished citizens who battle for justice for innocent Negroes . . . will do more than any other thing to show the North and the world that all southern white people are not as the Communists claim."[13]

38

The criminal cases show the ways in which the challenge from the left influenced Houston's role in the NAACP, and his sense of what the organization needed to strengthen itself against that challenge. Less celebrated than the Scottsboro case, the cases of Willie Peterson and George Crawford directly affected Houston's understanding of the relation between the NAACP and other more radical groups, and this understanding in turn influenced his decisions in the litigation against segregation.

In August 1931, as the Scottsboro case and its attendant interorganizational struggles were attracting great attention, three young women from prominent Birmingham families were raped. In a struggle for the assailant's gun, the women were severely wounded, and two of them died. The third provided a detailed description of the assailant. Two months later, as she was riding down a street in Birmingham, she pointed out Willie Peterson, whom she saw on the sidewalk, as the assailant. Peterson was moderately retarded, quiet, and well respected as a churchgoer in the black community. He also did not fit the description of the assailant that had been given earlier, and was probably physically incapable of both the assaults and the rapes. However, the victim insisted on her identification, and, after one jury could not reach a verdict, a second jury found Peterson guilty, and he was sentenced to die.[14]

The NAACP had monitored Peterson's case, but it did not become deeply involved until Peterson had been convicted. Walter White's letters reflect a pervasive concern with the competition offered by the ILD, and Houston explicitly drew the parallel to the Scottsboro case in a letter to R. R. Moton, head of the Tuskegee Institute. He characterized the Scottsboro and Peterson cases as an arena of struggle for leadership in the black community, and expressed concern that the ILD would undoubtedly win the Scottsboro case but that Peterson, whose case had been handled by the NAACP, was scheduled to be executed; the ILD, he wrote, was using those facts to show how "legalistic" methods would not work. Houston was sent to investigate the Peterson case, and the NAACP supported an ultimately successful effort to secure clemency for Peterson.[15]

Having been introduced to competition from the left in the Peterson case, Houston drew significant conclusions from his experience in the case of George Crawford. Crawford was indicted by a Virginia grand jury in January 1932 for the murder of a wealthy, socially prominent widow and her housekeeper. He was arrested in Boston a year later. The NAACP's national office usually received information about criminal cases of interest to the black community at a late stage, but the fact that Crawford had to be extradited from Massachusetts to Virginia gave the NAACP the opportunity to get in at the start, and it seized the chance. Walter White at first expressed "considerable doubt" that Crawford was guilty; a month later, he was saying that "the National Office is convinced of Crawford's innocence." White's judgment was based at least in part on a report from Helen Boardman, whom he had sent to investigate the murders. Boardman compiled scattered bits of gossip that suggested that the widow's brother might have been the killer; in addition, Crawford testified that he had been in Boston when the crimes were committed. By March 1933, after the NAACP had been involved for three months, indications of Crawford's guilt had come to White's attention, communicated to him in person by another brother of the widow, a man who clearly impressed White as an honest person.[16]

White was already concerned about the threat from the left. In the same month, Houston wrote White a long letter in which he noted his "hunch that if you skip out of the case, the I.L.D. will take it over," and White himself referred to the "fixed policy of the Communists now to try to horn in on every case the Association enters and try to gain control of it." Even after doubts had been raised about Crawford's innocence, White thought that the case was "of advantage to the Association as the Communists are working night and day trying to convince Negroes that we are a timorous, impotent organization."[17]

The NAACP's first step was to try to keep Crawford in Massachusetts. After appeals to the governor and the state court failed, an action was filed in the federal district court. The theory was ingenious: the indictment was void because Crawford had been indicted by a grand jury that had been selected in an unconstitutional manner by excluding blacks from consideration; any subsequent conviction would necessarily be reversed; therefore, sending Crawford to Virginia to stand trial would violate his constitutional rights. The theory was clever, but it was also rather obviously wrong; the proper remedy for an unconstitutional indictment was to challenge the defendant's conviction in the Virginia state courts and on appeal to the United States Supreme Court. Under the circumstances, the NAACP lawyers were understandably exhilarated when Judge James A. Lowell accepted their theory and granted relief. However, six weeks later, the victory was erased when the court of appeals reversed Judge Lowell's decision.[18]

After the Supreme Court denied the NAACP's application for further review, Crawford faced the prospect of an immediate trial in Virginia. Several weeks were spent in working out arrangements for representing

Crawford at the trial. White wanted Houston to be lead counsel, but thought that he should have a white lawyer associated with him so that, if racial tensions arose in the courtroom, the white lawyer could allay them. Houston insisted on an all-black trial team in order to demonstrate the ability of the black bar. He used his university's reluctance to release him from his continuing academic obligations as a bargaining lever; ultimately Houston prevailed by refusing to compromise and by explaining how important the issue was to black lawyers. The legal team developed a powerful challenge to the grand jury system, which was unsurprisingly rejected by the trial court. By the time the trial began, Houston had become convinced that Crawford was indeed guilty, and his defense consisted of an attack on the state's circumstantial case. He did not produce witnesses, even those who had given sworn affidavits in the Boston proceedings, who had previously supported Crawford's alibi. Houston pleaded for mercy if the jury found Crawford guilty, and the jury in fact gave Crawford a life sentence. Houston's performance was highly praised within the NAACP; he had shown that black lawyers could stand up in southern courts and fight tenaciously and with dignity for black rights. And once again the perceived threat from the Communists came into play. William Pickens, the NAACP's field secretary, wrote, "Take note: N.A.A.C.P. methods, with colored lawyers at that, saved a colored man who was clearly guilty, although the Communists with their methods seem unable to save nine Negroes, with the use of white lawyers who are supposed to have a better break with the courts, and although the nine Negroes are known by all the world to be innocent." [19]

Despite the strength of the grand jury challenge, Houston decided not to appeal the conviction, believing that a life sentence was the best Crawford could hope for; if Crawford were retried, the death sentence was a real possibility. But Houston's involvement in the Crawford case was not over. During the succeeding eighteen months, his handling of the case was challenged in an editorial by W. E. B. Du Bois in the NAACP's magazine and in articles in the *Nation* and the *New Masses*. The critics remained unconvinced of Crawford's guilt and thought that Houston had therefore been unjustified in failing to present Crawford's alibi witnesses. Houston replied that he could not have done so without suborning perjury. The most serious attack came in a pamphlet by Helen Boardman and Martha Gruening, which was distributed at a national meeting of the NAACP. [20] Houston saw this criticism as part of the ILD attack on the NAACP, and drew two related conclusions about the NAACP. First, the attack showed how shaky the existing structure of the NAACP was, for it was too easy for leftists in New York to dominate debate and decision. Second, as he noted to White, "all of this simply emphasizes in my mind once more the necessity for rearranging the structure of the organization so that the southern membership can come to your support." White and Wilkins expressed similar concerns about the NAACP's relative weakness in the South and pointed to the successes of the more radical Southern Tenant Farmers Union.[21]

The conflict Houston perceived with the Communists made him particularly sensitive to the implications of the campaign against segregation for the NAACP as an organization. Liberal intellectuals in the North provided one important reference group for several of the NAACP's leaders. The Communist party had some support in black communities nationwide, and it exercised some influence among liberal intellectuals and made repeated and sometimes successful efforts to control northern metropolitan branches of the NAACP. Houston's experience in the Crawford case confirmed his view that the campaign against segregation and especially its salary equalization component could be used to increase NAACP membership generally and, even more, to increase southern membership that could balance the leftist threat.[22] Houston was also deeply involved in the discussions of the NAACP's economic program, and persistently urged that that program be expanded.[23] Thus he was not seeking to develop a liberal program for the black middle class in the South to substitute for, and counterbalance, pressures for more radical programs. Rather, Houston wanted the NAACP to grow stronger throughout the black community. Litigation was the way to attract some new members; an economic program was the way to attract others.

Houston's conception of the litigation campaign had two substantive components, and each appears to have had different motivations. The problem was to specify how the "separate but equal" doctrine could be undermined. Challenges to segregation at the graduate and professional school levels were relatively easy to litigate and, if successful, would have the additional advantage of increasing the size of groups likely to provide leadership for the black community. Because teachers were the largest professional group in the black community, and because their incomes were more stable than those of other professionals who had to depend on income drawn almost exclusively from black patronage, salary equalization suits would strengthen the NAACP in the South.[24] Further, as we will see, Houston wanted to conduct his first lawsuits in the upper South. If

42

the litigation concentrated on teachers' salaries, Houston could focus on a simple measure of equality, the dollar amounts paid to the teachers. He would not have to be concerned about problems of compensating inequalities, which might have been troublesome, though perhaps not ultimately fatal, in the upper South. Houston may also have shared a common intuition, which did not, however, emerge into explicit consideration until after the litigation campaign was under way, that it would be easier to litigate and win lawsuits in the upper South. Personal relations between black lawyers for plaintiffs and white lawyers for defendants were likely to be less strained there than they would have been in the Deep South.[25] The black lawyers might find at least some places where white resistance would be weak enough to allow favorable settlements to be reached, and where concern among the white public might not be so great as to impede implementation of settlements and judicial decrees. The chance of finding white authorities who agreed in principle that discrimination was wrong was greater in the upper South. Also, Houston's permanent home was in the District of Columbia, and it was simply more convenient to litigate in Virginia or North Carolina than elsewhere.

But the most important part of Houston's conception was its flexibility within the framework set by the NAACP's long-term goals. Houston was reasonably self-conscious about his refusal to stick to a preordained plan; the litigation he conducted would be sensitive to pressures of the moment, to the opportunities provided and those foreclosed by shifting local circumstances. One factor supporting flexibility cannot be overemphasized. The Garland Fund and Margold devised their plans before litigation occurred. Houston actually had to conduct lawsuits, and the press of reality destroyed many possibilities imagined by the planners. The plans had rested on an image of "a lawsuit" as a thing, something like a block of wood, but lawsuits are processes. As we will see, this was most obviously true with what proved to be the fantasy of conducting forty-five, or even seven, coordinated lawsuits. It was hard enough to organize litigation for one lawsuit at a time; simultaneous filings were practically impossible.

As part of the litigation process, communities had to learn that they could not simply bring "a lawsuit," but needed to find proper plaintiffs and forums. The effort to educate the black community was substantial. Houston wrote many articles in *The Crisis,* with such titles as "How to Fight for Better Schools," and "Don't Shout Too Soon," in which he emphasized the need for "determination, persistence, brains and money." In the former he outlined the procedures blacks could use to agitate for better schools. He emphasized the importance of investigating the facts and preparing alternative proposals carefully, and listed voting as the step that followed litigating in attempting to alter discriminatory budgets. Houston's most detailed explanation of the litigation campaign was in an article published in October 1935 titled "Educational Inequalities Must Go!" He wrote: "The National Association for the Advancement of Colored People is launching an active campaign against racial discrimination in public education. The campaign will reach all levels of public education from the nursery school through the university. . . . Where segregation is so firmly entrenched by law that a frontal attack cannot be made, the association will throw its immediate force toward bringing Negro schools up to an absolute equality with white schools. If the white South insists upon its separate schools, it must not squeeze the Negro schools to pay for them." Houston emphasized that "the decision for action rests with the local community itself. . . . [T]he N.A.A.C.P. stands ready with advice and assistance." To Houston, "this campaign . . . is indissolubly linked with all the other major activities of the association." It was linked to the antilynching effort, he wrote, because education went to tragic waste when a black person was lynched; it was linked to the economic program because education improved the job prospects of blacks. Further, "[t]he N.A.A.C.P. recognizes the fact that the discriminations which the Negro suffers in education are merely part of the general pattern of race prejudice in American life, and it knows that no attack on discrimination in education can have any far reaching effect unless it is bound to a general attack on discrimination and segregation in all phases of American life." He concluded, "Fundamentally, the N.A.A.C.P. is not a special pleader; it merely insists that the United States respect its own Constitution and its own laws."[26] Houston thus urged the black community to take a broad view of the litigation campaign, to understand that it was not parochially concerned with teachers and aspirants to professional education, and to support it as part of a general political attack on the caste system of the United States.

Houston's travels and the later ones of Thurgood Marshall led them throughout the black community, where they proselytized and educated in large and small meetings. These educational efforts penetrated through several levels of community activity. It was easiest to work out graduate and professional cases, for the lawyers were dealing with educated and ambitious people as potential plaintiffs. Salary equalization suits were more difficult. The potential plaintiffs were educated but vulnerable to pressure from their employers. Lawsuits designed to equalize the facilities in elementary and secondary education were the hardest to organize. Entire communities of parents had to understand the importance of putting themselves and, even more important, their children on the firing lines. The educational process would necessarily take a long time.

The NAACP's litigation activities thus were shaped by a combination of personal preferences and organizational concerns. Houston simply felt more comfortable as a lawyer attacking targets of opportunity than as a long-range planner of litigation, and the conditions for conducting litigation, such as the need to have willing clients and community support, made it easy to follow that preference. Moreover, competition for the role of leading organization in the black community led Houston to devote much of his attention to cases that would increase the internal strength of the NAACP and thereby enable it to fight for leadership more effectively. These preferences and concerns made an approach broadly similar to Houston's perhaps the only one that could have succeeded in view of the extremely limited resources available to support litigation.

Houston's concerns led him to bring Thurgood Marshall onto the NAACP staff, to fold Marshall's own litigation into the NAACP "campaign," and to use Marshall's successes in Maryland as examples of the NAACP's successes. Marshall was born in Baltimore, in 1908. His father was a dining-car waiter and club steward; his mother had been a teacher before her marriage. Marshall was a tall, strikingly handsome, and gregarious young man. Indeed, his size and enthusiasm had led to a brief expulsion from Lincoln University in Pennsylvania because of the toughness with which he hazed younger students. After graduating from Lincoln, Marshall commuted between Baltimore and Washington while he attended Howard Law School. Immediately after his graduation in 1933 from Howard, where he had been first in his class and one of Houston's protégés, Marshall returned to Baltimore and established a private practice. Depression conditions and Marshall's sympathies made it difficult for him to earn a decent living. Like many ambitious young lawyers, Marshall quickly became involved in community activities as a way of making his name known to potential clients. But Marshall was far more devoted to those activities than most. The Baltimore branch of the NAACP was revitalized through the efforts of Marshall, Carl Murphy, the publisher of the Baltimore *Afro-American,* and Lillie Jackson, a homemaker who was active in community and church affairs. As Marshall's desegregation lawsuits developed, they were used as a focus for organizational activities.[27]

Marshall's devotion to the NAACP and to the struggle for civil rights took its toll on his private practice. In 1935, Houston cautioned him, "I do not advise that you drop everything for N.A.A.C.P. work. Keep a finger on your office practice whatever you do. You can get all the publicity from the N.A.A.C.P. work but you have got to keep your eye out for cashing in." By then, however, Marshall was deeply enmeshed in two major desegregation suits, to be discussed in the next chapter, and when Marshall got into a case he devoted virtually all of his attention to it. As a result, Marshall found himself in an increasingly difficult financial position. In May 1936, he described the tension to Houston: "Personally, I would not give up these cases here in Maryland for anything in the world, but at the same time there is no opportunity to get down to really hustling for business."[28]

Marshall began to look for other ways to earn a living while serving the community. He submitted an application to teach at Howard Law School, but the job he really wanted developed very rapidly in September and October 1936. In mid-September Marshall wrote Houston a plaintive letter saying that "something must be done about money," and suggesting that he receive a retainer of $150 each month for his NAACP work. Houston replied three days later that it made more sense for Marshall to join the NAACP staff in New York because his NAACP work would inevitably conflict with his obligations to private clients: "The very time your clients wanted you you would be out of the office. The time you had a private case on the docket, that day the Association would require your services." In addition, Houston found that he was overworked as the lawyer in charge of the litigation campaign, the general legal counsel to the NAACP, and an "evangelist and stump speaker." He thought the educational activities "necessary in order to back up our legal efforts with the required public support." But it kept him out of the NAACP office, which therefore needed another full-time lawyer. Marshall wrote by return mail that there would be no loss if he left private practice to work exclusively on the interesting NAACP cases.[29]

Houston then informed White of Marshall's financial situation and outlined an arrangement that would allow Marshall to join the staff. He said that "you can generally depend on [Marshall's] judgment, backed up by [Spingarn] until he has seasoned; and you can absolutely depend on his research." White replied that he was "much disturbed about Thurgood's situation, both for his personal sake and because he can contribute so much." He thought that financial arrangements could be made, though there were some risks that the NAACP would not be able to absorb the cost

46

of a second staff attorney. But he asked Houston to draft a letter urging Marshall's appointment to the committee administering what was left of the Garland Fund grant. Within ten days, Houston had done so. The committee already knew what Marshall had been doing, for a year earlier Arthur Spingarn had advised Walter White to defer another request to the fund until after one of Marshall's lawsuits had "show[n] something tangible" as a result of the first installment. Houston noted that Marshall had done the legal and organizational work for the Maryland suits. He bolstered his case with a handwritten note on a bill submitted by the Baltimore branch, which showed that from March to October 1936 Marshall had earned less than $200 for his NAACP work. Houston scrawled, "Not much for a year or half year's work. . . . You've always got to remember that Thurgood's practice had vanished and all he had was his NAACP work. Figure out also the moral effect on the Negro bar in general from rewarding one of our young lawyers who stripped himself for us. May lead others to work harder."[30] In mid-October, arrangements were completed, and Marshall moved to New York.

By placing Marshall on the staff, the NAACP had joined to its "outside man," Houston, an extraordinarily diligent "inside man." Marshall was concerned with the details of each lawsuit in a way that Houston was not, and was even more imbued than Houston with the need to nurture local branches carefully if the NAACP was to capitalize on its litigation for organizational purposes. In addition, the lawyers involved in the litigation found it easier to approach Marshall than Houston. For most of the lawyers, Houston had been their mentor, and he continued to act as a senior adviser to them. He also found it necessary on occasion to step back from the struggle in order to recuperate. He had developed a mild tubercular condition during World War I, and the energy he devoted to his legal work occasionally made the condition flare up and led to his exhaustion. In addition, Houston's marriage had deteriorated around the time he moved to the NAACP offices in New York, but shortly after he remarried in 1937 he returned to Washington. This removed him from the center of the NAACP's staff, and also brought him closer to his father, who persistently chided Houston for neglecting his duties to his family and his law practice for less lucrative activities.[31] All this combined to reduce Houston's involvement in the day-to-day operations of the litigation campaign. His protégé Marshall was easy-going and open, as is perhaps indicated by the host of nicknames—"Nogood," "Turkie," and the like[32]— that his friends used, and he seemed to thrive on throwing himself into the black community. In many ways, indeed, Houston's greatest contribution to the litigation campaign crystallized in the person of Thurgood Marshall: Marshall really believed in a coordinated litigation strategy, and though, as we will see, he was no more successful than Houston in actually implementing it, his dogged persistence and enormous energy in pursuing possibilities as they cropped up allowed the campaign to take shape along pragmatic rather than strategic lines. By the time *Sweatt* v. *Painter* was litigated in the late 1940s, it was possible to look back on a decade of litigation and piece together a path on which each next step was both clear and achievable.

4. Thurgood Marshall and the Maryland Connection

The NAACP's early desegregation cases displayed all the variations on the tactical choices that Houston and Marshall had to make. Their first decisions had to be about remedy—to seek mandamus or injunctive relief—and about forum—to go into state or federal court. Those decisions were made in light of both legal analysis and staff needs.

Initially, the choice between mandamus and injunction was framed along two dimensions. Mandamus was thought to be more appropriate for individual relief, injunctions more appropriate for class relief; mandamus was thought to be more appropriate for relief that would direct officials to take certain positive actions, injunctions more appropriate for directives to refrain from other action. This analysis led the lawyers to favor mandamus in the graduate and professional cases, where they were trying to force university officials to admit individual applicants to their schools, and injunctions in the salary cases, where they sought to force officials to refrain from paying discriminatory salaries to the entire black teaching staff in a district.

Analysis fails to reveal substantial differences in the forms of relief. In a graduate case, for example, the NAACP was not simply seeking to get one applicant admitted, and lawyers of course relied on the precedential effect, within the covered jurisdiction, of a successful mandamus action to create benefits for all potential black applicants. Thus, mandamus could have a classwide effect. In addition, the distinction between affirmative and prohibitory relief is untenable. The NAACP was contending that the school officials had a duty under the Constitution to treat black and white alike. That duty could be enforced by directing the officials to give the blacks what whites had, or by directing them to refrain from taking race into account when making their decisions. The former looks like mandamus, the latter like an injunction. But, partly as a result of the NAACP's success, we now know that affirmative injunctive relief is possible.[1]

The lawyers' choice of the remedy they should seek was therefore not as important to the litigation program as it migh have seemed. Yet, as litigators, the lawyers had to be concerned about the possibility that judges hostile to their claims would use ambiguities about procedure to derail the lawsuits. Thus, detached legal analysis was less important than the development of cases in ways that forced judges to decide them on the merits. The lawyers had some useful tactical flexibility, because they could reach their goals by a number of routes.

Still, some remedy had to be sought in each case, and the decision about remedy was closely linked to choice of forum. There were good organizational reasons for the forum choices that the lawyers made. Mandamus was a relatively unusual type of relief, hedged around in many states with curious procedural prerequisites. The substantive conditions under which mandamus was available were probably not very different from those under which as a practical matter injunctions were available. But injunctions had long been the primary remedy over a wide range of controversies outside the field of civil rights, and procedures for seeking injunctions were relatively easy to master. In addition, as a distinct remedy, mandamus was essentially available only in state court because the remedy was designed to require state officials to do their duty. Because those duties had to be defined primarily by state law, federal courts would be reluctant to use mandamus to direct officials to take actions that state law did not authorize them to take.

Such considerations made mandamus a more difficult remedy from the point of view of litigators on the NAACP's national staff. If the NAACP staff lawyers sought mandamus, they would be litigating in state courts, and would have to learn each state's special procedures for that remedy. If the staff could coordinate the lawsuit by using reliable local counsel, the problems were manageable. But as the lawsuits became more complex, coordination became difficult. Those considerations effectively ruled out mandamus in the salary cases, where there had to be detailed investigations over which the staff needed significant control. In contrast, the preliminaries to a graduate case were rather cut and dried, and the procedural details might be more easily left to the local lawyers. As Houston put it in a slight overstatement, "all the court work, travel, propaganda have been handled by staff counsel—local counsel have been used in court fights chiefly to take care of local peculiarities of court procedure."[2]

Thus, organizational considerations supported the choice of injunctive relief in the salary cases, but did not affect the choice of mandamus in the graduate cases.

When injunctions were sought, the NAACP could use either state or federal courts. Organizational factors similar to those just discussed made federal courts more attractive. Especially after the Federal Rules of Civil Procedure were adopted in 1938, the staff lawyers in the national office knew what procedures would be used in the federal courts in any state where they decided to litigate. If they sued in state courts, they would have to familiarize themselves with the procedural rules in each state, which might vary considerably, and then rely even more on local counsel. One factor that appears to have played no role in the choice of forum, and ought not have, was an assessment that the state or federal judges in a jurisdiction might be more favorable to the interests of blacks than those of the other forum. The fact that until the late 1940s the graduate cases were generally conducted in state courts at the same time that the salary cases were litigated in the federal courts located in the same state shows that such assessments did not matter to the NAACP lawyers, though they apparently did not discuss the issue in detail. The reasons are clear: federal judges and, at least, state appellate judges were similar sorts of people, drawn from the same segments of the white bar and white society. Thus there could be no systematic advantage, but only random variation, in choosing one forum over the other.[3]

I have said that organizational factors supported seeking injunctive relief in federal courts in the salary cases. One additional element must be added to fill out the picture and explain why the graduate cases tended to be mandamus actions in state courts. Simply put, Marshall won the first graduate case in a state mandamus action, and he won the first salary cases in federal injunctive actions. The type of relief and the forum may in fact have been irrelevant to those successes, but it was psychologically attractive to stay with procedures that had worked before. Other procedures might have worked just as well, but Marshall knew that the ones he had used had in fact produced the results he sought.

The fact that choices of remedy and forum were more strongly influenced by internal organizational requirements than by elements in a coherent legal strategy actually raises some questions about the very existence of a strategy. Because the NAACP staff remained under the influence of the Margold Report's idea that a systematic campaign was needed, they tended to justify litigation choices in terms of broad legal strategic concepts. Yet at least the legal components would have justified any choice they made. It seems likely that the staff had in mind little more than the general approach of attacking segregation whenever they could: any positive outcome was seen as a victory, whether or not strategic analysis suggested that the particular result would have a domino effect or make any other contribution to the accomplishment of the long-term goal.

The Maryland cases were the NAACP's first successes, but some instructive failures preceded and followed them. The failures show how the lawyers' litigation choices in the Maryland cases make sense in light of concerns about the effective use of the NAACP staff, and provide a background against which to identify the features that made the Maryland cases more likely to succeed.

In early 1933, two North Carolina lawyers, Conrad Pearson and Cecil McCoy, informed Walter White that they were about to file a challenge to the state university's failure to admit black applicants. After graduating from Howard Law School in 1932, when he was thirty years old, Pearson had begun practicing law in Durham. He was thus one of the first products of the revitalized Howard Law School under Houston, who regarded the increasing presence of talented black lawyers throughout the South as one of his primary accomplishments. In March, Pearson and McCoy filed a state court mandamus action on behalf of Thomas Hocutt, an applicant for admission to the state university's school of pharmacy. Hocutt had a B average as an undergraduate and, according to Pearson and McCoy, had "a hue closely approaching ebony." Houston suggested to White that William Hastie, Houston's colleague at Howard Law School, be sent to North Carolina to oversee the litigation. Hastie discovered a great deal of dissension within the black community over Hocutt's suit: the state's leading black educator opposed it because agitation on the issue threatened legislative support for black schools, and the local NAACP branch voted not to support the lawsuit. McCoy wrote White, "Those upon whom we had counted for our staunchest moral support have been found leading the attack against us and a few loyal supporters." McCoy attributed "this dissension" to "the pressure of few white politicians upon our so-called Negro leaders." Although he and Pearson found themselves "almost alone after being promised the unqualified support of almost every influential man of color in our city," they were encouraged by "the sympathy of the Negro in the street, as well as many other Negroes and well-thinking white people," and by their success in reorganizing the local branch. Unfortunately, they found the branch "already in control of a group of spineless persons who have disappointed us by scuttling to cover at the first stage of the action."[4]

Applicants to the university had to submit recommendations and a complete transcript from their undergraduate schools. Because of the opposition of James Shepard, the president of the North Carolina College for Negroes, Hocutt could not provide that material.[5] Hocutt also turned out to be not an ideal candidate; his high school grades were not very good, and, despite his college record, he appeared to be marginally literate when he took the stand in his lawsuit. But these obstacles had no obvious bearing on the state court's decision. The trial judge denied the relief requested. The complaint had sought an order directing that Hocutt be admitted. The judge held that, because mandamus was available only where the officials who were defendants were under a legal duty to take the requested action, and because the officials had discretion to admit applicants, the only form of mandamus that was proper would have been an order that Hocutt's application be considered without regard to his race. Because the complaint did not request that precise relief, the suit was dismissed. No appeal was taken, perhaps because Hocutt's record was so unattractive that the prospects of success either on appeal or on retrial were slim, and Pearson became "bitter" about the fact that the NAACP "ran out" on the case.[6] *Hocutt* demonstrated the importance of central control over litigation, and the difficulty of obtaining such control where the staff was geographically far away from the state and where litigation could be aborted by what state judges could treat as technical errors of various sorts. As we will see, it also shows the correlation between local support and legal success, a correlation whose explanation is an important part of the story.

Similar problems of coordination arose later in graduate cases in Tennessee. There the national staff could not control enthusiastic local attorneys, with the result that the NAACP lost every graduate school lawsuit that it handled. The national office first learned of the possibility of a Tennessee suit in August 1935, when J. Reuben Sheeler, a high school teacher in Athens, Tennessee, wrote Houston that he had brought his desire to go to law school to the attention of Carl Cowan, a black lawyer, the year before. Cowan, a graduate of Harvard Law School, was then thirty-three years old and had been in practice in Knoxville for four years. Houston immediately asked if Sheeler was still interested in a legal career, and when Sheeler asked for advice about choosing between law and teaching,

Houston wrote back: "[T]here is an unlimited field in the law for young Negroes who are willing to make the fight. The lawyer is going to be the leader of the next step in racial advancement." But Sheeler eventually backed out because he did not want to lose his teaching position.[7]

Meanwhile, however, William Redmond of Franklin, Tennessee, had taken the initiative in applying to the state's pharmacy school. Houston's plans required that applicants pursue their remedies within the university system, and Redmond began the process by appealing to the university's president and board of trustees. Because the available spaces in the entering class were being eliminated as white applicants were admitted while the board of trustees held Redmond's appeal without acting on it, a state mandamus action was filed in late April 1936. During the trial in June, the state's lawyers tried to intimidate Redmond and to show that the suit was devised by the NAACP. No decision was rendered immediately, and Redmond enrolled in Fisk University, where his work was an academic disaster. By the end of 1936, Walter White regarded the situation as "both tragic and dangerous," because the NAACP had invested a great deal in Redmond's case and because it was hard to find "the combination . . . of competence and courage" needed for a successful fight. When the trial judge ruled against Redmond in April 1937, on the ground that the action had been filed prematurely—that is, before the trustees had reviewed Redmond's appeal—Houston decided that further litigation should be avoided. Although the NAACP usually opposed legislation providing out-of-state scholarships for black students, Houston encouraged the local lawyers to support a pending scholarship bill and to use that bill as a lever in negotiating with the state over an appeal. When the bill was enacted, Redmond's case was not appealed.[8]

Roy Wilkins had identified the problem of defining the NAACP's policy when Redmond's academic difficulties became public. He wrote the editor of the *Memphis World,* a black newspaper: "We are trying to be careful . . . in the publishing not to say that these suits are planned and instituted by the Association. As a matter of fact they are not. We simply stand ready to assist any eligible candidate who exhausts the ordinary means of entering these schools in the event he wishes to go forward with a Court fight."[9] But the reactive posture meant that Houston might be saddled with litigants whom he thought were unqualified and whose prospects for success in court were not great, and that the NAACP staff had less control than they needed in shaping the litigation. For example, Houston surely would have tried to allay Redmond's impatience and to delay filing until the trustees acted; as it was, the failure to do so was fatal.

The second round of Tennessee cases, begun in mid-1939, illustrates another difficulty. Carl Cowan found several qualified applicants, whom Houston insisted must be seen and evaluated by Leon A. Ransom, Houston's close associate. Ransom, a native of Ohio, had received his law degree in 1927 from Ohio State University, where he was first in his class. After working with Houston at Howard, he practiced law for most of his career in Columbus, Ohio, where he was active in the affairs of the Republican party. Houston also wanted to keep Z. Alexander Looby informed about the cases. Looby, who was born in the British West Indies in 1899, was a graduate of Columbia University Law School. He had moved to Nashville in 1926, and had been a member of the NAACP's Legal Committee since 1932. According to Houston, Cowan and Looby were the only black lawyers in Tennessee whom the NAACP could use. An immediate problem arose over a purely legal question. Cowan, Looby, and Ransom disagreed over a question of state law regarding who should be sued and served as defendant: was the University of Tennessee, a corporate entity, the appropriate defendant, to be served through its agent, or must the members of the board of trustees be served individually? Lacking expertise in Tennessee law, the national office could not resolve the dispute. The wrong decision was made, and the mandamus action, filed in November 1939, was dismissed in June 1940. When the action was filed again, with the proper service, it lay dormant for one year, during which the state developed graduate programs at its black colleges. The case was then dismissed and, after the dismissal was affirmed by the state appellate court, the NAACP abandoned the case.[10]

The failures in North Carolina and Tennessee show the importance of national control and of knowledge of local law. Conflicts among the lawyers could have been managed more easily if all the lawyers had been members of the national staff. Perhaps more important, variations in procedures could trip up even well-thought-out cases. The initial cases in Maryland worked their way around these problems precisely because Marshall was a native of Maryland and also a member of the national staff as associate counsel after 1936. Maryland was therefore an extraordinarily favorable site for the first successful lawsuits, both because it was Marshall's home ground and, as we will see, because the black community was well organized in support of the litigation. Those facts were, not surprisingly, related to each other. In addition, the political climate in Maryland, where blacks were not completely denied access to those holding power, reduced the degree of white resistance, though important pockets of strenuous opposition were discovered as the litigation developed.

Throughout 1934, blacks in Maryland had been pressing toward a graduate school challenge. A number of applicants seemed ready to sue, and in December the perfect plaintiff appeared. His suitability was clear especially in comparison with the *Hocutt* case. Donald Murray was a member of a prominent Baltimore family and had graduated from Amherst. By the end of March 1935, Murray had pursued his application to law school through an appeal to the state university board of regents, and the mandamus action was filed in state court in April. Early in the litigation, the *Baltimore Evening Sun* commented that the case "may cost the State a lot of money before the thing is over." Marshall handled the preparations for trial, while Houston examined the witnesses at the trial. The trial went smoothly, and relief was granted in late June.[11]

Murray was scheduled to enroll in the University of Maryland Law School in the fall, but two problems arose. The state sought to advance its appeal so that the case could be decided before Murray's registration; the court of appeals refused the request. More seriously, Murray found himself in financial difficulty; Houston and Marshall arranged for loans to be made by Carl Murphy, publisher of the *Baltimore Afro-American*, and by a black fraternity so that Murray could enroll. Marshall consulted closely with Houston in preparing their appellate brief; Marshall wanted time to abstract every relevant case "so that we may have a brief which may be used in all subsequent cases," and Houston wrote a detailed critique of the brief Marshall prepared. Houston called Marshall the "real counsel" in the case, and said that he himself had only "giv[en] it, perhaps, the weight of greater experience." But Houston was then acting on Marshall's behalf, thinking that to give recognition to Marshall would encourage other young blacks to engage in service to their communities. It seems fair to regard *Murray* as a collaboration in which Marshall had perhaps slightly more of an eye on precedent building and a litigation campaign.[12]

In January 1936 the Maryland Court of Appeals affirmed the decision ordering that Murray be admitted to the law school. The first part of the opinion dismissed the law school's claim that because it relied largely on tuition, it was a private agency not subject to constitutional commands. The opinion examined the background of the school, which had been a private institution until 1920. In that year it was consolidated with a state

college of agriculture, which the state had taken over in 1914 by foreclos-
ing the mortgage it held. The court said that the law school was clearly
a public agency. It then addressed the argument that by providing a
scholarship for out-of-state study, the state did all that the Constitution
required of it. The scholarship system provided $200 to defray tuition
costs of not more than fifty students. Of the 113 applicants for scholarships, only one had sought a scholarship for legal study. Further, the
court noted, the scholarship, if Murray received it, would cover tuition at
Howard University Law School. But Murray, a resident of Baltimore,
would have to commute to Washington or resettle there. Either course
would involve "considerable expense," according to the court. "This
rather slender chance for any one applicant at an opportunity to attend
an outside law school, at increased expense, falls short of providing for
students of the colored race facilities substantially equal to those furnished to the whites in the law school maintained in Baltimore."

But the court had a deeper objection to the scholarship system. "The
requirement of equal treatment would seem to be clearly enough one of
equal treatment in respect to any one facility or opportunity furnished to
citizens, rather than of a balance in state bounty to be struck from the
expenditures and provisions for each race generally. We take it to be clear,
for instance, that a state could not be rendered free to maintain a law
school exclusively for whites by maintaining at equal cost a school of
technology for colored students." Pursuing that line of analysis would inevitably raise questions about the "separate but equal" doctrine itself, for
if a technology school was not a "facility or opportunity" equal to a law
school, perhaps a segregated law school was not an equal "facility or opportunity" either. Not surprisingly, the court ended its opinion simply by
noting that its analysis gave the state a choice between opening a new law
school for blacks or admitting Murray to the existing school. Because
Murray was entitled to immediate relief, he had to be admitted. Of
course, the opinion left open the possibility that in the future, if a law
school for blacks was created, the university's law school could be re-
segregated. However, that was not a realistic possibility given the state of
race relations in Maryland.[13]

After Murray entered law school, the state legislature substantially expanded the out-of-state scholarship program, apparently believing that
the state courts would eventually disregard the deeper objections they
had raised to the program. The state attorney general ruled that Murray
remained entitled to attend the state law school because the expanded

program applied only to new applicants for admission. While Murray was in law school, he received encouragement and assistance from the NAACP. Just before he registered, Walter White wrote him: "Work hard; make the most brilliant record of which you are capable; conduct yourself with dignity and naturalness. By your very manner you will create, if you wish to do so, a new concept of the Negro in the minds of your fellow students and professors." When Murray was uncertain about his upcoming examinations, Ransom coached him. When a survey of Maryland law students disclosed an unexpected amount of hostility, White asked Carl Murphy to refrain from publishing a story about the survey.[14] Those facts, as well as the essentially trouble-free course of the litigation, illustrate the close connection between support from both the locality and the national office and successful litigation. The connection was made through the person of Marshall.

The same connection characterized the successful efforts from 1936 to 1940 to equalize the salaries of black and white teachers in Maryland. As in the university case, success in Maryland was preceded by failure in North Carolina. As early as 1933, Cecil McCoy told Walter White that teachers in North Carolina would be interested in equalization. His colleague Conrad Pearson similarly thought there was a "great deal of interest." But both noted difficulties: McCoy wrote that "petty local politics . . . [had] embittered . . . the Hocutt [university] case," and Pearson thought that the national office should become involved in order to galvanize local activity that had previously started and then failed. White was interested enough, and concerned enough about the potentially disruptive role of the International Labor Defense, to set William Hastie to work on a North Carolina lawsuit. The state provided the occasion when, as an economy measure during the Depression, it cut teachers' salaries by 32 percent, with a disproportionate cut for black teachers. Hastie found some local support for an equalization challenge, but also had difficulty in locating potential plaintiffs. The state association of black teachers was in accommodationist hands; its president J. N. Seabrook, for example, was the head of a segregated state college. The association was seriously divided, with the leadership opposing the intervention of an "outside" group such as the NAACP. Though the NAACP naturally thought that it had a role in the teachers' fights, and though North Carolina seemed to present a good place to fight because of opposition by white teachers to the salary cuts, the fact of the divided local community meant that here as in *Hocutt* the salary challenge fizzled out.[15]

Marshall had some additional advantages in Maryland that had gone unnoticed in the development of plans. In general, Maryland school boards were not that deeply committed to maintaining unequal salaries. Indeed, at an early point, Marshall and the board in Calvert County agreed not to publicize their negotiations unless a lawsuit became necessary.[16] In a significant number of counties, equalization occurred rather quickly through settlements after a lawsuit was filed and a pro forma defense had been rejected at the initial stages. Perhaps more important from the NAACP's point of view, Maryland had a strong teacher tenure statute. If the NAACP could find a plaintiff who had taught for three years, it could assure the litigant that filing the lawsuit would not lead to discharge.[17] These characteristics arose in large measure from the nature of racial politics in Maryland. Blacks had migrated from rural areas to the cities, where they were able to exercise some concentrated political power. Though voting districts were gerrymandered to minimize the numbers of black elected officials, blacks had some impact on statewide politics. The *Baltimore Afro-American* claimed that the black vote had been essential to the victory of Republican governor Harry Nice in 1934, and indeed Nice was said to have been "more willing to break the color line in appointments."[18]

Despite these advantages, the litigation did not proceed without complication. Marshall began his efforts in October 1936. He felt out Judge Morris Soper of the federal district court about the prospects of a federal challenge. Soper, a liberal judge sympathetic to the interests of blacks, urged him to use the state courts because Soper was the head of a state commission on black higher education and might have to disqualify himself if the case came to federal court. Over the next month, Marshall was pressed by Carl Murphy and Enolia Pettigen of the state's association of black teachers to get a lawsuit started. The teachers' association had been lobbying for legislative action to equalize salaries, but was discouraged at the repeated failures it had suffered. Marshall wanted the association to present him with a plaintiff, so that "we will not be guilty of stirring up litigation." But the association found it impossible to do so, apparently because of an informer within its ranks.[19]

However, in late October, William Gibbs, the principal in a four-room school in Montgomery County, wrote Marshall directly to volunteer as a plaintiff. Marshall developed a trust agreement, which he thought was probably unenforceable, in which a joint committee of the NAACP and the teachers' association arranged to indemnify any plaintiff who was fired, with funds to be raised by the teachers' association. Once the committee was established and Gibbs was available, the lawsuit took shape. The procedure involved a petition by Gibbs to the county board and an appeal to the state board. The state superintendent of education had agreed to immediate disposition of the appeal, which Marshall hoped would allow him to file the lawsuit just after the legislature convened. He expected that the suit would encourage the state board to place pressure on the legislature.[20]

A state mandamus action was filed on December 31, 1936. Marshall found the attorneys for the board quite courteous; one wrote him that he had received "a favorable impression of [Houston's] personal character and professional ability." The case seemed to drag on, although later experience would show that it actually moved along rather quickly. The delays allowed Marshall to push Gibbs into organizing a branch of the NAACP and to get the Baltimore branch to write legislators in support of equalization. But, particularly in light of the degree of militancy among the teachers who wanted salaries equalized quickly, the delays forced Marshall to pacify that constituency, and he eventually wrote the judge to urge an early hearing on the board's motion to dismiss the action. The NAACP had little to fear from that motion, and indeed very little research on possible problems was done. The only issue discussed within the NAACP seems to have been whether salary differentials could be justified by differences in the cost of living for black and white teachers. In this the lawyers were surely influenced by the NAACP's successful efforts to combat attempts to place cost-of-living differentials in the codes of industrial organization under the National Industrial Recovery Act.[21] The hearing was held on June 9, and less than two weeks later, the NAACP's position prevailed. The board's attorney immediately wrote Marshall, explaining that personnel changes on the board made a quick settlement possible. Indeed, the case was settled on July 30, 1937, with an agreement to equalize salaries over a two-year period; the plaintiffs accepted the delay in receiving full relief because they realized that the board could not immediately secure the necessary money, which would have to be raised by a bond issue. In August, Walter White received a letter containing a pledge that members of the association of black teachers in Montgomery County would take out five-dollar memberships to encourage the NAACP's work.[22]

By 1938 equalization efforts were occurring all over the state. For example, Elizabeth Brown, a teacher in Calvert County, wrote Marshall on August 31, 1937, that the head of the black teachers' association had advised her to send her record to him. Within four months of this initial contact, a settlement agreement was signed. Petitions were filed in January and February 1938 in five more counties, and a press release on April 1 announced twenty coordinated filings. The state organization of county superintendents of schools recommended that salaries be equalized, and settlements were reached in at least three counties by May 1938. Governor Harry Nice and the platform of the state Democratic party supported equalization. Governor Nice stated: "There can be no possible question but that this discriminatory legislation is totally unconstitutional." He urged the legislature to repeal the discriminatory laws, and had a budget prepared that would increase state assistance so that counties could equalize salaries. Governor Nice expressed concern that a judicial decision holding the statutes unconstitutional would require "immediate and mandatory equalization," which in the absence of state aid would require reducing the pay of white teachers. This, he said, "is a result not desired by the colored teachers, and certainly would be deeply resented by the white teachers." Marshall had indeed avoided "stir[ring] up litigation," and "the initiative [came] from the local [black] state teachers associations."[23]

Yet although the equalization efforts substantially improved the financial position of many black teachers, they were not entirely successful when seen as part of a litigation campaign. In a sense, the victories were too easy, for Marshall did not get a judicial opinion that had significant precedential value.

Cases in Prince Georges and Anne Arundel counties promised greater precedential impact, for there the school boards fought hard on all fronts and were determined to obtain a court decision rather than a settlement. In Prince Georges, in fact, the school board fought so hard that it delayed the lawsuit for two years, by which time Marshall had won the case he had later filed against Anne Arundel County. The Prince Georges case started smoothly enough. In January 1938, every black teacher in the county signed an equalization petition, and three of them agreed to be plaintiffs. In February, Marshall reassured the teachers and kept them committed to the case after rumors of a three-year equalization plan circulated; the state mandamus action was filed in March. Then things began to fall apart. The board forced Marshall to sue for access to its records, and asserted that it did not have a salary schedule at all, a claim that could be answered only by inspecting the records. In June, Houston told White that "the forces of repression are beginning to strike back in the effort to intimidate the teachers through economic coercion." The contracts of probationary teachers were not renewed, and elsewhere the dismissal of William Gibbs, although for reasons that Marshall agreed were not retaliatory, made the teachers' situation seem less secure. A "stooge" among the black teachers seemed to be manipulating the group for personal ends, and "the teachers [were] much disturbed, anxious, and in a state of apparent unrest and fright."[24]

Although Marshall had thought in June that a two-year equalization plan would not be accepted by the board, by October negotiations were in progress, with a two-year plan as the key. Marshall informed Enolia Pettigen: "I have done all I possibly can to keep the teachers in line, to prevent them from accepting a compromise which will endanger the entire fight." He resented the school board's use of politicians rather than lawyers to make settlement offers, particularly because the teachers weakened from time to time and would sometimes be ready to accept a settlement that would reduce the existing salary differential by 50 percent but would not lead to full equalization. Again, however, the teachers managed to hold firm, and nothing whatever happened in the pending lawsuit for the next year. In January 1940, Marshall sent the school board the court's opinion in the Anne Arundel case, and the board immediately voted to equalize salaries as of September 1, 1940. The lawsuit was over, but the teachers' problems were not: in May, the superintendent of schools reclassified all but eleven black teachers, effectively denying them the raises they had expected.[25]

Unlike the Prince Georges case, the case in Anne Arundel County was simple and resulted in an important published opinion that did indeed advance the equalization campaign. After a petition was filed, settlement negotiations broke down in June 1938. Marshall now tried a new legal theory. Because some money for teachers' salaries came from the state, it might have been possible to secure statewide relief to replace the time-consuming county-by-county lawsuits, if the state board of education and other state officials could somehow be compelled by an injunction to distribute the state funds in a manner that would equalize salaries. Marshall therefore decided to sue the state officials in federal court.[26]

In March 1939, this lawsuit failed. Judge W. Calvin Chesnut held that salary determinations were made exclusively by the local boards, and that state funds were used only to achieve educational minima; the state officials thus were not responsible for, and could not be directed to remedy, the existing differentials. After describing the statutory scheme for state payments to local school boards, Judge Chesnut continued, "If therefore the state laws prescribed that colored teachers of equal qualifications with white teachers should receive less compensation on account of their color, such a law would clearly be unconstitutional." The same would be true under the principle of *Yick Wo* v. *Hopkins,* if the statutes were applied in a discriminatory manner. Though Mills, the plaintiff, might have stated a valid claim against the county school board, which was responsible for discriminatory administration, he had sued state officials. If he succeeded and obtained an injunction against the unlawful distribution of state funds, the judge said, "the only definite effect . . . would be to tie up the [state fund] and prevent its distribution to the Counties who are the beneficiaries of the fund." If that happened, Mills would suffer, rather than benefit, because the funds available to pay his salary would be reduced. Further, some of the counties that received state aid had already equalized teacher salaries. "To withhold the [fund] from all alike would be to punish the innocent along with the guilty. From every point of view it is evident that the problem is local and not statewide, and that the remedy of the plaintiff and others of his class is properly against their respective County Boards." Judge Chesnut concluded by demonstrating his understanding that the NAACP did indeed desire a statewide solution to the problem of discrimination: "From a realistic point of view it may be that the embarrassment to the Counties by withholding the Equalization Fund would result in political pressure on the legislature . . . to increase the amount of the Fund sufficiently to enable the Counties, without cost to themselves, to equalize salaries; but this is a political consideration which the court is not at liberty to entertain."[27]

Judge Chesnut made it clear that he would be sympathetic to a suit against the Anne Arundel County board, and that suit was begun. Marshall relied on Benjamin Kaplan, a recent graduate of the Columbia Law School and an associate at Morris Ernst's law firm, for advice about some apparently complex issues that the county raised under the new Federal Rules of Civil Procedure, and once again spent time persuading the teachers to reject unfavorable settlements. Judge Chesnut ruled in favor of the teachers on November 22, 1939, holding that the salary disparities were not in fact justified by differences in the levels of achievement of black and white teachers but rested on racial discrimination alone. Judge Chesnut noted that the average salaries of white teachers in the state as a whole had in the recent past been almost twice those of black teachers, and that the disparity, though decreasing, persisted. In Anne Arundel

County, white and black teachers of equivalent qualifications and experience received $1,250 and $700 respectively. Mills, a principal, received $742 less per year than three white principals. Indeed, Judge Chesnut dismissed the school board's claim that the whites headed larger schools and had more complex administrative duties by pointing out that Mills received $492 less than the board's minimum salary for white principals. He found the board's justifications for the salary differences "really unsubstantial," and concluded that the differences were based on race alone. Although Judge Chesnut expressed concern about the burdens equalization would place on the county, and praised county officials for their efforts to reduce salary disparities, he said, "these financial considerations cannot control the supreme law of the land."[28]

More maneuvers were needed to secure the fruits of this decision. Because Marshall also acknowledged the board's financial problems, he agreed to have the effective date of the injunction postponed until the next budget was prepared. The board then proposed to delay equalization until September 1941, and the judge seemed sympathetic. Kaplan urged Marshall to insist on immediate equalization. That might provoke the school board into appealing Judge Chesnut's decision, and the fact that the NAACP had won in the trial court meant that the prospect of winning in the court of appeals, and securing a statewide precedent, was good. The teachers voted to accept equalization as of the next school year, beginning in September 1940, but, recognizing problems the board might have in raising money, they proposed to accept retroactive payments in January 1941. The board initially resisted the idea of retroactive pay, but the teachers, with their bargaining position enhanced by the trial court's decision, insisted and prevailed.[29]

In one sense, the Anne Arundel decision was the precedent the NAACP needed. It meant that, in relatively favorable environments like Maryland, if the NAACP had the resources to develop a factual record showing significant disparities in pay that were explicable only on the basis of race, its lawsuits could succeed. A comment in the *Harvard Law Review* suggested that school boards might soon put forward the defense that the salary differentials resulted not from considerations of race but from market factors: the salaries were "the market value for the services . . . bought, and . . . negro teachers of equal capabilities could be obtained at a lower salary." But this, the author said, was "quite unrealistic in view of the well-known counterdiscrepancies in the other facilities which constitute an educational system." Further, the market discrepancy resulted from private discrimination based on race, which the state could not adopt. In suggesting that subtler defenses might be met by looking beyond salaries to "counterdiscrepancies," however, the author failed to appreciate Houston's successful effort to keep his theory of the cases simple. Anything more would have placed strong pressure on the NAACP's capacity to conduct litigation. Fortunately, in Maryland the NAACP's resources were not stretched to the limit: in April 1941 the state legislature mandated equalization.[30] But the resources were strained even in the relatively receptive climate of Maryland, where some school boards were not adamantly opposed in principle to the NAACP's goals. In particular, Marshall spent large amounts of time in Maryland. Other states did not have the advantage of being Marshall's family home. Especially after he joined the staff in New York, he found it difficult to stay as close to the ground as he had been in Maryland. That reduced his ability, notwithstanding his tremendous talent at the job, to show the teachers that their interests coincided with those of the NAACP.

Marshall's third desegregation case in Maryland began in 1935. Baltimore County surrounds the city of Baltimore. The county's dual system had no black high schools. Black students from the county who wanted a high school education were allowed to attend the black high school in the city. The city charged tuition to non-residents, but if a black student from the county passed an entrance examination, the county would pay the tuition through the eleventh grade. However, only about one-third passed the examination. In the summer of 1935, Carl Murphy gave Marshall the names of black county students who might be plaintiffs in a suit challenging this system, and Marshall had them apply to the city school. Houston advised Marshall to develop two suits, one directed at the city to force admission to the black school there and one directed at the county to force integration of the white schools. In terms reminiscent of the Margold Report, Houston said that such a course would be "in substance leaving it up to the county whether it will admit Negro children to the white school or provide separate but equal high school facilities for the Negro child." By not specifying the remedy desired, Houston argued, the suits could minimize the adverse impact within the black and white communities of actions that appeared to be designed only to integrate existing white schools: blacks wishing to strengthen black schools and whites wishing to avoid integration could rely on the suit directed at the city to allay their fears. The NAACP's activities in the Baltimore County case had two immediate consequences: the county agreed to pay the tuition for black twelfth-graders in the city schools, reversing the prior policy, and a Baltimore County branch of the NAACP was organized and solicited memberships at meetings devoted to the case.[31]

Because Marshall regarded the case as one in which "we can experiment, try out the different remedies and discover which is the best to be used in subsequent cases in other States," he conducted an extremely detailed investigation of the facts. For example, he knew that black county students failed the entrance examination at a high rate. One of his plaintiffs received a grade of 244 on her second try, when 250 was the minimum grade. Perhaps anticipating a defense that such applicants were unqualified, Marshall developed a powerful case that, if black students were unqualified, the fault lay in the unequal facilities in the county's black elementary schools. In one sense, these investigations were unnecessary, and they may perhaps have led Marshall, who consulted closely with Houston, down the wrong path. The basic argument should have been quite simple: black seventh-graders in the county schools had to pass an entrance examination to get a high school education, and white seventh-graders did not. There were supporting details: white seventh-graders took practice examinations and received scholastic coaching before their final examination that would determine whether they could graduate, whereas black students took only the final examinations. But the basic disparity was simplicity itself. Unfortunately, the trial judge did not see the case that way. Either because the judge willfully misread the complaint or because Marshall's concern about disparities in the county's facilities led him to err in his brief, the judge held that the crucial issue, as the case was pleaded, was whether the plaintiff had in fact passed the entrance examination. It was clear, of course, that she had not.[32]

On appeal, the Maryland Court of Appeals first suggested that Marshall had erred in seeking the remedy of admission to the city schools. If the entrance examination was not authorized, it said, the remedy should be "payment of tuition in the city colored schools without the examination requirement. And the remedy for refusal to admit the child after her failure of a test which is authorized by law but defective would seem to be, not admission without a test, but a better test to determine whether she is qualified. For error of the authorities in either respect correction would not be by the remedy sought now, admission to the white children's school." Since segregation was the general state policy, admission to the county school "could be required only upon a showing . . . that equality of treatment is not obtainable separately."

The court of appeals then turned to the examination policy. Here it construed the record in a curious way. Everyone acknowledged that white students took final examinations before they graduated from seventh grade. The court of appeals treated these final examinations as entrance examinations for high school admission. It did note "some differences in administration." The white students took their tests in their own schools, just as if these tests were like other classroom exercises, whereas the black students "are gathered in central places at a distance from home for many, and strange to them." In addition, the school authorities designed the tests in light of white students' school assignments, and gave final grades based on the class performance and the test results for white students. Black students, in contrast, received final grades based solely on the test results, and may have had curricula that were incompatible to some extent with what the examinations were designed to test. These differences, the Court of Appeals said, were "insufficient to show unconstitutional discrimination. . . . [T]he allowance of separate treatment at all involves allowance of some incidental differences, and some inequalities, in meeting practical problems presented. And . . . the differences here amount to no more." The plaintiffs argued that "inequalities in the separate elementary school teaching" had the effect of "deny[ing] the colored children equal opportunities to qualify for the examinations, and thus equal access to the high school course, but this could not be remedied by admitting to a high school a child who is not fitted for it. The remedy would have to be one reaching farther back."[33]

What lessons did the NAACP lawyers draw from their experiences in Maryland? They learned, obviously, that they could win desegregation cases. But they were hardly so blind as to believe that they won only because of the merits of their claims. Thus, they had to figure out those conditions that supported success which were not at the same time linked to the peculiarities of Maryland. That Maryland, a border state, was involved was not insignificant, however. The Garland Fund proposal and the Margold Report had focused on discrimination in the Deep South. Though they had pursued the litigation more vigorously in Maryland than elsewhere, Houston and Marshall had done so largely because it was convenient. No record indicates that they chose Maryland because it was a border state. But they concluded from the Maryland experience that lawsuits could more easily be organized and judges more quickly persuaded in the border states. A letter from Marshall to the president of the NAACP branch in Richmond spoke of the Gibbs case in Montgomery County in organizational and strategic terms:

This case not only means that the salary of teachers will be equalized and is a definite step in our campaign to equalize educational opportunities but also has a much wider effect on our entire program. This type of case has, perhaps, one of the greatest appeals to a larger NAACP program in Maryland and this case means that it is the opening fight to give to Negroes a half million dollars a year because that is the amount of the difference between white and colored teachers' salaries in the state of Maryland. Here, we are actually giving material benefit to Negroes in general. This money will eventually get into the hands of Negro physicians, dentists, lawyers and other professional and businessmen. It will do much to raise the standards of living for Negroes; it will also break down the age old tradition that Negroes are not entitled to the same salaries as white men, even though equally qualified to do the same work.

We believe that this program should next go into Virginia and North Carolina. Other southern states farther down are desirous of filing such cases but we would prefer to go from Maryland into Virginia, then into Carolina and Kentucky and on down.[34]

Thus, the success in Maryland crystallized an intuitive sense that victories would be easier to achieve in the upper South than in the Deep South.

The staff did, however, suffer from the endemic problem associated with "learning by doing," given the small amount of experience available. They fell into a classic *post hoc ergo propter hoc* fallacy. Thus, in 1940 Marshall discouraged a facilities equalization suit in Pittsylvania, Virginia: "I am not at all sold on the question of mandamus on a case like this because we lost such a case in Baltimore County, Maryland."[35] More subtly, the lawyers tended to confuse the existence of local support and cooperation, which the contrast between the North Carolina and Maryland university cases had correctly shown was crucial, with the forms that such support took. They tended to be unhappy with teacher cases in which a committee of teachers and NAACP members was not formed, for example, although that was partly explained by their concern to avoid charges that they unethically stirred up litigation. The choice of forums and remedy, discussed earlier, also seems to have been affected by the models of Maryland.

In June 1939, Marshall drafted an outline of procedure in salary equalization cases. It set forth what he had done in the Maryland cases: investigate, petition the school board, ask for a hearing, and the like. The

68

general procedures, which were added two years later, insisted that the national office be informed of "all steps *before* they are taken"; proposed pleadings, for example, should be reviewed so that local attorneys could receive advice based on other cases in which the national staff was involved.[36] This outline embodied what the staff had learned: the Maryland model worked. So long as Marshall's energies could be harnessed elsewhere, the prospects were indeed bright.

It is now possible to summarize the development of the litigation campaign in more general terms. The NAACP chose the course of action that appeared likely to minimize the costs of conducting successful litigation. The staff lawyers could conduct lawsuits in two ways. They could litigate the cases themselves, or they could supervise local attorneys who would conduct the day-to-day litigation. Staff litigation would be cheaper in federal than in state courts; supervision of local attorneys was cheapest of all, from the staff's perspective. But supervising local attorneys was difficult in complex cases, because complexity introduced the procedural ambiguities on which hostile judges might seize. Finally, litigating first in Maryland and then in the upper South reduced the expenses of travel and lodging. Those costs thus could justify decisions about where to bring the lawsuits, and in what order. They also could justify the allocation of the salary cases to federal courts and the graduate school cases to state courts, because the salary cases required more complex procedural development, which in turn made supervision by a national staff, familiar with procedures in federal courts, more important. In addition, costs could be kept down by using old strategies until they failed, rather than by continuing to innovate.

5. Securing the Precedents:
Gaines and *Alston*

To understand the course of the litigation campaign, we must now examine what happened in the first salary and university cases to reach the federal appellate courts: a salary case from Norfolk, Virginia, and a university case from Missouri. At the time those two cases were initiated, there was no reason to single them out as likely to be particularly important. The NAACP lawyers were doing no more than litigating the cases at the pace imposed by the litigants and the local courts; they were not selecting cases to pursue on the basis of any long-range strategy—except, of course, the strategy of eroding "separate but equal" at every opportunity. There were reasons why the Norfolk salary case followed the Maryland cases in the campaign, although nothing in the circumstances guaranteed that it would create a broader precedent than had the Anne Arundel case. But there was no reason at all that the Missouri law school case rather than any other should yield an important Supreme Court decision. University cases were bubbling up through the South, and it is only in retrospect that we can see in the Missouri case a significant restriction on the doctrine of "separate but equal." The details of the Norfolk and Missouri cases are extremely instructive, for in them we can see foreshadowed the difficulties that emerged over the next decade and that produced the final, major shift in the NAACP's strategy.

Immediately after the victory at the trial level in the Maryland law school case, Houston wrote Sidney Redmond, the leading black attorney in St. Louis, asking him to investigate the situation at the University of Missouri. Redmond had attended Harvard College and Law School. After practicing law in his native Mississippi for a few years, he had moved to St. Louis in 1929, where he became active in NAACP affairs and local politics. In August 1935, Redmond suggested that Houston consider the case of Lloyd Gaines, the president of the senior class at Lincoln University in Jefferson City, Missouri. Gaines, then twenty-three years old, wanted to go to law school. Redmond also indicated interest in a salary suit. Houston's response was rather cool. He wanted Redmond to find more applicants, and to avoid litigating until they had an "air-tight case"; the issues were "so big that we cannot afford to omit any detail of preparation in a hasty attempt at grandstand play." By December, the national office advised Redmond that preparations had bogged down "for lack of suitable candidates," although the objections to Gaines remained unclear.[1]

Gaines turned out to be the only plaintiff available. When he applied to the state law school, his application caused university officials some difficulty. Missouri's segregation statutes appeared to be inapplicable to colleges, and the university had no admissions criteria other than scholastic ability. The university's board received a letter from the dean of the law school suggesting that it would be unconstitutional to deny Gaines's application solely because of his race. Nonetheless, the board rejected the application. It gave Gaines two choices: accept a scholarship to attend an out-of-state law school or apply to Lincoln University, a major institution of black higher education that would, the state said, create a full-scale law school on demand. The NAACP opposed scholarship programs both in principle—they embodied the segregationist view that contact between blacks and whites in a segregated state was intolerable—and for practical reasons—the Missouri scholarship, for example, would have paid the excess tuition Gaines might be charged, but would not have paid his extra expenses for living away from his home state. Missouri's position made it possible for the NAACP lawyers to work out a next step. If they could establish that the scholarship was an unconstitutional option because it did not satisfy the "separate but equal" doctrine of *Plessy* v. *Ferguson*, the state would either have to desegregate or have to carry out its promise to create a new black law school. But then, they thought, it would be easy to establish the actual inequality between the older white school and the new black one. As it turned out, it was not easy at all, but a coherent line of development could at least be seen.[2]

Houston, who regarded the university cases as his territory, traveled to Missouri for the brief trial, which went off uneventfully. The state courts ruled that the Constitution had not been violated because either option would discharge the state's duties. While the NAACP's appeals were pending, Gaines decided to get a graduate degree in economics at the University of Michigan, and, because his undergraduate record was too erratic for him to get a scholarship, the NAACP raised money to pay his tuition. The NAACP's appeal to the United States Supreme Court succeeded in December 1938, when the Court held that Gaines had, at the time he applied, a right to opportunities for legal education equal to those made available by Missouri to whites.[3]

Chief Justice Hughes's opinion for the Court relied on the *Murray* decision in holding that Missouri's failure to provide a law school for blacks "manifest[ly] . . . constitute[d] a denial of equal protection."[4] It dismissed Missouri's stated intention to create a law school at Lincoln University "whenever necessary or practical" because "a mere declaration of purpose, still unfulfilled, is [not] enough." But the opinion indicated that the case might have been different had Missouri been firmly committed to opening a law school for blacks even if only "a very few students, [or even] one student," had requested it. The opinion then turned to the only real option available to Gaines, the provision for out-of-state scholarships. Here the opinion was not marked by logical rigor. It treated as "beside the point" Missouri's claims that a black student could get as good a legal education in Kansas or Illinois as in Missouri, even though the curricula in none of the other states specialized in local law. "The basic consideration is not as to what sort of opportunities other States provide, or whether they are as good as those in Missouri, but as to what opportunities Missouri itself furnishes to white students and denies to Negroes solely upon the ground of color." The Court said that the "separate but equal" doctrine "rests wholly upon the equality of the privileges which the laws give to the separated groups within the State." As in the railroad case of 1914, the issue was the state's "duty when it provides [legal] training to furnish it to the residents of the State upon the basis of an equality of right." Missouri gave whites a "privilege" that was "denied to Negroes by reason of their race. The white resident is afforded legal education within the State; the negro resident having the same qualifications is refused it there and must go outside the State to obtain it. That is a denial of the equality of legal right to the enjoyment of the privilege which the State has set up, and the provision for the payment of tuition fees in another State does not remove the discrimination."

The Court assumed that a separate legal education for blacks in Missouri could be equal to that for whites in Missouri. But if, as the Court conceded for purposes of analysis, education for blacks in Kansas could be equal to that for blacks at a hypothetical separate black school in Missouri, it is hard to understand why the scholarship system did not satisfy

constitutional requirements. The Court's opinion was forced to emphasize the inevitably arbitrary facts of geography. "Manifestly, the obligation of the State to give the protection of equal laws can be performed
only where its laws operate, that is, within its own jurisdiction." Missouri
could not satisfy *its* burden by "cast[ing]" it on another state. The "separate responsibility of each State within its own sphere is of the essence of
statehood maintained under our dual system." According to Chief Justice
Hughes, Missouri's argument implied that if Kansas, for example, did not
have a law school, Missouri would have a "constitutional duty" to open a
law school for blacks. To Hughes, this showed that Missouri had that
duty "independently of the action of other States." He could not "conclude that what otherwise would be an unconstitutional discrimination,
with respect to the legal right to the enjoyment of opportunities within
the State, can be justified by requiring resort to opportunities elsewhere.
That resort may mitigate the inconvenience of the discrimination but cannot serve to validate it."

Responding to the Court's decision, the Missouri legislature appropriated $200,000 to improve and extend graduate instruction at Lincoln
University. Although the NAACP thought the plans inadequate, the state
court, on remand from the Supreme Court, sent Gaines's case back to the
trial court to see whether the new law school at Lincoln would be equal
to the white school by September 1, the date that the next term would
begin. Then things began to fall apart. According to Redmond, Lincoln's
trustees were proceeding in good faith, and "all indications are that it will
be a[s] good in many respects as money, handicapped by the limited time,
can make it." William E. Taylor, acting dean of the Howard Law School,
was appointed dean of the law school of Lincoln University. The school
was located in St. Louis and shared a building with a hotel and movie
theater. Three full-time teachers and a librarian were hired, and initial
orders for library books were placed. By September 1939 the adviser to
the American Bar Association's accreditation committee found after an
informal inspection that the school fully complied with the association's
requirements. The school opened on September 21, with an enrollment of
thirty, rather than the sixty Taylor had anticipated. The small enrollment
suggested that the state would not really make the law school at Lincoln
equal to that at the University of Missouri. Blacks, later joined by white
students from the University of Missouri and Washington University, established a picket line, carrying signs that said "Don't Be a Traitor to Your
Race" and "I Have Self-Respect; How About You?"[5]

With the prospect of an accredited black law school came tactical problems. Walter White had found it easy to urge blacks to apply to the white law school, to "make it perfectly clear . . . that we are fighting not only the question of equal facilities but are actually fighting against all attempts at segregation." Houston, who had returned to his family's law practice in Washington in mid-1938, was perhaps more attuned to the interests of the named client and was certainly sensitive to charges that the NAACP had manipulated the applicants. He expressed his concern that "if we try to keep [Gaines] back we add fuel to the charge already made against us that we are not really interested in getting Negroes graduate and professional education, but in creating problems for propaganda purposes." Houston asked Marshall to "have the office give this matter serious consideration." Because Marshall left the office for a rest, Houston was answered by White, a nonlawyer who was not as sensitive to the questions of legal ethics raised by the NAACP's activities:

[I]t is most definitely not our function to advise Gaines to go to a jim-crow school. If you should so advise him, please make it very clear that you are doing so as an individual and not as acting for the N.A.A.C.P. Instead, it should be made clear that we very strongly oppose his going to Lincoln since it is manifestly impossible for many years to come to assume that the Lincoln University Law School would be substantially equal to the University of Missouri.

As to your second point . . . I do not think that should deter us in the slightest. Regardless of what we do or say the charge is going to be made and, frankly, I do not care. Our position, as I see it, is to stand unremittingly and without any faintest suggestion of compromise for complete equality. With this position I know you will agree.[6]

The crushing problem lay ahead. Houston, confident that victory in the trial court was "around the corner," asked Marshall to have Redmond "get a hold of Gaines," who had not been heard from for over a year. After working as a clerk and at a filling station, Gaines had gone to Chicago and stayed at a black fraternity house. Then he simply disappeared. Registered letters to his last address failed to locate him before the end of August. In October 1939, Houston noted that the state's attorneys had "hit [the NAACP] in our tender spot" by requesting that Gaines appear for a pretrial examination in preparation for the trial on equality of facilities. According to Houston the NAACP had last heard from Gaines in April 1939. By the end of the year, Houston gave up. "Since we cannot find Gaines we cannot go on," he wrote, and the NAACP was forced to accept a dismissal of the case because it could not pursue it any further.[7]

Despite this conclusion to *Gaines,* the NAACP had secured its first Supreme Court decision eroding the principle of "separate but equal." The Supreme Court's decision attracted a significant amount of public and scholarly comment. Virginius Dabney, a liberal white from Virginia whose position as editor of a prominent Richmond newspaper gave his views special weight, wrote in the *New York Times* that the decision had "severely jolted" southern educational systems, which were on notice that they had to make "far-reaching readjustments." Southern educators, he said, were "holding hurried conferences" to appraise the situation. Though white educators were virtually unanimous in supporting separate black institutions—and, Dabney wrote, "a good many Negro leaders agree"—they were concerned that it would be too costly to maintain separate programs for the small numbers of black students who would be interested. "[S]ome Negro leaders are known to be anxious to avoid stirring up the inter-racial friction which would follow" the filing of applications by blacks to southern universities. According to Dabney, "there [was] talk" that states in the Deep South would "even refuse to do anything, and then would make it so uncomfortable for any Negro applying . . . for admission that the practical effect of the court's ruling might be virtually nil."[8]

The observations in the law reviews tended to focus on the decision's likely effects. The *University of Chicago Law Review* was typical in noting that "[i]n equalizing the facilities three choices are open to the state: Abolition of professional schools for whites, which would disadvantage the latter to no gain for the colored. Admission of Negroes to the existing institutions, which would foment the prejudice which the system of segregation is designed to obviate. Construction of separate higher institutions, which would entail expense alleged to be disproportionate to the limited number of Negro students on these levels." It predicted that the third course was the most likely to be followed; but, despite the Court's "bold and laudable affirmation of Negro rights," the commentator expected few "far-reaching consequences," because "[t]he principle of segregation is preserved. . . . Skepticism may therefore be expressed whether the facilities furnished will as a practical matter equal the opportunities for acquiring a professional education on a liberal out-of-state scholarship plan." Another observer praised the Court for penetrating the fiction that segregation was "the will of the people" to see that it was "more properly . . . the will of the white people," and yet another praised the Court's "determination to prevent discrimination, however camouflaged or sugar-coated, which is to be commended by all who desire to end prejudice and prejudicial actions."[9]

Commentators in border-state law reviews were unhappy that the Court had rejected the scholarship system, which they called "a sane and acceptable answer to a difficult situation," and "the only solution to a very difficult, perplexing and embarrassing problem which has arisen out of the adoption of the Fourteenth Amendment." The *Tulane Law Review* concluded that "although the negro's right to have educational facilities equal to those of whites is recognized, as a practical matter the negro is greatly limited in demand [*sic*] his rights by the technicalities and expense of judicial process." *Gaines* might motivate southern states "to create actual and not merely theoretical equality."[10]

The *Fordham Law Review* published the most carefully argued criticism of *Gaines,* which concentrated on the Court's attention to state lines and by inference suggested that the logic of *Gaines* could be extended in the directions the NAACP desired: "[T]he majority of the court . . . has treated the problem as though it had arisen in the Colonial era rather than in modern times. Their decision is rooted deeply in a view of the Union as a collection of strange countries. It seems concerned with some mythical impregnability of state borders." Because of the ease of transportation, the commentator wondered why crossing a state line should make any constitutional difference.[11] This logic is persuasive and suggests that *Gaines* had the potential to undermine the idea that separate facilities within a state were constitutional. The Supreme Court's willingness to invalidate Missouri's system by pinning its decision to an irrelevancy suggested that its real motivation was hostility to segregation.

The black press, of course, praised the Court's decision. To the *Pittsburgh Courier* it was "the greatest decision" since the Court held unconstitutional efforts to deprive blacks of the vote through grandfather clauses. The *Chicago Defender* was more restrained; it emphasized that the decision was "limited" and that it had relied on the "separate but equal" doctrine. Several newspapers saw the decision as shifting the burden to those who wanted to preserve segregation, and predicted that it would begin a series of attacks on "the citadels of prejudice and discrimination in the Southern States," as the *Amsterdam News* put it.[12]

Because southern states had relied on scholarships to dissipate pressure for graduate instruction for blacks, there were few adequate graduate programs within those states. With the *Gaines* decision in hand, the

NAACP could turn its attention to litigating the question of equality in fact. As Houston's confidence about the trial in *Gaines* indicates, the legal staff had little doubt that they could win on that question. They were both right and wrong; they could indeed win, but the problems were immense. The NAACP had not anticipated the kinds of delays that the states could successfully interpose, nor did it expect problems with plaintiffs to arise. But, despite the difficulties that later appeared, the Supreme Court's decision in *Gaines* made a difference, by forcing the courts to take seriously the question of the equality provided by separate facilities. In this sense, *Gaines* was one facet of what the Garland Fund plan and the Margold Report had sought to accomplish, though the route to that result had not been laid out in the plans.

Gaines ended in disarray because of difficulties in a case that posed a simple legal question and had a single plaintiff. The salary cases presented much more substantial problems of management. Even as Marshall had been litigating the Maryland salary cases, he had been encouraging teachers in Virginia to organize their own challenge. Virginia had many of the same advantages that Maryland had as the next locale for litigation. All of its major cities were relatively close to Washington. This eased logistical problems because Marshall's personal ties to a number of black lawyers in that city allowed him to count on them both to assist him while he was in New York and to provide him with places to stay and work when he came to Washington. Marshall could visit for short times and have all the resources in Washington available for the litigation. In addition, the issue of race per se was not central to Virginia politics. The white primary was held unconstitutional in 1929, and by 1940 blacks found few racially based restrictions on registration. Virginia politicians were more concerned about issues of class than those of race, and did not attempt to preserve their power by mobilizing the white community as a whole against blacks.[13]

In late 1936, the black Virginia Teachers' Association set up a committee and raised $1,000 as a fund to support teachers who might be fired for suing their employers. When Marshall won the Montgomery County case in mid-1937, activity in Virginia accelerated. Marshall wrote the presidents of several local branches of the NAACP that he would visit the state soon and "would like to get something started"; he thought that the teachers were anxious to sue. Houston solicited an invitation to speak at the state teachers' association convention. As they had earlier, NAACP activists again saw equalization suits as providing a "good opportunity to have [teachers] become members providing we have something tangible to lay before them."[14]

Once again coordination difficulties intervened. In March 1938, Marshall thought that the cases were "almost ready to start." But by October, nothing concrete had happened, and the teachers were said to be "whispering it around that they are not going to put any money in our [membership] drive, because we haven't started on their case." At first, Marshall thought that he lacked plaintiffs, and he urged a newspaper editor to "impress . . . upon the teachers that they should take active part in this fight." After spending two weeks in Richmond, Marshall was more confident but still cautious. Although he wanted the potential plaintiffs to have signed contracts so that they could not be fired, he was concerned that courts might find that the teachers had waived their objections to unequal salaries by signing contracts. The trip to Richmond generated several possible plaintiffs, and in October Marshall finally satisfied his critics by filing a petition for Aline Black, a Norfolk teacher, seeking equalization.[15]

Within a week, the NAACP received information that a supervisor had "already begun to 'check up' on Miss Black's classroom work and to make complaint," and in the spring of 1939, the school board voted against renewing her contract. The lawsuit filed in Black's name was thereupon dismissed, and Marshall informed the Virginia committee overseeing the litigation that he saw no way of getting her job back. The committee paid Black one year's salary, as had been agreed, and she went to New York to obtain a graduate degree. The NAACP organized a mass demonstration to protest the dismissal. The Norfolk *Virginian-Pilot* praised those who protested and regretted the problems Black faced, but commented that her difficulties showed that no one could "force improvement at too swift a pace."[16]

Marshall thought that he had another plaintiff available. When the teachers had expressed dissatisfaction with the pace of the NAACP's efforts, Melvin Alston, the president of the Norfolk Teachers' Association, had volunteered. Marshall decided that Black was "by far the better plaintiff" but asked Alston to "keep . . . in readiness." After Black's suit was dismissed, Marshall asked Alston if he was still willing to sue; apparently because he was under some pressure, Alston said that he was not. In September 1939, Marshall met with Alston and convinced him to become a plaintiff, and on September 28 a new petition was filed.[17]

Concern and dissension flared up again among the teachers. They were disappointed and confused about the outcome of Black's case, and the teachers' association intially refused to join the new case as a plaintiff. The teachers were also troubled that Marshall did not seem to them to be spending enough time on their case. On Marshall's behalf, Walter White pointed out that the Virginia case was "an integral part of a nation-wide campaign," to which Marshall was devoting all his energy. At the end of October, Marshall went to Virginia once more, and explained to the teachers' satisfaction why he had dropped Black's case in the state courts and had begun Alston's in the federal courts; he emphasized that the NAACP was engaged in "experiments" and had to feel its way along. This quieted the teachers' concerns, but internal division remained near the surface, grounded in conflict between impatient teachers and traditional accommodationists who used Black's dismissal to illustrate the hazards of militancy.[18]

Marshall was then able to concentrate on the lawsuit itself. In February 1940, the district judge dismissed the case on the grounds of waiver: Alston, he said, could have refused to sign the contract giving him an unequal salary and could then have sued, but having signed it he had accepted the inequality. The NAACP lawyers had worried about this issue for several years, but their concern was soon alleviated when, in June, the court of appeals reversed the district court. It rejected the waiver defense because Alston sought only to increase his salary in future years and did not "insist . . . upon additional compensation for the current year." The complaint described salary differentials between black and white teachers that were based solely upon the impermissible ground of race. Alston alleged that he received $921 per year, whereas white teachers with the same duties and qualifications received $1,200. The court of appeals quoted the Norfolk salary schedule, which showed dramatic disparities. In the elementary schools, black teachers in their first year with certificates from normal schools received $597.50 and those with degrees received $611.00, whereas white teachers with certificates received $850.00 and those with degrees received $937.00. In the high schools, newly hired black women teachers received $699.00 and white women received $970.00; black men teachers received $784.50, white men, $1,200. The court then continued, "That an unconstitutional discrimination is set forth in these paragraphs hardly admits of argument. The allegation is that the state, in paying for public services of the same kind and character to men and women equally qualified according to standards which the state itself prescribes, arbitrarily pays less to Negroes than to white persons. This is as clear a discrimination on the ground of race as could well be imagined and falls squarely within the inhibition of both the due process and the equal protection clauses of the 14th Amendment." The school board sought review in the Supreme Court, which was denied in October 1940.[19]

The decision still had to be translated into a decree equalizing salaries, and the divisions among the teachers were exploited by the school board as the terms of the decree were negotiated. The board presented "leaders" among the teachers with a partial equalization proposal. Those teachers, without consulting Marshall or any other attorneys for the plaintiffs, urged that the board's plan be accepted. At first the teachers refused, but a second vote indicated that they would accept what Marshall thought was a worthless compromise: equalization would be abandoned and the lawsuit would be dismissed outright, leaving the teachers without the enforcement mechanism that a consent decree would provide. Marshall therefore threatened to withdraw. The threat kept the compromise from being accepted, and although negotiations dragged on for two more months, the decree that resulted was one that Marshall could live with: it was a consent decree, not a dismissal, and provided for full equalization over three years.[20]

Walter White, looking at the confusion engendered by what should have been a triumph for the NAACP, was puzzled by the apparent hostility toward the NAACP among the teachers. Alston shared White's views, saying that he would not have gone through with the lawsuit "had I not a larger objective in mind." It probably was not irrelevant that the school board, apparently flexing its muscles, had fired three black principals unconnected with the litigation. Alston thought that this had fatally weakened the NAACP.[21]

In September 1941 the NAACP published a fifteen-page pamphlet titled *Teachers' Salaries in Black and White*. It was designed to generate support for the equalization litigation by pointing out the disparities and by describing the lawsuits that had been brought. After stating that the disparities amounted to $25 million, the pamphlet listed the salary scales in the South, showing that black teachers earned 32 percent of the average white salary in Mississippi and that in most southern states the ratio ranged between 40 percent and 50 percent. "Wherever the fight has been concluded," the pamphlet said, "it has resulted in a victory for the teachers." In Norfolk the teachers won $129,000, and in Maryland as a whole they won $500,000. Although school boards had engaged in "intimidation, chicanery and trickery of almost every form imaginable," including firing teachers and proposing meaningless settlements, "the fight for full salary equality goes on." The pamphlet called equalization "a critical step in the progress of Negro Americans toward cultural and economic equality" because it would establish the principle of equal pay for equal work. It praised the courage of the teachers involved and criticized the "Uncle Tomism" that had occasionally been voiced. The pamphlet concluded:

> It has been an uphill climb, but the fight can be won. It can be won through the persistence, organization and continued cooperation of the teachers, both those for whom salary-equality has been achieved and those for whom it must be achieved. It can be won through the moral and financial support of all intelligent citizens, Negro and white. And it can be won through the united resolution of all of us to fight until full equality is established within the jurisdiction of every school board in the United States.
> The National Association for the Advancement of Colored People is determined to gain for Negroes full educational equality on every front. But the speed and effectiveness with which we can fight depends upon YOU! What are you going to do about it?
>
> IT IS YOUR JOB TOO!![22]

But just as the disappearance of Gaines symbolized the final result in a successful university case, the dissension in Norfolk symbolized the outcome of successful equalization suits: victories could indeed be won in the courts, but the benefits to blacks and to the NAACP as an organization were problematic. Over the next ten years, the victories themselves became harder to win. In the university cases, litigating equality in fact proved to be extremely time-consuming, a defect that made it even more difficult to sustain the interest of the few individuals who wanted to attend white universities; in the salary cases, school boards developed methods of perpetuating unequal salaries for black and white teachers in which the criterion of race was submerged enough that successful attacks would be difficult, though not impossible. Before turning to the next group of cases, however, we must note one absence: there was no early case that the NAACP could see as a successful facilities equalization suit at the elementary and secondary levels. As we will see, there were reasons for this too.

6. The Campaign in the 1940s:
Contingencies, Adaptations, and
the Problem of Staff

Favorable appellate decisions are only an intermediate stage of a litigation campaign. As *Gaines* and *Alston* indicate, implementing such decisions is often difficult even in the very cases in which the appellate victory was won.[1] It is even more difficult to use the appellate decisions as precedents to affect the behavior of those who were not a party to the initial lawsuit. The same contingencies that attended the initial litigation recur: plaintiffs are hard to find and, once found, can disrupt the negotiations that are an essential part of the use of precedents by accepting settlement offers for less than they could win by litigating, or by rejecting offers for more than they could win. In addition, nonparties can read precedents too, and can adapt what they do so as to escape the direct force of the appellate decision. Contingencies and especially adaptation can in turn force those directing the litigation campaign to spend as much energy on the follow-up cases as they had on the initial ones. The NAACP faced exactly those difficulties; and though it could declare a sort of victory in the salary cases by the late 1940s, the victory was quite equivocal. The litigation was draining the NAACP's resources, with increasingly small returns for the effort. The decision to attack the "separate but equal" doctrine directly was significantly affected by those organizational factors.

Before *Gaines* was decided, Houston and Marshall kept their eyes on potential university cases in North Carolina and Virginia. But in both states the actions were aborted. For example, the applicant who might have become the plaintiff in North Carolina received a very low score on the medical aptitude test, and, though Houston thought that a ruling requiring nondiscriminatory consideration of applications could benefit others, he had to tell the individual involved that the lawsuit would probably not help him.[2]

Later university cases in Missouri, Kentucky, and South Carolina provide the best examples of the NAACP's problems. Though Missouri had provided a disappointing plaintiff in Lloyd Gaines, it also generated a nearly perfect plaintiff in Lucile Bluford. In 1937, at the age of twenty-six, she became managing editor of the *Kansas City Call,* a leading black newspaper—a position earlier held by Roy Wilkins, who had moved from the newspaper to the NAACP staff as assistant executive secretary in 1931. Because Lincoln University in Missouri did not offer an undergraduate course in journalism, Bluford had attended the University of Kansas on a state scholarship. Seven years later, after the Supreme Court's decision in *Gaines,* she decided to seek an advanced degree in journalism and simultaneously to test Missouri's policy of segregation. Houston encouraged her by invoking feminist as well as racial concerns. Her suit, he said, would "focus attention on Negro women," and would "keep public attention focused on the University problem" by showing that the state could not eliminate its difficulties simply by opening a black law school.[3]

In a long memorandum to Bluford and Sidney Redmond, the NAACP's local counsel, Houston explained his view of the significance of Bluford's case and of the litigation. His first point was that admission to the graduate program was in his client's interest. Then he turned to broader issues. Missouri would learn "the utter futility of trying to establish separate schools for every Negro who demands graduate and professional work" and that it had not "silenced . . . Negro demands by furnishing a law school" for a single black applicant. The NAACP would also "show the country" the breadth, variety, and inevitability of the black community's "demand for training." He concluded by alluding to the international situation: "Finally, in these days of stress at home and abroad we want to focus ever sharpening attention of the people of the United States on the discriminations and injustices heaped on the Negro citizens in this 'democracy,' and to show the country that the danger to democracy in America does not lie so much in Hitler's aggressions as in the repressive and unjust attitudes and practices here in this country; that the 'acid test' of America democracy [*sic*] is not defense against foreign enemies but domestic injustice. That being so we must be thorough and prepare the case with a board [*sic*] sweep. . . ." By "illuminat[ing]" the race issue, the NAACP would provide "a blue print" of what had to be eliminated "before facing the foreign enemy." Thus, Bluford's case had to be seen in "its framework" of challenges to all other types of discrimination.[4]

Bluford applied for admission to the University of Missouri's program in journalism in January 1939, and was accepted for the second semester when the university authorities failed to note her race. After she was not allowed to register in January, she reapplied for admission in August and was told that *Lincoln* University would not offer a journalism program that semester. Houston had still not resolved the persistent questions about proper procedure, and in the fall of 1939 he filed actions for Bluford in both federal and state court. As a matter of tactics, Bluford had not demanded that the trustees of Lincoln establish a journalism course, but simply applied for admission to the University of Missouri. She claimed that a separate course would be inadequate, arguing that though she was employed by a newspaper directed at a black community, she had to understand how general circulation newspapers operated, because in some ways her newspaper competed with them.[5]

The tactical decision to forgo a demand proved fatal—that is to say, the judges failed to appreciate the force of Bluford's argument that, in this context, separate could not be equal. The federal action, seeking damages for the school's refusal to admit her, and the state action, seeking an order admitting Bluford to the University of Missouri, were both dismissed for failure to make a demand on Lincoln. The federal judge noted that Bluford claimed that because she was entitled to immediate relief, and because Missouri had no journalism program for blacks, she therefore did not have to demand that a separate program at Lincoln be established. Thus, Bluford argued, even if a program was created in the near future, she would not get the immediate relief she desired. The judge held that the Missouri Supreme Court had been correct in its disposition of the *Gaines* case on remand from the United States Supreme Court. The state had to have a "reasonable opportunity to provide facilities, demanded for the first time." The judge was concerned that, unless Lincoln University was given an opportunity to comply with a demand, the members of the Board of Curators of the University of Missouri would be liable for damages if someone demanded that a program be created at Lincoln on one day and sought admission to the University of Missouri on the next. He did not believe that the Constitution required that Lincoln "keep and maintain in idleness and non-use facilities . . . which no one had requested or indicated a desire to use."[6]

The Missouri Supreme Court reached the same result a year later, although it first rejected as unfounded the university's argument that Bluford should not prevail because she wanted only to pursue a test case and did not really want to attend the university. The court then relied on evidence that the board of Lincoln University had decided to institute a journalism program in February 1941, which, it said, "would have de-layed [Bluford] for two semesters." It did not think that requiring that a demand be made a reasonable time before Bluford sought to attend school was itself unreasonable, for such a demand would have allowed her to enter school promptly. The court noted that, like many applicants, Bluford "had formed the purpose to take a graduate course in journalism many months before she made her application, but her purpose was to take it at Missouri University, not at some other school in Missouri." The board had to be given a chance to open a new department, because it had to "allocate its funds to the courses most needed," and should not be "re-quired to maintain departments for which there are no students." But the court left open the possibility of desegregation. "If, upon proper demand, the Lincoln Board had refused to establish a course in journalism within a reasonable time, or had informed appellant that it was unable to do so, appellant would have been entitled to admission to that course in the Missouri University."[7]

After the state court issued its opinion saying that Lincoln had to have a "reasonable time" to set up a journalism course, Bluford drafted a state-ment noting that her application had been pending for over two years. Because the opinion was issued in July 1941, the state took the position that a "reasonable time" meant at least until the beginning of the second semester in January 1942 or even until September 1942. The legislature appropriated $60,000 to establish a journalism school at Lincoln, which opened in February 1942 and had an enrollment of fourteen the next year. Bluford, who had refused a position on the staff of the NAACP be-cause taking the job would feed the false claim that she was not interested in the degree but was only seeking to destroy segregation, maintained her interest in the suit.[8]

In early 1942 Missouri took the alternate route to equalization and closed the journalism school at the University of Missouri. Houston be-lieved that the school was closed because the new course at Lincoln, which had been criticized by an advisory accreditation committee, was obviously inadequate, but he noted that the draft had severely reduced enrollments at the white school. What was left in Bluford's suit was a claim for damages, which went to trial in April 1942. The state made racist appeals to the jury, which held against Bluford, perhaps only be-cause it believed that the closing was not caused by the impending need to admit Bluford. The NAACP remained interested in Missouri's university system and came up with another plaintiff, also a journalist, at the end of

1943. She seemed to have a strong case, because the state had announced that Lincoln's law and journalism schools would be closed, but Missouri was up to the challenge. A month after the new plaintiff came to the NAACP, the state announced that Lincoln's journalism school, but not its law school, would continue to operate, using faculty members from the white university.[9]

The Kentucky university case petered out in part because of the state's tactics, as in Missouri, but also because of difficulties in organizing the litigation. Prentice Thomas, who had established his own practice in Kentucky after serving an informal internship with Houston and Marshall, received detailed instructions from Houston: Thomas should identify a program at the University of Kentucky that was not offered at the black colleges; the program should, if possible, be a laboratory course or one requiring physical equipment so that the state could not readily establish a separate but nominally equal program; Thomas should find a qualified plaintiff to apply to the black schools, demand that the program be given at a black school, and then apply to the white university. It took Thomas eighteen months, but by June 1941, he had two plaintiffs, one for social work and one for engineering. Thomas, somewhat impatient with the lack of organizational support, quickly filed suit in state court on behalf of the engineering student. Marshall counseled him to be less precipitate, and Thomas then withdrew the state lawsuit, filing instead a federal action seeking classwide relief.[10]

Now contingencies and adaptation began to whittle away at the lawsuit. Northern supporters of black organizations had usually been sensitive in Kentucky to the interests of Berea College, which had retained its commitment to integration until, at the turn of the century, state law prohibited integrated education even at private institutions. But the president of Berea questioned the wisdom of an attack on the state university's policy because it would heighten racial tensions, noting that some integrated continuing education courses had already been stopped. Berea's objections caused only a minor flurry of concern within the NAACP, because it had already received a substantial contribution to finance suits to challenge the university's segregation and the statute prohibiting integration at Berea. After the university lawsuit was filed, the state managed to force extended delays centering on confusion about who should receive process in the case; Thomas' inexperience undoubtedly opened the way for such maneuvers on a technical issue of state law, about which the national staff could give no guidance. The legislature also appropriated $20,000 for an engineering program at a black school, but the amount was not enough to pay for the equipment needed and would support a faculty for only a two-year program. Those tactics succeeded in their intended object of discouraging the plaintiff. By March 1943, the plaintiff had understandably lost interest. He had forgone a full year of education, had not been supported by leaders in the Kentucky black community, and had even been offered money to leave the state. All this led him to attend Howard University. In January 1945, the case was dismissed for lack of prosecution after the plaintiff signed an affidavit saying that he was "not particularly interested in further continuing the litigation."[11]

It is not surprising that the university lawsuit in South Carolina did not start until 1946, nor that it was shot through with dissension arising from within the black community. Harold Boulware, the local black attorney affiliated with the NAACP, received a sample complaint in September 1946. A 1938 graduate of Howard Law School, Boulware had been admitted to the South Carolina bar in 1940, when he was twenty-seven. From 1942 on, he was counsel to the South Carolina organization of NAACP branches. In November 1946, the president of the state conference of NAACP branches complained to the national office that the failure to file the lawsuit was hurting the organization. Robert Carter, a young black lawyer who had joined the national office at the end of his service in World War II, explained that the apparent delay was due to overwork. The lawsuit was filed in January 1947, and, although the state appropriated money for a black law school in February, nothing had been done by the time of trial in June. The state was then given until September to open the black law school. When the state acted, the school was obviously unequal to the white school, with poor facilities and only three teachers. The NAACP of course filed a motion for further relief. When Marshall learned that local NAACP officials had advised the plaintiff to go to the black school, he exploded. Simultaneously, the plaintiff decided to abandon the lawsuit; he could not get a job from white employers because of his involvement in the suit, and he was going to enlist in the Army. Although Boulware persuaded him to reconsider, these difficulties dampened the national office's enthusiasm for the suit. Marshall advised Boulware to withdraw the motion for further relief, calling the plaintiff unreliable. In July 1948, the court held that the black law school was equal to the white one.[12]

The university cases posed several difficulties for the NAACP. First, *Gaines* held out the possibility that a separate but equal graduate program would satisfy the courts. Southern states seized the opportunity and created separate programs. Though the NAACP lawyers knew that these programs were obviously unequal and therefore inadequate under *Gaines*, they were forced to litigate the issue at length. Yet as the campaign extended through the South, the national staff, faced with other demands on its time, found it impossible either to conduct the litigation or to supervise it closely. Second, the university suits usually had a small number of plaintiffs. As the litigation dragged on, these plaintiffs were vulnerable. Economic pressure or the simple desire to get on with one's life made it hard to sustain the interest of individual plaintiffs, and in some instances lack of local support contributed to even greater disaffection.

The 1940s brought no major victories in university cases. Although there were victories in salary cases, they entailed analogous difficulties. School boards abandoned salary schedules that were overtly discriminatory, only to adopt schedules that reproduced discriminatory results by seeming to rely on nonracial factors; penetrating the facade of objective merit measures was almost as hard as demonstrating inequality in graduate programs. Instead of individual defections, the salary cases raised complicated problems of internal politics, as factions formed within local teachers' groups around many issues. A direct attack on the principle of "separate but equal" might temporarily escalate the problems of holding plaintiffs to the lawsuit by increasing the obvious risks of participating. But it promised to alleviate the difficulties over the longer run by opening the benefits to the entire community and by eliminating the need to confront school board claims that facilities were equal—if the direct attack could succeed.

The NAACP's Annual Report for 1941 listed fifteen salary equalization actions pending during that year; in 1947, a list was prepared showing that thirty-one salary cases had been brought, of which only four were unequivocally lost.[13] It would be unduly repetitive to work through each salary case in detail, as the basic elements can be seen in a few selected cases. But selection has its limitations, for it tends to underemphasize the substantial burdens that were imposed on the national staff by the delays, evasions, and divisions that occurred almost everywhere. No strictly chronological account can bring out the important details, for suits in several states were pursued almost simultaneously. Somewhat arbitrarily, I have organized the selection on the basis of the date of the NAACP's first efforts at salary litigation in each state; I have then traced the developments within each state. The sequence shows that the campaign can be characterized as having two stages. The first began in the upper South, Florida, and Louisiana in the late 1930s and early 1940s; the second extended the campaign to the Deep South, from which Florida and Louisiana may perhaps be excluded because of their atypical racial politics.[14]

At an early point in the litigation effort, the NAACP explored the possibility of conducting salary suits in Tennessee as well as in Maryland and Virginia. On January 4, 1935, Houston wrote three black attorneys in Nashville: "Is there any agitation in Nashville on the part of the school teachers for equal salaries? If so, what procedure would you suggest in order to raise the question? Are there any teachers available for test plaintiffs? Would any of you or other lawyers in Nashville be interested in handling such a case?" Nothing happened there until 1941, because the teachers were apparently so intimidated by the strength of the political machine that they could not mobilize to fight. When the suit was filed, it proceeded without complication to a judgment in favor of the plaintiffs, in July 1942. Salary differentials ranged from $25 per month to $55 per month for teachers, and reached $150 per month for principals. The school board argued feebly that the differentials were based on the schools in which the teachers taught, not on the race of the teachers. But the judge rejected that argument because no black teachers had ever been appointed to teach in white schools. This was especially significant, he said, because of the board's second defense: "that the differential in the pay of the salaries to the teachers was based solely upon an economic condition in that, colored teachers were more numerous than white teachers, their living conditions less expensive, and that they could be employed to work at a lower salary than white teachers." If that were so, a cost-conscious board would have used black teachers in white schools. The board, though, was race-conscious, not cost-conscious, and lost the law suit.[15]

The successes in Maryland encouraged the national office to pursue equalization cases with some vigor and, sometimes, without difficulty. In Chattanooga, for example, the teachers hired their own lawyer in 1941 and elicited a proposal from the school board of an annual 10 percent reduction in the salary differential. Marshall advised the local lawyer to reject the offer; the school board quickly responded by establishing a nondiscriminatory salary scale, allocating to black teachers 62 percent of the money for salary increases to reduce existing differentials and promising to eliminate the remaining differences as quickly as it could. The case was placed on the inactive docket of the court only six months after the lawyer was hired and three months after the case was filed.[16]

The case in Louisville proceeded almost as smoothly, although occasionally it languished for lack of attention by the NAACP. In January 1938, Victor Perry of the Louisville Colored Teachers Association asked for information on methods of eliminating the explicit salary differential of 15 percent between white and black teachers. Marshall asked the president of the Louisville branch "what plans [were] being made" for a salary suit in June 1939, a year and a half later, and sent advice on forming a committee. When the support committee was established, Marshall wrote Prentice Thomas that it was "splendid" to add Kentucky "to the snow-ball." A slight embarrassment occurred when NAACP officials realized that Thomas had acted before he had consulted Charles Anderson. Anderson, who had graduated from Howard Law School in 1931, had been elected to the Kentucky legislature in 1935, when he was twenty-eight. He was the first black elected to a southern legislature since the end of Reconstruction, and the NAACP's desire to work with existing black leadership ought to have led it to secure Anderson's assistance from the start. Fortunately, the embarrassment passed when, after being asked, Anderson declined to bring the suit and registered no resentment of Thomas or the national NAACP. Indeed, Anderson cooperated by first writing Marshall that the lawsuit had not been filed because only 25 percent of the teachers contributed to the committee that was to support the litigation, and by then using Marshall's response to revive interest in the suit.[17]

With Thomas in charge, the case went forward. In January 1941, the school board, after some political skirmishing with the city's mayor, voted to equalize salaries, and at its April meeting set September 1 as the date. All this was satisfactory, but the board insisted that its resolutions justified dismissal of the pending lawsuit. The NAACP wanted to obtain a consent decree as a protection against repudiation of the promise to equalize, but once the new contracts went into effect, it accepted a dismissal of the suit.[18]

The most important salary suit of the 1940s was brought in Little Rock, where the teachers organized themselves and then sought NAACP assistance, leading Marshall to comment, "Boy, these southern teachers have acquired brand new backbones." Although Arkansas was part of the segregationist South, it is important to note that the federal appellate court that heard cases from Arkansas covered Iowa, Minnesota, Nebraska, and the Dakotas as well. The suit was filed in February 1942 and tried that fall. Fourteen months later, in January 1944, the trial judge ruled against the NAACP. He found that the school board maintained no salary schedules but paid teachers on the basis of a merit rating, and that the rating system had not been administered in a racially discriminatory manner. He insisted that the school board had the right to adopt an individualized merit system rather than rely on "arbitrary standard[s]" based on college degrees and seniority. So long as they "do not fix these salaries solely on race and color, their discretion and judgment cannot and will not be interfered with by the courts. They are human agencies, hence fallible, and have made mistakes, and been guilty of errors of judgment. This they frankly admit." But the judge believed that these errors did not amount to constitutional violations.[19]

The fundamental findings about the way the merit system actually operated were factual findings, which were harder to challenge on appeal than legal rulings, and the NAACP staff initially thought that reversal was extremely unlikely in light of the skill with which the trial judge had made the fact-findings. While the appeal was pending, the school board voted to increase the appropriation for salaries by $140,000, some of it to be used to close the gaps between white and black salaries, but it tried to shield its action from public attention to minimize the effect publicity might have on the appeal.[20]

To their surprise, the NAACP lawyers persuaded the court of appeals that the trial judge's findings of fact were "clearly erroneous." The appellate judges agreed that the evidence failed to establish that Little Rock maintained a salary schedule, but they were convinced that it did have a discriminatory rating system. For example, the court cited resolutions by the board of education in 1928 and 1929 increasing the salaries of white teachers by $100 and those of black teachers by $50. The appellate judges were struck by what had happened in 1941 and 1942, when surpluses were distributed to the teachers. The board established a point system, based on training, service, and present salary. It seemed to be a merit system, like that said to underlie the salary system in general, but the board then decided to give $3.00 for each point to the white teachers and $1.50 per point to the black teachers. The court said that salary differentials based on merit were permissible, but those based on race were not. "The crucial question in this case is whether the evidence demonstrates that there existed in Little Rock . . . a policy or custom of paying negro teachers less for comparable service than was paid to white teachers solely on the basis of race or color." The court found that the evidence did not support the explanation that "substantially all colored teachers are worth less than substantially all white teachers." Rather, the explanation "seems to be an after-thought designed to meet the exigencies of a defense." Although a few individual disparities might have been based on individualized determinations of merit, the system as a whole was, the court said, "based upon race and color." After this decision, all salaries in Little Rock were equalized in 1946.[21]

That the Little Rock case was a victory is, of course, obvious, but it was victory that had to be won on very unfavorable terrain. Challenging merit rating systems was far more difficult than challenging a system like Louisville's, where the racial discrimination appeared on the face of the salary schedules. Challenges to merit rating had to be heavily fact-based, which had two consequences: the difficulties of investigating and preparing for trial increased substantially,[22] and unfavorable lower court decisions would be harder to overturn on appeal, for episodes with the force of Little Rock's point system were likely to be rare. In addition, the complexity of the fact-based cases allowed unsympathetic judges to delay their decisions, as happened in Little Rock. Each of these matters made the NAACP's job more difficult, as the experiences in South Carolina, Alabama, Florida, and Louisiana show.

In South Carolina, the source of the NAACP's problems was easy to identify: delay eroded local support. Teachers first approached the national office in late 1940 and early 1941, but no plaintiff was found until February 1943, and he had to be replaced in October. The president of the Columbia branch wrote Marshall that the organization was losing prestige because people thought they had been deceived about what the NAACP could do. The lawsuit was filed in late October, about a week after the branch president had expressed his concern. When a consent decree providing for equalization was signed in February 1944, an uproar arose. The state legislature passed a bill requiring teachers who challenged their salaries to proceed through an elaborate administrative system before going to court.[23]

But South Carolina had ready at hand an even more effective barrier to equalization, the use of an apparently objective merit system. The Court of Appeals for the Fourth Circuit, which had decided *Alston,* the Norfolk salary case, in 1940, had authority over federal cases from South Carolina. The state legislature immediately responded to *Alston* by appointing a committee in 1941 to review the certification and compensation of teachers. The committee urged a thorough study of the possibility of using the National Teacher Examinations, a set of objective tests on specific subjects thought to be relevant to teacher competency. The use of such tests, the committee concluded, might reduce problems in certification that were caused by variations in the quality of teacher-training programs. The state board of education studied the issue for two years and issued a four-volume report in 1944. The report recommended that the tests be used to develop a four-tier system of certificates. The best certificate would go to those who scored in the upper 25 percent of those taking the test, B certificates would go to the middle 50 percent, C certificates to the next 15 percent, and D certificates to the bottom 10 percent. Pay scales would be based on the type of certificate a teacher held. In 1945 the board made a preliminary decision to use this system. Before the decision was implemented, the board tested half of the state's teachers. The pretest showed that 90 percent of the white teachers and 27 percent of the black teachers would get A or B certificates, whereas the remaining 10 percent of the whites and 73 percent of the blacks would get C or D certificates. Not surprisingly, the results did not lead the board to change its initial decision to rely on the tests.[24]

The delays in Alabama were even longer, and the cases consumed more of the lawyers' attention. A teachers' committee was established in Birmingham in 1938, but was moribund until Marshall prodded people in Alabama after the appellate decision in the Norfolk case. However, he found that the teachers were confused about the meaning of that decision and that local officials were threatening, as they often did, to equalize salaries by lowering those of white teachers. Local NAACP officials were so uncertain of support from the teachers' association that they wondered if the NAACP could act without that support. Marshall discouraged independent action, and was vindicated when the teachers raised $2,000 for a defense fund. By then, though, it was mid-1941. Several months passed before a plaintiff was found, and two months were consumed in futile discussion with the school board, which had equalized minimum salaries and promised to do more but set no date for full equalization. The lawsuit was filed in March 1942, the plaintiff was drafted into the army in May, and the suit then lay dormant until a pretrial conference was held in November 1944. Trial was set for April 1945, at which time the suit was settled, with equalization to occur that fall.[25] Over the course of the five years in which this lawsuit was more or less active, Marshall in the national office had to nurse it along, encouraging the teachers, giving advice to the attorneys, and, once, meeting with the Alabamans in Birmingham.

Without a major expansion of the national staff, it would have been impossible to supervise many salary suits to that extent. Houston had hoped to generate a cadre of black lawyers dispersed throughout the country. As he told the NAACP's National Conference in 1935, "the most hopeful sign about our legal defense is the ever increasing number of young Negro lawyers, competent, conscientious and courageous, who are anxious to pit themselves against the forces of reaction and injustice." Houston, aware of what he had accomplished at Howard, thought that "we are gradually developing a staff of good lawyers who can take over at any point so that the program will not lag regardless of personnel casualties."[26] But experience showed that delegating the campaign to local attorneys led to victory only by luck, caused at least one disaster, and created serious problems in the relations among the national legal staff, the national office of the NAACP, the local attorneys, and the local NAACP branches. Here the cases from Florida and Louisiana are the most instructive, for they spanned the period from the Maryland cases to the late 1940s and draw together nearly all of the strands that complicated the litigation campaign.

Teachers in Florida took the initiative, informing Walter White in August 1937 that they were ready to file an equalization petition. Although Marshall urged Houston to support the case, Houston was alarmed. Saying that "we will have to go very carefully here and be sure of each step before we move," he outlined the various matters that had to be decided: whether the plaintiffs should be taxpayers or teachers, what administrative steps had to be taken, and how they could meet the defense that lower salaries were justified by a lower cost of living for blacks. Houston thought that it was unwise to skip from Maryland to Florida; "clean[ing] up" the upper South first would mean that "we won't dissipate our money, and we will be working in states where the public won't be afraid to support us." Houston's fears that teachers in Florida would be too timid were confirmed by difficulties in lining up support and then in reassuring the plaintiffs who were located by S. D. McGill of Jacksonville, the black lawyer handling the case in Florida. Unlike most of the NAACP's lawyers, McGill was an older man, nearly sixty years old, who had been practicing law for almost thirty years. He was a successful lawyer in accident cases, but that did not necessarily make him a suitable attorney for the purpose at hand. Although he had been active in NAACP litigation for many years, he may have been unfamiliar with the methods of civil rights litigation that Marshall and Houston had developed, and he seems to have been unwilling to accept guidance from the younger men. Nonetheless, Marshall pressed McGill forward.[27]

Unfortunately, McGill chose to file state court mandamus actions, which were defeated on the grounds that school boards had no duty to use salary schedules and that mandamus to equalize discretionary salary schedules was therefore unavailable. Meanwhile, several teachers were fired—some not even connected with the lawsuit—and Marshall gave up. He criticized McGill for failing to present the courts with the statutes authorizing salary schedules, and made a more general point, once again based on the Maryland experience: "Mandamus just will not work in those states where they fire the teachers without cause or refuse to give them new contracts. It is not our fault that they do these underhand things but it ruins the cases. Our only hope is in the Federal courts to seek injunctive remedy." [28]

Because the state association of black teachers strongly supported the equalization drive, efforts in Florida persisted. In mid-1940, teachers in Jacksonville informed McGill of their interest in pursuing litigation. Marshall tested the waters, reminding them that "at the beginning of this fight I told the teachers of Florida that they were in for a long fight. This is not a single battle but rather a real war in which we will lose some battles and win others." The Jacksonville suit was filed in April 1941, and although Marshall was "thoroughly disgusted" at one point when he learned that some teachers had tried to negotiate their own settlement, the case resulted in the entry of a strong consent decree in 1942. A memorandum from a Florida attorney to White, Marshall, and Hastie gives a flavor of what the management problems were like in Jacksonville and elsewhere:

The handling of this case by the local committees and local counsel has resulted in utter confusion. In the first place, Mr. J. L. Williams, head of the Steering Committee, is highly emotional, an alarmist, and has a temper that often gets out of control. It is said that he threatened Counsel McGill with bodily harm, on one occasion. The committees have constantly consulted with the Board of Education without counsel being present. Also, they have talked with counsel for the defendants without Mr. McGill's being present. There are rumors abroad that the lawyer for the School Board is an associate of Fleming & Fleming, attorneys who have been associated with Mr. McGill in several cases, and that there had been a general sell-out concerning the way the teachers would be rated. McGill's version is that the teachers and the several committees have tried to settle the case without his advice, and have held meetings and conferences without his knowledge; that the teachers have conferred with the lawyer for the School Board more than they have conferred with him. On the other hand, the teachers say that McGill has never met with them at any time, even when they have requested him to do so;

and that McGill has refused to answer their questions concerning the case, replying in every instance that he was the lawyer and that they had no business inquiring about legal procedures.

Apparently the teachers do not trust themselves, or him, or any of their committees. Some of the citizens claim that Williams, too, has sold out the teachers. Generally, it appears that none of the teachers have any confidence in McGill.

On the day that I arrived in Jacksonville, September 23, Mr. McGill said that he could not be present for the final hearing on the case because he had to go to Tallahassee on a criminal case. I announced this at a meeting of the Steering Committee on that night. I understand that the chairman of the Citizens' Committee called McGill and told him that the opinion was general that he was selling out the teachers, and that his leaving town would confirm this rumor. . . .[29]

When school boards discovered that a merit rating system could be used as a device to avoid equalization, problems of internal dissension among black teachers became even more severe. In Ocala, for example, the school board combined threats of dismissal with merit rating to demoralize the teachers. L. E. Thomas, the lawyer who had been retained by the teachers, wrote Marshall, "There is a great lack of courage in the ranks over there, and I have to combat it as best I can from within." The rating system that the board adopted seemed acceptable when viewed from the national office. But when the lawyers presented the teachers with a draft decree incorporating the system, the teachers objected, because they thought that the system had been used to discriminate. Now the NAACP was trapped: the moving force behind the Ocala challenge had been made up of black principals, and the rating system had those principals rate black teachers. The principals thus lost interest in the suit, and the consent decree simply mirrored the rating system.[30] Similarly, in Palm Beach, the teachers won only a reduction in the number of steps in the rating system. The system was subjective, but the teachers seemed most upset over the specific black person named to the rating committee; once they were assured that she would be replaced, the teachers were satisfied.[31]

The real blows in Florida came when the courts approved rating systems that the NAACP had challenged. The federal district court upheld the system used in Tampa, which established three salary classifications incorporating twenty-nine factors, many of which were subjective. As implemented, the racial breakdown of the categories was clearly discriminatory: 84 percent of the white teachers were in the best-paid group and only 1 percent in the lowest paid, whereas 80 percent of the black teachers were in the lowest-paid group and only 6 percent in the highest. The judge concluded that "the fact that 80 percent of the negro teachers fell into A-3 and 84 percent of the whites into A-1 may be significant," but he thought that the proportions "represent[ed] the fair and conscientious effort" to apply the rating system uniformly. He relied on testimony that "the members of the Committee did not give any consideration as to what effect their ratings might have upon the ultimate salaries to be received by either the white or negro teachers." [32]

Although the case illustrated the problems that rating systems posed for the equalization campaign, the NAACP might have drawn some hope from the appellate court's decision in the Little Rock case. That hope was dashed in a case from Miami, where the teachers hired their own white lawyer, who used pleadings developed by the NAACP but otherwise had no contact with the organization. The trial judge approved the board's rating system, and the United States Court of Appeals for the Fifth Circuit, whose rulings governed all actions brought in federal courts in the Deep South, affirmed. The trial record was very slim, and the teachers' attorney had not attacked assertions about the inferior quality of black colleges or about the "negro [being] an undeveloped race, as we know him in the South." The court of appeals concluded: "Where all rating is on an individual basis, it is impossible that there should be a class discrimination except against members of the class. No case of individual unfairness has been revealed . . . and no witness has testified to any, though unintended errors are admitted." [33] The decision was a disaster: unless school boards made grotesque errors like the one in Little Rock, they could use rating systems that had significant subjective elements to reproduce with only modest changes the prior discriminatory salary patterns.

Action in Louisiana began in May 1939, when J. E. Perkins, a non-lawyer who was the secretary of the Regional Conference of Southern Branches of the NAACP, wrote White seeking information about salary cases. Marshall said that he would help, but he failed to proceed with the case when investigation disclosed that Perkins's reputation was uncertain and that his work on the case was inadequate and "dangerous," presumably to the long-term prospects of the litigation effort. Political divisions within the New Orleans branch impaired further progress, and New Orleans teachers finally had to use an intermediary, the editor of the local black newspaper, to approach the national NAACP. Donald Jones, the editor, thought that "a gradual build-up" of support was needed because the black teachers were apathetic about, and the white teachers opposed to, equalization. He decided to use the state teachers' association to raise funds, which was accomplished by February 1941. These actions generated some tension with the local NAACP branches, who found that their fund-raising efforts were faltering because of the competition. Marshall went to New Orleans in March, and, after he received a telegram in May saying that the teachers were restive, an equalization petition and a lawsuit were filed.[34]

Once again, initiatives by the teachers threatened what the national staff thought was appropriate. With at least tacit support from their local attorney, A. P. Tureaud, they planned to propose a two-year equalization program, which Marshall regarded as the minimum acceptable resolution and therefore inappropriate as the first proposal in negotiations. Almost a year later, after the school board's motion to dismiss the suit had been denied in February 1942, the board responded with a five-year program that Tureaud thought would ultimately benefit a larger number of teachers than the shorter one. Marshall told Tureaud that the proposal had too many catches and extended over too long a period, and the teachers agreed. But Tureaud, apparently unhappy at the degree of control that Marshall was imposing on him, continued to try to move on his own. He wanted to tell the board what the teachers would accept as the maximum time for equalization, but Marshall rejected that approach because the board was the party pushing for settlement and would come up with increasingly favorable terms if the teachers stood firm. When Tureaud seemed to endorse the board's next proposal for equalization over three years, because the board's budget would not allow a shorter period without cutting the salaries of white teachers, Marshall found it "alarming" that Tureaud supported a proposal playing black against white. Finally, in August 1942, a two-year decree was agreed upon.[35]

For our purposes, the most significant events came after the settlement. Tureaud had graduated from Howard Law School in 1925 and became one of only four black members of the Louisiana bar in 1927. Before 1941 Tureaud had held a Republican patronage job and had no significant private practice. He had resigned from the local branch of the NAACP in 1929 when it hired white attorneys for a voter-registration case, and he may have regarded the teachers' suit as an ordinary fee-generating case. When Tureaud presented his bill for $3,500, the teachers' committee became angry and offered him a much smaller "donation" in lieu of full payment. Tureaud rejected the donation, writing to Marshall that, like the teachers, he was angry and bitter that his hard work was not appreciated. Eventually the dispute was ironed out, with Tureaud receiving $2,000. Marshall had told the teachers that fees for local attorneys were not controlled by the national office and therefore varied; Tureaud's bill, he said, was not wildly out of line.[36]

The dispute over Tureaud's bill was one of a recurring series of disputes that can be understood only by placing them in a broader framework. Because litigation figured so centrally in the NAACP's actions, Walter White, as executive secretary, took a great deal of interest in what the lawyers did. Yet he was not a lawyer, and his point of view was affected by his organizational position and by his belief that as a result of his position he ought to participate in the litigation decisions being made by the lawyers. For example, he understood that the lawyers wanted "desirable" plaintiffs if they could be found, but he once reported to the board of directors that the lawyers were "still waiting for an ideal [university] case. We want to get a qualified student as near as white as possible."[37]

White was part of the background against which the lawyers acted. He had coordinated the NAACP's legal work in the 1920s skillfully, but the development of a professional legal staff meant that his skills in that area would go unused. The branches sometimes directed their expressions of concern about litigation to him, and the legal staff had to be able to respond to his occasional, and occasionally erratic, interventions. Further, as the NAACP's litigation garnered more publicity, some personal rivalry for community leadership developed between White and Marshall. White's strength lay in his abilities as a publicist.[38] He made major contributions to the NAACP's antilynching campaign. As the legal challenge to segregation took shape in 1936, he had attempted to preserve a sphere for his special talents by proposing that both campaigns join in a fund-raising effort. By late 1939, however, the legal program had replaced the antilynching campaign in the organization's priorities. Although White, sometimes described as egocentric, of course supported the legal program, he also wanted to protect his position within the NAACP and the black community; he therefore took actions that the legal staff viewed as intrusions on their proper domain.[39]

In addition, as the lawyers in the national office attempted to farm out the litigation, the national office had to satisfy the demands of its own broader constituency, the NAACP membership. The branches had two complementary interests. First, they needed to conduct their own fund-raising drives. As the New Orleans case shows, however, those drives competed with efforts by joint NAACP-teacher committees to create a defense fund for salary cases. Second, they preferred assistance from Houston and Marshall. Not only were these men the most prestigious black lawyers in the country, whose presence in a lawsuit would enhance the branch's image and fund-raising ability, but they were salaried and therefore would not present the branch with a bill for service.

Thus, the interests of the NAACP executive staff were in some tension with those of the national legal staff. In some ways, that tension was inadvertently institutionalized in 1939. During the 1920s and 1930s the NAACP engaged in a major effort to secure the passage of a federal antilynching law. That effort entailed lobbying activities. Federal law allowed contributions to "charitable and educational" organizations to be deducted from the contributor's income before calculating his or her taxes. The NAACP's lobbying activities led the commissioner of the Internal Revenue Service to deny this tax benefit to the NAACP's contributors in 1925, a decision that was reaffirmed in 1934 and 1938. The NAACP asked the commissioner to reconsider this last decision, which had led three large contributors to withhold their usual donations, totaling about $2,000, but the request was denied. Acting on a suggestion made by tax officials during the 1938 negotiations, Marshall proposed that a separate fund be set up to handle lobbying only. The NAACP's board of directors apparently realized that the NAACP's membership was the surest source of money for unrestricted purposes, and in September 1939 it resolved instead to incorporate a fund for tax-exempt activities such as education and litigation. At its inception, the NAACP Legal Defense and Educational Fund shared directors with the NAACP itself, to assure contributors that the "Inc Fund" would carry on the familiar work of the NAACP.[40] Although the "Inc Fund" and the NAACP shared the same office space until 1952, after 1939 the lawyers were no longer institutionally a part of the NAACP, and separate fund-raising by the "Inc Fund" led in 1941 to the selection of directors for the fund who were not all members of the NAACP Board of Directors.[41] The institutional separation undoubtedly bred some psychological distance as well.

By 1942 the expansion of the NAACP's program led to difficulties in administering its activities. Walter White explained his problem to the members of the Committee on Administration of the NAACP Board of Directors: "As far as personnel and pressure of work would permit these instructions from the Board have been or are being carried out by the Staff. But the volume of work and problems which grow in number and perplexity prevents members of the Staff, particularly the Secretary, from having the time or detachment from details of the work to do the job as it should be done. Perhaps even more pertinent is that those of us who are engaged in the day-to-day work cannot wholly achieve the objectivity necessary for such shifting of program and revision of machinery." The committee accepted White's recommendation that William Hastie be hired for four to six weeks to prepare "an objective analysis of our work and methods." Hastie's report had the effect of suggesting that the ties between the NAACP and the legal staff be loosened. His primary recommendation was that the NAACP rent additional space. He recognized that this would lead to the "physical separation" of the department concerned with contact with NAACP branches from the legal department, though the branch department often received inquiries that ultimately had to be answered by the legal staff. Hastie also recommended that the legal staff be expanded so that Marshall and Milton Konvitz, Marshall's only assistant, could devote their time to "actual litigation" and legal research on the major NAACP cases. A new staff member could "handle routine correspondence and interviews." Further, Hastie wrote Konvitz that "it seems to me that it is not sound tactics to handle a technical legal problem which is presented to the National Office by writing to members of the National Legal Committee and asking their opinion. It seems to me that the first job of the legal staff is to work out a tentative analysis of the problem on the basis of such preliminary research as is feasible." Marshall and the Committee on Administration approved of Hastie's recommendation.[42] Taken together these steps began to separate the legal staff from the rest of the NAACP's national staff by creating a legal bureau specializing in the litigation effort. It is inaccurate to see what happened as a complete divorce between the "Inc Fund" and the NAACP, but it can be fairly described as the institutionalization of certain professional and personal differences that probably exerted a subtle psychological effect on the legal staff, who could begin to think of themselves as independent actors in the politics of the black community.

Several examples of difficulties between the NAACP and its lawyers can be drawn from the NAACP's early school cases. One, astonishingly, caused a rather harsh exchange of letters between the NAACP and Houston himself. Early in the Bluford journalism case in Missouri, which Houston handled after he left the national staff, Roy Wilkins told White that independent fund-raising for the case would hurt the NAACP's membership drive. Houston then tried the case. When the bill he submitted had not been paid two months later, he wrote a curt letter to Marshall saying that lawyers who were not on salary needed to be paid promptly. Wilkins immediately replied with a stern letter. He said first that during the time Houston was paid from the Garland Fund appropriation, he had centered the litigation effort on himself and had received extensive publicity as a crusading warrior for black rights. The program was continued after the fund money was gone, Wilkins added, not because it benefited the NAACP directly—indeed, he said, membership drives conducted in conjunction with litigation had not been productive—but because it gave some prestige to the NAACP. Wilkins thought that the litigation campaign was something of a luxury, and concluded by noting that Houston had used his staff title in the Missouri case, even though he was privately retained. Houston replied with a letter that lowered the level of controversy but that did point out the differences in perspective between the national legal staff and the national executive staff: he told White and Wilkins to ask Marshall how much complaints about slow pay from the NAACP hurt the organization. Marshall too was sensitive to the concerns of the NAACP's affiliated lawyers. In October 1939 he sent a memorandum to Wilkins on "inaccuracies in press releases," one of which was the failure to mention the name of Leon Ransom, chief counsel in the University of Tennessee cases and "associate counsel" in the salary cases. "He is serving without fee and the least we can do is to give him the publicity to which he is entitled."[43]

Two less highly charged incidents illustrate the ability of the branches to move around the lawyers and appeal to the executive staff. Several members in Florida questioned the NAACP's reliance on S. D. McGill, who was called on because he was a member of the NAACP's legal committee. When McGill presented his bill, White was told that some teachers thought that it was too high, an objection that White endorsed. Marshall suggested to White that McGill, who Marshall thought was the only suitably qualified black lawyer in Florida, might lower his fee if William Hastie hinted at that solution subtly enough.[44]

One other conflict can serve as a final example of the difficulties facing the legal staff. In August 1941, the black teachers in Richmond proposed a five-year equalization plan, a much more extended one than Marshall typically sought. The school board rejected the proposal and countered with an eight-to-ten-year plan. The teachers, infuriated, filed suit on December 24, 1941. Six days later, the board voted to equalize in five years if the suit were withdrawn. The legal staff advised the teachers to accept the five-year proposal because the board had met the teachers' original demands. Several teachers wrote White of their disgust at the position of the staff, and Marshall told White that the staff had made a mistake in becoming involved in the case, because now it would be blamed for a settlement on terms that the staff had not set or even influenced.[45]

The NAACP's leaders had always thought that the legal attack on segregation would increase its cost beyond the point where the practice was economically viable. In 1946 a journalist observed that it had cost Missouri $500,000 to graduate one student from the black law school and ten students from the black journalism school in Lincoln University. He noted that the effects of the NAACP's lawsuits had been delayed by the war, but that every southern state "must now find a solution." Similarly, when school officials from several states met in the aftermath of *Alston,* they estimated that equalization would cost $10 million.[46] These participants and observers were too sanguine about the inevitability of compliance with what at the outset seemed the clear requirement of law. Clarity became obscurity, as state officials began to construct definitions of equality that preserved the status quo and that judges were willing to accept. Compliance with the law as it was applied by the courts was then accomplished, but little changed.

At the end of 1946, Robert Carter drafted a speech for White, in which he suggested that White say, "The teachers' salary fight is now about over." Equalization had occurred in some states, but average salary differentials, though smaller than they had been in 1930, remained significant. Taking the South as a whole, black teachers in 1931−32 received approximately 50 percent of what whites received. By 1935−36, the ratio had increased to about 55 percent, and by 1945−46 to perhaps 65 percent. These gains resulted from the NAACP's litigation and southern responses, but the lawsuits were concentrated in urban areas. Recalcitrant school boards outside the cities, where litigation would have been difficult, could be fairly confident that they would not soon be compelled to increase the salaries of black teachers. Thus, Carter's comment had a somewhat different meaning than first appears. In one sense, the campaign was an investment in a particular type of activity, which had to be justified by its return. That return was the erosion of segregation, "to compel the states to pay for their 'luxury' by compelling complete equalization which will inevitably destroy segregation," as Marshall put it in the enthusiasm after the victory in the Little Rock case.[47] By the late 1940s, however, investing in university and salary suits seemed less likely to generate a return that would justify the investment. The minimum unit of investment, to pursue the metaphor, was rather large: each case consumed a great deal of time and effort, as school boards adopted merit rating systems and as teachers sporadically lost enthusiasm over the long haul, and each suit threatened serious ruptures among the segments of the black community interested in eliminating segregation. In addition, the returns on the investment were decreasing, at least on the margin: it had been easier to work in the South's cities, and mopping-up operations, though they probably would have succeeded, would have increased the costs of segregation only slightly.

The NAACP had not reached the Supreme Court in a segregation case since 1939. By the mid-1940s the staff understood that anything short of a major victory there would have the same effect that strategic litigation was designed to avoid: it would fritter away the NAACP's limited resources without significantly eroding segregation. These organizational factors played into the decision to abandon the equalization strategy and to attack segregation directly. The staff had persisted in Houston's twofold strategy, but by 1945 the costs of continuing further far exceeded the benefits that would accrue. The NAACP lawyers made no real decision that has to be explained in this period. What mattered was that the NAACP's expectation of substantial increases in the costs of segregation as a result of litigation had been disappointed. It had proven difficult to coordinate the litigation, especially in the face of evasive maneuvers that school boards developed. The coordination problems in turn caused difficulties within the NAACP, which were compounded by the attempt to rely more heavily on local attorneys. For all these reasons, a change in direction would seem inevitable. But the change did not come until 1950, because Marshall first had to lay some crucial political groundwork.

7. The Strategy of Delay and the Direct Attack on Segregation

The Margold Report had focused on the unequal expenditure of funds for black and white elementary and secondary schools. It had suggested that attacking unequal expenditures would destroy segregation directly, if the states chose to equalize spending by merging the systems, and indirectly, if the states were forced to bring the black separate schools up to the level of the white schools at so great a cost as to make segregation a fiscally intolerable policy. Yet through the 1940s the NAACP's national staff became involved in only a few cases involving inequality of facilities in elementary and secondary schools.

In early 1940, Houston, acting as a private attorney, investigated the situation in Loudoun County, Virginia, in which the facilities at the black schools were inadequate. But the black populaton was divided over the wisdom of suing, and Houston wanted to keep the NAACP as an organization out of the situation, to avoid the charge that it "trumped up" litigation.[1] In 1946 and 1947, the black community in Lumberton, North Carolina, complained about the dilapidated condition of black schools and the absence of gymnasium and playground facilities. The youth branch of the NAACP sponsored a mass meeting in October 1946 to protest the unequal facilities, and the discontent escalated significantly before the national office of the NAACP even learned of the situation. By February 1947, local activists were beginning to feel that the national office had let them down by failing to begin litigation. Marshall responded that "you don't run into court with a legal case overnight. I, personally, get sick and tired of people in our branches who wait 81 years to get to the point of bringing legal action to secure their rights and then want the lawyers to prepare the case, file it, have it decided and have everything straightened out in fifteen minutes." After a boycott of the black schools

gained wide support in the black community, a suit seeking equal facilities was filed in July 1947. Robert Carter indicated that the NAACP national office did not plan to make the Lumberton case a major one: "We
merely intend to show the inferiority of the school and of the facilities . . .
in comparison with those offered in white schools." Perhaps because of
the accommodationist cast to the leadership of the North Carolina black
community, and perhaps because of the national office's difficulties in
bringing suits to equalize facilities, discussed later in this chapter, this
lawsuit was not vigorously pressed.[2]

A similar local initiative in Hearne, Texas, protesting disparities between a white school with a physical plant worth $3,000,000 and an
average class size of twenty-seven and a black school worth $300,000 and
an average class size of sixty, resulted in a boycott that kept 75 percent of
the black students out of school. Eventually a suit was filed against the
school district. Elsewhere in Texas, W. J. Durham filed and immediately
settled a lawsuit in 1949 that brought a well, bus transportation, and fur-
niture to a black school. Other suits in Texas generated needed repairs
and laboratory equipment for black schools.[3]

The NAACP found it difficult to support actions even as limited as
these. In regard to the Hearne case, Marian Wynn Perry, an assistant to
Marshall, praised "the courage of the 'little Joes' in the South." But she
suggested that the complaint be modified to omit a request for "a modern, fireproof school plant for Negroes" as relief. The national staff preferred to seek admission of blacks to white schools. Although Perry recognized that it was not "always possible to take such a position in view of
the temper of the local community," she recommended a strategy proposed in the Margold Report: the complaint should seek elimination of
discrimination and leave it to the defendants to decide how to accomplish
that. Similarly, Perry suggested that the equalization claim in Lumberton
be expanded to include "material on the general inequality of Negro
schools," and in another later case Carter discouraged a "limited" equalization suit.[4]

In light of the Margold Report, it is initially surprising that the NAACP
engaged in so little activity involving elementary and secondary facilities
until the late 1940s. The issue has three parts: why was there so little
activity before 1950, why did elementary and secondary cases suddenly
become central in 1950, and why at that time did the NAACP challenge
segregation directly instead of seeking to equalize facilities? These questions do not deny that from the start the NAACP wished to attack segrega-

tion in elementary and secondary education. Rather, they ask why it took so long to bring the challenge, and why the challenge ended up taking the form that it did.

In many ways all these questions have a single answer. Facilities cases posed extraordinarily delicate political problems for the NAACP. Because the problems of internal politics were so severe, decisions about elementary and secondary cases were postponed for a few more years. By 1950, the decisions could not be put off, nor did Marshall want to postpone them further. He had used the period to lay the groundwork for a direct attack on segregation by demonstrating to various constituencies that the direct attack was an attractive though not costless choice. Successes in university cases that reached the Supreme Court, for the first time in nearly a decade, played an important part in that demonstration, as did a sense that the general political climate was receptive to a direct attack. Further, though some of Marshall's constituencies were hesitant about directly attacking segregation, other important elements in the NAACP had been urging the strategy on Marshall for several years. All things considered, the timing, and to a lesser degree the substance, of the direct attack decision appear to have been most significantly affected by organizational politics.

The national staff was reluctant to pursue an equalization strategy for both ideological and organizational reasons. The former were developed in detail in a series of increasingly bitter letters between Marshall and Carter Wesley. Wesley was an attorney and editor of an important black newspaper published in Houston. He was described as militant and as having strong willpower, and, as the exchange with Marshall makes clear, Wesley was not an easy person to get along with. He had been involved in an earlier dispute with the NAACP over strategy in challenging the Texas white primary, and the arguments in 1945 and 1946 were rather similar to the earlier ones. In both Wesley was concerned with questions of control by the national office as well as with questions of strategy.[5] In 1946 Wesley set up the Texas Conference for the Equalization of Educational Opportunities. The conference, which may well have existed almost exclusively on paper, was said to be concerned with "prosecution of such cases as do not come within the NAACP's segregation field." That is, it was to fight "on the segregated side" for equal though separate facilities. Marshall expressed concern that, if the conference did not necessarily duplicate the NAACP's efforts, it would "work . . . toward the establishment of segregated educational facilities" and therefore "compet[e] with the principles of the N.A.A.C.P." He said, "You just simply cannot have a little segregation; you cannot rationalize on the necessity of segregation at all." One letter to Wesley concluded:

Every segregated elementary school, every segregated high school and every segregated college unit is a monument to the perpetuation of segregation. It is one thing to "take" segregation that is forced upon you and it is another thing to ask for segregation. I still believe that if the opposition finds that there are *representative* and *respectable* Negroes who cannot be bought and who have standing, who are in favor of segregation, then they will consider that as a much better victory than any legal case that they can win against us.[6]

Wesley presented his case, after personal relations with Marshall had become strained, in a long letter of October 8, 1947. He agreed that direct attacks on segregation were appropriate, but objected to "making this an exclusive remedy." Instead, equalization suits should be brought; it did not "invite the establishment of segregated schools to insist that those schools already established be equalized." To Wesley, "the N.A.A.C.P. [was] fooling itself" in thinking that a direct attack would "knock down segregation at one fell swoop." Wesley pointed to the salary equalization cases as models, and thought that Marshall could not simultaneously support those cases and attack facilities equalization suits. Wesley found no inconsistency between direct attacks in university cases and equalization suits elsewhere. The latter simply accepted the existing fact of segregation, without adopting it as a principle, and sought to make "separate but equal" a reality. He concluded by noting that the *Gaines* case and other university suits had resulted not in the desegregation of existing facilities, but in creating "shameful makeshift" separate programs, with no real equality. If such farces were to be avoided, equalization suits had to be brought: "In Mt. Pleasant, Texas the whites are taking most of the money and giving Negroes makeshifts in the form of inadequate buildings, short school terms, no bus service, and no lunches. You know as well as I that you aren't going to get a Negro with nerve enough in that mean East, [*sic*] Texas town, to sue to have his child go to a white school. But you will get plaintiffs to sue to make their school equal, because that follows the pattern that the white man himself has set up."[7]

Marshall's response came a week later. NAACP suits in elementary and secondary school cases "point . . . out the inequalities" and seek an order that would bar the school board from "denying to the Negro the equal facilities furnished to the white student." Marshall contrasted Wesley's procedure as seeking a different form of relief, "the establishment of equal facilities by raising the Negro school to the level of the white school." A lawsuit seeking an injunction against discrimination "would be answered . . . by either the admission to the white school or the type of relief you request." Thus, Marshall argued, "in our proceedings we get either the type of relief in your case or the breaking down of segregation" and could not "get less." Yet the NAACP's approach "would be constantly hitting at segregation." Marshall thought that his analysis reduced the disagreement to one over a relatively minor procedural point. He acknowledged that there had been changes in the NAACP's approach, due to "a carefully worked out legal attack which we have been working on for several years; . . . a realization that the procedure formerly followed was not gaining the results we expected; and most important, the terrific support for an all-out attack on segregation through the people in Texas." The salary cases were not a precedent for Wesley's approach, for there the issue was "not the school but the race of the teacher," an issue applicable to mixed as well as segregated systems.[8]

Marshall's position, then, was that relief in the form of equalization of facilities was subsumed under the request for an end to discrimination, and would be acceptable as a fallback position. But he rejected equalization as the sole form of relief to be sought, because that would implicitly accept the position that segregated schools were legally tolerable and could be made equal in fact. Marshall seems to have had the better of the argument, and indeed it was later noted that the basic desegregation cases were developed in ways that "left all options open," and that "some of these cases look suspiciously akin to the old equality approach with the direct challenge thrown in." But it was not just the contest with Wesley for leadership in the black community that led Marshall to tell the Texas Conference of Branches of the NAACP that " [i]t no longer takes courage to fight for mere equality in a separate school system," and that the NAACP would not seek to enforce segregation statutes.[9] The reality of the litigation process meant that the difference between equalization and the direct attack could not be blurred once the cases moved past the stage of pleading, and it was certain that, given a choice, school boards would equalize rather than desegregate.

These ideological concerns were augmented by organizational factors. Investigating inequalities was likely to be time-consuming, especially in systems where black schools might be as good as white ones in some respects—for example, by having been constructed more recently—but worse in others—for example, in lacking laboratory facilities. The salary equalization cases had shown how serious a drain on the NAACP's limited resources one fact-laden case could be, and how difficult it was to use such a case as a lever in securing victories in other cases. Marshall explored these problems by reproducing what he had done in the 1930s. In late 1947 he arranged to pay a young Virginia lawyer, Spottswood Robinson, for a one-year effort to establish a litigation program for elementary and secondary schools. Robinson, a native Virginian, had received his law degree from Howard in 1939, and had practiced law in Richmond with two other black lawyers. Most of Robinson's effort was devoted to "getting things lined up for court action" by investigating, petitioning school boards for general relief, and applying for admission to white schools. When the year ended Robinson had explored the situation in seventy-two districts, and had "active" cases at some stage in thirty-eight. But by October 1950, three years after the program began, Robinson reported that only three of fifty-one active cases were in court. The reasons were obvious: as Robinson reported to Marshall in a memorandum apparently solicited as part of Marshall's effort to persuade doubters that the direct attack was preferable to equalization litigation, the cost of a single equalization case in which only two schools were compared was $5,000. Investigation required substantial investments of attorney time, and, as Robert Carter pointed out, whereas equalization cases had to proceed school district by school district, the direct attack would require only a single case for each jurisdiction. If, as Marshall desired, a concentrated attack leading to real progress were to occur, it would have to take the form of a direct attack. The NAACP lacked the resources for any other course.[10]

The national staff had been expanded, but this, instead of making more attorneys available for the time-consuming equalization cases, actually increased the pressures for the direct attack. The staff at first consisted of Houston and Marshall. Houston resigned as special counsel in 1939 and became the most important member in a sort of "shadow" staff that conducted occasional investigations and litigation. Typically, Marshall supervised the investigation and did the litigation himself. As he had before 1939, Marshall handled most of the salary equalization cases after he succeeded Houston. But for some time after 1939, Houston, though not formally on the NAACP staff, litigated a number of important graduate school challenges. By the mid-1940s Houston's direct contributions to litigation had substantially diminished, but his place was taken by a number of salaried staff lawyers. The expansion of the staff, which included at various times Milton Konvitz, Edward Dudley, Robert Carter, Marian Wynn Perry, Franklin Williams, and Constance Baker Motley, allowed Marshall to claim that "we are now in a position to broaden out our legal program."[11]

The new attorneys enthusiastically favored the direct attack. Although Carter and Dudley had been born in the South, they and the others had moved to New York before they became associated with the NAACP, and they may not have fully appreciated the difficulties that litigation caused for blacks in the South. Some of their impatience can be glimpsed in a memorandum Carter wrote to Marshall in April 1948 after a meeting with Robinson in Virginia. Carter said that the only problem was "the old [one] as to whether or not an all-out attack on segregation will be made or whether counsel will be satisfied with a settlement which provides for steps toward equalization." He had told Robinson that a settlement giving the schools time to equalize was probably inevitable; there were not enough resources to pursue a direct attack. But he questioned the typical request for relief, an order prohibiting further discrimination. Carter said that Robinson agreed with the view that such an order would allow school boards to escape from further obligations by taking minor steps in the direction of equalization. He acknowledged that the NAACP did "not have sufficient funds to make the all-out attack on the elementary and high school level," but he chided Marshall for having "caused some confusion" about the NAACP's position:

However, you realize, of course, that unless you attack these cases on the ground that segregation itself is unlawful—and unless you refuse to accept any settlement short of that—you are taking steps in these cases which . . . are short of the goals which you have set. . . . You and the national office will have to do some very careful thinking on this proposition by the time you hold your general education conference in order that there can be some clear-cut, well-defined policy in this regard.[12]

Though the pressures to attack segregation directly were strong, they were partially offset by others. One was a diffuse sense that the direct attack was premature; the NAACP had not, after all, secured a major school decision from the Supreme Court since the *Gaines* case in 1939. More important, black teachers and principals, who had provided the primary support for the litigation until then, were extremely nervous about the direct attack strategy. A study of the 1950 *Who's Who in Colored Amer-*

ica indicated that educators, including those in elementary and high schools, formed the main professional group in the southern black leadership. Their sense of southern mores and some painful experiences had shown them that the jobs of all black teachers, not just those of a few who took active part in litigation, were threatened by the direct attack. They knew that southern whites would not tolerate a situation in which black teachers, especially men, taught white children, especially girls. The threats did not materialize until after the decision to pursue the direct attack was made, but by the end of 1951 it was clear that these fears were "one of the greatest factors contributing to opposition to integrating the public schools" within the black community. In 1953 the superintendent of the Topeka schools refused to renew the contract of a black teacher, because the school board believed that "the majority of people in Topeka will not want to employ Negro teachers next year for white children." Earlier a branch member whose wife was a teacher expressed concern that "in Kansas when such cases are brought for integration of students . . . the Negro Teachers are cut adrift without any consideration."[13]

The most extensive discussions of threats to the jobs of black teachers came in connection with a decision by white authorities to close the black Louisville Municipal College when desegregation occurred in 1951. The college was founded as a segregated branch of the University of Louisville in 1931, after the black community had spent ten years lobbying for its creation. Although it became accredited in 1936, the college suffered serious declines in enrollment during World War II. Even with curtailed programs, the college lost money after the war. In the fall of 1949, the trustees of the university, responding in part to threats that lawsuits would be filed, studied desegregation of the university. When the state legislature authorized the admission of blacks to the university, the trustees voted to desegregate it as of the fall of 1950 and to close the college in June 1951. Initially the trustees planned to terminate the contracts of all faculty members, including the four tenured professors and the three with contracts running through June 1952, giving them two months' terminal pay. The black faculty members at first insisted that they receive either positions at the University of Louisville or one year's pay. Eventually a compromise was worked out. One tenured faculty member became a member of the university's faculty. Four others received fellowships that allowed them to improve their credentials while seeking other positions; the tenured faculty member in this group also received one semester's pay. The other two took jobs elsewhere, one of which was arranged through the trustees' political influence, and accepted a financial settlement.[14]

The NAACP took a "very avid interest" in the situation, because "we cannot hope to secure the full-hearted support of the teaching faculty of Negro institutions in our fight against segregation in education if the successful results of such a fight will be the loss of jobs." The staff tried to allay fears by pointing to experiences in New Jersey and Indiana, where no wholesale firings occurred, and by developing legal strategies to challenge as discriminatory the firing of black teachers in the course of desegregation. Dean Charles Thompson of the Howard School of Education argued that there would be no "wholesale dismissal" because there were not enough white teachers to serve the combined school populations and because residential segregation would permit the continued employment of black teachers in black neighborhood schools. But those associated with the campaign knew that the remedies after dismissal were, in a practical sense, of limited value, and that the threat of dismissal would be carried out in some places. Dean Thompson concluded that black teachers should accept the sacrifices entailed by desegregation: "the elimination of legally-enforced segregated schools should outweigh in importance the loss of teaching positions even by a majority of the 75,000 Negro teachers who might conceivably be affected."[15]

The response was available, though, only after the decision had been made to seek desegregation rather than equalization. Because black teachers as a class were not threatened with loss of jobs until that decision was made, there is little indication in the documents that actual threats affected the NAACP's decisions. But the members' knowledge of the white South and the staff's understanding of the role of black teachers in providing community leadership in the campaign up to that point made it inevitable that these problems would weigh heavily against a direct attack decision.[16] Margold had proposed, and Marshall sometimes advocated, a "leave it to the defendants" strategy. But the members and staff had the sophistication to recognize that such a strategy was only a fig leaf for an underlying decision in favor of the equalization approach.

These countervailing pressures could have resulted in organizational paralysis. It is true that the choice between equalization and direct attack was postponed from 1945, when the issue surfaced, to 1950. But the period was not one of paralysis. Rather, it gave Marshall the time to use his skills as brilliantly as he ever did throughout the campaign. He combined a consistent rhetorical commitment to the direct attack with a conscious strategy of temporizing. The delays were used to prepare the organization for the direct attack decision that Marshall preferred all along.

In late 1945 Marshall expressed concern to Walter White about "our inability to get cases started on the equalization of educational opportunities in the South." The lawyers were available, the cases were important, and they were easy to win. He suggested that a planning conference be held. In May 1946 the lawyers met in Atlanta for an informal review of procedures. Although much of the discussion focused on the university cases, it did explore the theoretical problems entailed by seeking a general injunction rather than the elimination of specific inequalities. By the end of the year Marshall was able to write Carl Murphy a letter that combined support for the direct attack with reasons for delay: "Frankly, and confidentially, and just between the two of us, there is serious doubt in the minds of most of us as to the timing of an all-out attack on segregation per se in the present United States Supreme Court. We are now working on the problem of having a complete study made of the evil of segregation to demonstrate that there is no such thing as 'separate but equal' in any governmental agency. . . . When this is complete, it might then be possible to make an all-out attack. However I do not know how long it will take to complete this study. . . ."[17]

A long memorandum from Marshall to Roy Wilkins in 1947 demonstrates Marshall's personal commitment to the direct attack, and shows that his hesitancy served the purpose of balancing pressures within the NAACP:

I had assumed that the NAACP really meant business about an all-out attack against segregation, especially in the public school system. I had assumed that we not only realized that segregation was an evil but had come to the conclusion that nothing can be gained under the doctrine of "separate but equal." I had assumed that the Board of Directors, as well as the branches and branch officers, were in agreement on this. I had assumed that the resolutions adopted at the Annual Conference and the beautiful statements made at Board and staff meetings meant exactly what they said. On this basis, we have proceeded to develop the legal techniques for this all-out attack on segregation.

. . . [W]e propose to file these cases on the theory that facilities are unequal and to request an injunction by the court to enjoin the maintenance of the policy of discrimination. This will bring about either equal facilities or the breaking down of segregation. All of this was explained in the memorandum on policy, which concludes with the following . . . paragraph . . . : "Finally it must be pointed out that because of the reasons set out above, the N.A.A.C.P. cannot take part in any legal proceeding which seeks to enforce segregation statutes, which condones segregation in public schools, or which admits the validity of these statutes. . . ." You will note from this procedure that the real difference is that we do not at any place admit the validity of segregation statutes and we do not call for the enforcement of these illegal statutes.

. . . I am beginning to doubt that our branch officers are fully indoctrinated on the policy of the NAACP in being opposed to segregation. It is therefore obvious that we need to educate our branch officers and in turn the membership, and finally, the people in the need for complete support in this all-out attack on segregation because it will be impossible for our branch officers to do a good job unless we first sell them.[18]

The Board of Directors and the Annual Conference of the NAACP endorsed Marshall's position in 1948. The board stated, "it is our policy that the N.A.A.C.P. will not undertake any case or cooperate in any case which recognizes or purports to recognize the validity of segregation statutes or ordinances; the N.A.A.C.P. will likewise not participate in any case which has as its direct purpose the establishment of segregated public facilities." The conference "urge[d] the National Office and the Branches to engage in a campaign to remove narrow thinking within the ranks and eliminate any internal opposition to the elimination of segregation." Spottswood Robinson reported on his activities in Virginia to the lawyers' conference held in conjunction with the 1948 annual conference. He noted uncertainty in the community about "what they want. . . . There were many . . . who had gone no further than the question of a new Negro high school or accredited elementary schools for Negroes." It was clear, though, that Robinson preferred the direct attack. The next year the lawyers went to the annual conference firmly supporting the direct attack. The national office had called the lawyers together to discuss how "to have all governmental enforced segregation declared invalid." The lawyers agreed that the cases should seek injunctions against discrimination *and* admission of blacks to white schools. They recommended that cases "in each instance should make a direct challenge of the segregation statutes involved."[19]

The staff had thus become committed to the direct attack rather quickly, but no action followed from that commitment. Although the lawyers rejected equalization as a remedy that the NAACP should seek, they accepted the practical equivalent of "leave it to the defendants" relief in cases that were actually filed, which would of course eliminate the pressures from those who feared a direct attack. But that pragmatic approach left the staff vulnerable to attacks from two other directions. Those, like Carter Wesley, who seemed to prefer equalization litigation saw nothing happening. To them Marshall offered Robinson's exploratory survey as a reason for the staff's failure to act. First the survey had to be completed, and its results then showed how expensive the strategy would be. The other source of pressure was the constituency that desired an immediate direct attack. Marshall's letter to Carl Murphy gave one response, but far more common were references to the pending university cases in Texas and Oklahoma. For example, the Topeka branch of the NAACP expressed interest in 1948 in starting a direct attack on segregation there, believing that the schools were "physically substantially equal." Marian Wynn Perry replied that the national staff would not handle the case until the university cases reached the Supreme Court, "presenting a picture from which it could be argued that inequality inevitably results from segregation."[20]

The most elaborate explanation was given to the president of the North Carolina State Conference of Branches by Edward Dudley. Dudley wrote that the national office would not pursue additional university cases until the Supreme Court had ruled on "the question of segregation per se." The national office lacked the financial and physical resources to supervise more cases, although Dudley said that it would check the papers in cases prepared by the state conference's legal committee. The NAACP, he wrote, believed that "there can be no equality in a segregated set-up." But if the Supreme Court disagreed "at this time, we can then fall back and rely upon the 'separate but equal' theory and file as many suits as we are financially able to do so seeking to equalize every single facility offered to the public by virtue of state monies." The state conference should act only "in continuous cooperation" with the national office. But the NAACP might not be able to appeal some cases "because of the number of cases presently pending and the further fact that it only takes one good case to set a precedent."[21]

Marshall and the staff had thus bought time, which they could use to work out the problems associated with the direct attack strategy that they wanted to pursue, and to persuade their constituency that the course the staff preferred was the correct one to follow. They were also able to take advantage of changes in the political climate between 1945 and 1950. Blacks, North and South, formed an important part of the New Deal coalition that was beginning to experience internal strains. Liberal Democrats, and Harry Truman, needed to solidify the support of an increasingly militant black community. Truman established a Committee on Civil Rights, whose 1947 report *To Secure These Rights* forthrightly called for "the elimination of segregation . . . from American life." International policy joined with domestic politics in the new atmosphere. In addition to moral and economic reasons for eliminating discrimination, the committee gave an "international reason." Discrimination was "a serious obstacle" to making the country "an enormous, positive influence for peace

and progress throughout the world. . . . Those with competing philoso-
phies have stressed—and shamelessly distorted—our shortcomings. . . .
They have tried to prove our democracy an empty fraud, and our nation a
consistent oppressor of underprivileged people. . . . The United States is
not so strong, the final triumph of the democratic ideal is not so inevitable that we can ignore what the world thinks of us or our record."
Shortly after *To Secure These Rights* was issued, Truman's attorney general, Tom Clark, decided to file a brief supporting the NAACP's position in
cases then pending that challenged judicial enforcement of the racially restrictive housing covenants.[22] Opponents of the direct attack had been
able to couple the fear of mass firings with a sense that the direct attack
was unlikely to succeed. By reducing the risk of failure, the changes in the
general political climate strengthened the position of Marshall and the
staff. The direct attack strategy, they could now say, was not only right, it
was likely to succeed.

The brief of the United States in the restrictive covenant cases had another significant facet. Its legal argument was prefaced by a detailed
analysis of the implications of restrictive covenants as a matter of public
policy. Although the policy analysis formally functioned to provide the
reasons for the government's participation in a lawsuit between private
parties,[23] it also suggested the ways in which Legal Realism had affected
the process of constitutional decision making. Legal Realism had its origins in the work of Oliver Wendell Holmes, Jr., who developed his intellectual position in the late nineteenth century. At that time legal thought
was dominated by a theory now called formalism. According to formalism, rules of law were justified because they were consistent with or,
in its strong versions, were deduced from abstract concepts like "freedom
of the will" or "sovereignty." These abstractions were the foundation of
the American legal system. In a sense, the Supreme Court's opinion in
Gaines was a late expression of formalism, in its reliance on what by
1939 appeared to be the arbitrary concept of "the state" as something
significantly defined by its geographical borders. Holmes and later Legal
Realists attacked formalism in two ways.[24] First, they argued that formalists were simply wrong in thinking that particular rules could be deduced from the abstract concepts, or that any particular rule was more
consistent than its negation with those concepts. Second, they augmented
this critique of formalism with an alternative ground on which rules of
law could be justified. Legal rules, said the Realists, inevitably promoted
some social policies and hindered the achievement of others. They could

be justified only by identifying the social policies implicated by the rules and then by defending the policies the rules advanced as themselves sound and wise. By collapsing law into policy, the Realists almost inevitably were drawn to examining the operation of legal rules in their social context. Formalists had to worry about how the rules fit together within the abstract categories of the legal system; Realists had to worry about how the rules fit into the actual operation of the social system. They therefore were interested in the sociology and psychology of law.

Howard Law School, with its emphasis on using law to advance the interests of blacks, was in one sense a center of Realist thinking. For example, William Hastie evaluated the law school in a memorandum to Howard's president in 1936, saying that it sought to develop lawyers who have "an intelligent understanding of the law and its nature and ends in the social order."[25] But Howard existed outside the intellectual core of academic law. By the early 1930s, Legal Realism had become a major intellectual movement in law. Law students at such leading institutions as Yale and Harvard could not escape exposure to Realism. Further, Realism had an important political effect. Formalism was almost inevitably conservative, because of its attachment to the idea that innovations had to be reconciled with the existing set of legal principles. Legal Realists argued that the effort at reconciliation was intellectually empty, because any innovation—no matter how radical it seemed—could fit into "the law" as formalism described it. Legal Realism was thus politically liberating: the wisdom of a proposed policy was all a Realist had to be concerned with. Realists, and the students whom they influenced, were inclined to favor the politics of the New Deal, and their jurisprudence placed no obstacles in their way. Recent graduates of law schools brought to the postwar NAACP and Department of Justice the conviction that the constitutional argument against segregation could be keyed to facts and policy. Analytical distinctions could be drawn between, on the one hand, factual and policy analysis to inform legislative choice or to uphold legislation as constitutional, and, on the other, similar arguments to support a decision finding a practice unconstitutional. But intellectual currents do not always follow the lines that analysis would lay down. What came to be called the sociological argument against segregation gained at least some of its force as a legacy of Realism.

The sociological argument was Realist to the core. Law, even constitutional law, was social policy. Social policy had to be understood as it actually operated. Schools that had equal material endowments might nonetheless operate differently. The sociological argument was that, if one looked beyond material endowments to social consequences, separate schools were inevitably unequal. Whites had social opportunities unavailable to blacks in separate schools no matter how new or well staffed the black schools were; separate schools induced a sense of superiority in whites and a sense of inferiority in blacks, which in turn influenced what each race could make of the education they received in materially equal facilities. In a curious way the sociological argument had its roots in the Margold Report, too. Noting that state laws created the possibility of unequal expenditures on black and white schools and simultaneously failed to provide mechanisms by which disparities could be eliminated, the report argued that desegregation could follow from the fact of irremediable inequality. To Margold, "irremediable" referred to the absence of legal remedies for inequality. The sociological argument understood "irremediable inequality" differently; in that argument it meant that no matter what a state did to provide facilities that were equal in monetary or physical terms, an unconstitutional inequality in intangibles would remain. The move from a legal-analytical meaning to a social factual one, which one might characterize in terms used by those who analyze rhetoric as an equivocation, was precisely the effect of Realism.

The generous reception that followed the 1944 publication of Gunnar Myrdal's *An American Dilemma* made the sociological argument still more attractive. The book collected a large amount of information that drove home to readers the degree to which blacks were oppressed. This information was not only made available to NAACP litigators. It entered public consciousness and confirmed for many the arguments that political liberals had been making for years. *An American Dilemma* said nothing new to the NAACP, but it certified to the general public that people should pay attention to what the NAACP said. It was only natural for the NAACP lawyers to find satisfying an argument that allowed them to draw upon something as highly regarded as *An American Dilemma*.

The NAACP had its first opportunity to use the sociological argument in 1946. Mexican-American parents in Orange County, California, had filed a lawsuit in March 1945, challenging the local practice of segregating their children from those of whites. Neither they nor their attorneys informed the NAACP of the original proceedings. Although the NAACP "did not anticipate" the case, when the staff learned of it they understood the opportunities it gave them. The trial judge found the practice unconstitutional, and the school board appealed. The NAACP and other organizations filed briefs supporting the parents. The NAACP relied heavily on the sociological argument, drawing on published material detailing the harms caused by segregation per se. William Hastie, still serving as a counselor to Marshall, read the brief and wrote him that the argument must be developed "fully with as little delay as possible. . . . The point is clearly developed, but I believe we will be able to sustain it only when we make an exhaustive investigation." He suggested using "people in the field of education" to "assembl[e] and organiz[e] practically the entire body of available material." He closed by noting that "there may come some other case sooner than we anticipate in which we will have to make a decisive fight upon this issue."[26] Because the NAACP was not a party to the California case, it was able to experiment with the sociological argument at no cost whatever. Though the appeals court agreed that the practices were unconstitutional, it neither adopted nor rejected the sociological argument. The NAACP staff thus began to put the argument into shape, suffered no defeat with implications for its own cases, and expressed its commitment to the direct attack without threatening its own constituency in the South.

As Hastie guessed, the sociological argument had to be put to work sooner than Marshall expected. In early 1946 the NAACP prepared to bring cases seeking the admission of black students to the state law schools in Oklahoma and Texas, where no law schools for blacks had been established. The authorities in Oklahoma were sufficiently antediluvian in their actions that though the NAACP won its first education case in the Supreme Court since *Gaines,* the victory involved only a restatement of the rule set out in *Gaines.* The Texas authorities, though, were surprisingly agile, and their maneuvers forced Marshall to work out the details of the sociological argument under some pressure.

From the beginning Marshall believed that he could have won the Oklahoma case "in Mississippi." Ada Lois Sipuel decided to apply to the law school in Oklahoma when she was a junior at the State College for Negroes in Langston, Oklahoma. After a meeting of the state NAACP in September 1945 produced an announcement by Marshall that the University of Oklahoma would be sued, Sipuel sought the assistance of the NAACP. The university's board of regents adopted a resolution directing that blacks be denied admission. Sipuel and Roscoe Dunjee, an attorney and the publisher of a leading black newspaper in Oklahoma, met with the university's president, who carried her application through the admission office and promised that she would be denied admission on the ground of race and not on the ground that the State College for Negroes was unaccredited. Some students at the university supported Sipuel; an editorial in the student newspaper said, "[S]eparate school systems are impractical, undesirable, and unnecessary."[27]

The case was attended at the start with the usual delays, but the suit was filed in April 1946. In July the state trial court dismissed the action, holding that a plaintiff could not use mandamus to challenge the constitutionality of a statute. Sipuel appealed, and one year after the lawsuit started, the state supreme court affirmed the decision. It discovered some ambiguities in the NAACP's complaint, briefs, and oral arguments, which led it to conclude that Sipuel did not clearly seek admission to the white law school but might be satisfied if the state established a separate but equal black school. However, the court said, a demand on the state was required before it was compelled to set up a black school. Although the NAACP sought review in the United States Supreme Court, Marshall was not entirely happy when the Court agreed to hear the case. Because the case had been disposed of without any evidence having been heard, the record was so thin that a reversal of the state courts might simply but, Marshall feared, openly reaffirm the "separate but equal" doctrine. He therefore took care to mount a direct attack on *Plessy* in his brief to the Supreme Court; the Court might then treat the case as a simple one but be scared away from relying directly on or reaffirming the "separate but equal" rule. While the Court was considering Marshall's application for review, the *New York Herald-Tribune* editorialized, "The subject is one for practical judgment and specific application. But progress is inescapable, and a jolt by the Supreme Court is about due. We decline to believe that higher education can be both separate and equal."[28]

On January 12, 1948, in what the *New York Times* called "a move of startling suddenness" four days after argument, the Supreme Court reversed the state courts. Its opinion consisted of three paragraphs, and relied exclusively on *Gaines*. After stating the facts, the opinion said: "The petitioner is entitled to secure legal education afforded by a state institution. To this time, it has been denied her although during the same period many white applicants have been afforded legal education by the State. The State must provide it for her in conformity with the equal protection clause of the Fourteenth Amendment and provide it as soon as it does for applicants of any other group."[29]

The NAACP's lawyers thought it significant that the Court had decided the case so quickly and had directed that its mandate, the document directing the lower courts to act on the case, be sent immediately to the state courts. Registration at the white law school was scheduled for January 29. Sipuel, her lawyers, and other observers assumed that the Court wanted Sipuel admitted. However, the state supreme court, in an opinion issued on January 17, took the escape route that *Gaines* seemed to permit, and directed the university authorities to open a "substantially equal" black law school. Two days later the regents of the university met. They established a black law school in three rooms of the state capitol. Students had access to the state law library, which had more volumes than the university's law library. Within a week the regents had hired three white attorneys as the faculty of the law school. Because of the United States Supreme Court's mandate, it seemed to the NAACP lawyers that the black school had to open by January 29, too. That was manifestly impossible, which meant, the lawyers decided, that the state supreme court had blatantly defied the United States Supreme Court. Invoking the standard but rarely employed procedure for challenging direct evasions of the Court's mandates, they therefore filed a motion for permission to file a petition for an order directing the Oklahoma courts to comply with the original decision by ordering Sipuel's admission to the white law school.[30]

Marshall's earlier strategy now turned back on him. The Court was unwilling to face challenges to the "separate but equal" doctrine. Marshall's strategy gave the Court a way to avoid the issue: if Sipuel had in fact indicated that she was willing to attend a separate but equal school, the proper forum for exploring the issue of substantial equality should be the state trial court. Over two dissents, the Court rejected the NAACP's motion on the ground that Marshall had not attacked "separate but equal" in the state court, nor, the opinion said, was that "an issue here" as the case was submitted to it. Rather, the Court said, all that it had decided was that the state courts had erred in dismissing Sipuel's initial lawsuit "on the ground that she had failed to demand establishment of a separate school and admission to it." As the case stood, Sipuel could apply directly to the white law school, but the state could respond either by admitting her or by closing the white schools or by opening a black law school, so long as it moved quickly if it chose the third option. Justice Rutledge's dissent argued that *Sipuel* required Oklahoma to "end the discrimination . . . at once, not at some later time, near or remote." Oklahoma could close its law school, or it could give Sipuel a legal education that was "equal . . . in fact, not in legal fiction," to that given whites. Because Oklahoma "obviously" could not create an equal law school "overnight," it had to admit Sipuel immediately. Rutledge believed that "delay . . . would continue the discrimination." Oklahoma did open a law school for blacks, and a trial on substantial equality was held later in 1948. In the eighteen months the black school operated, only one student attended. After the black school closed, Sipuel was admitted to the previously white school in August 1949, from which she graduated in 1951.[31]

There was little public or scholarly comment on *Sipuel*. The *New York Times* thought that the Court had "begged the issue" of the constitutionality of segregation, though it of course approved the decision. "The very fact of segregation makes [facilities] unequal," said its editorial. In a segregated school with only one student, "classroom discussion . . . [,] a part of the educational process," was impossible. The editorial concluded by invoking the international scene: "If the United States is to stand before the world as an exemplar of equality of rights, if it is to urge with integrity the acceptance by the rest of the world of the tenets and practices of a democratic society, then it would be well if we set our own record straight. It seems to us that the language of the Fourteenth Amendment must be tortured out of common meaning to make segregation practices in education anything except unconstitutional." The University of Oklahoma received letters expressing similar sentiments: "It is incidents such as the Sipuel case which furnish fuel for disparaging comments by the Russian press. The Russians seize upon anything which is undemocratic or discriminatory and vilify our way of life." The *Chicago Defender*, a black newspaper, welcomed the decision in *Sipuel* as showing that "the props of Jim-Crow are buckling," but acknowledged that it was not "the death knell" of segregated education. The black press roundly criticized efforts to create new black institutions of higher education, in part because new schools could not possibly equal old ones, and in part because they were efforts to give segregation a sounder legal basis.[32]

Law reviews noted the case and almost uniformly saw it as a precursor of broader inroads on segregation. Thus, Edward Brooke, a black who was later to be a senator from Massachusetts, wrote a student note in the *Boston University Law Review* in which he concluded that the Court "apparently felt that the time was not opportune" to decide whether separate law schools could ever be equal. The case "which at first blush loomed as an important case in Federal Constitutional Law turned out to be a mere 'dress rehearsal' for the 'big show' which will undoubtedly follow in the near future." A student writing in the *Southern California Law Review* cited the California case in which the sociological argument had first been made and concluded, "More than the measurement of physical factors, [the issue of equality] presents a difficult problem in value judgment of such intangibles as comparative teaching ability and the relative merits of instruction. . . . On the question of equal educational opportunity under the Constitution, therefore, what is most significant in [*Sipuel*] . . . is not what has been said but rather what remains to be said by the Court." Others understood that what remained to be said concerned elementary and secondary schools as well, because they concluded their comments on the equality of separate facilities by citing disparities not in professional schools but in the elementary and secondary schools.[33]

In contrast, comments in southern law reviews tried to limit the scope of the Court's decision. One emphasized the Court's implicit adoption of a rule allowing a state to take one semester to establish a separate school, but acknowledged that achieving substantial equality, especially in a short time, would be extremely costly. The author suspected that applicants would frequently try "to harass the state into providing *identity* (not equality) of facilities," both by challenging the asserted equality of facilities and by keeping the numbers actually attending separate professional schools low, and suggested that some sort of sharing of facilities might be adopted: a law library might be "located conveniently between both separate schools . . . with separate reading rooms," and the same faculty might be used in both schools "with class schedules harmonized." Another author declared, "Manifestly the Supreme Court is not prepared to declare segregation unconstitutional. It is equally certain, however, that the economic obstacles which the Supreme Court has placed in the path of segregated education will make it increasingly difficult for a state to maintain this policy in all levels of the educational system. . . . Prior decisions indicate that the Supreme Court, believing the problem to be more social than judicial, will allow the people to set their own pace in teaching the mental attitude necessary to the recognition [that "the Negro must . . . cease to be *distinguished* because of his color."]" He hoped that "the Supreme Court will . . . allow the state and the individual members of both races to iron out their difficulties in the spirit of cooperation and realization of mutual benefit." John B. Harris, writing in the *Georgia Bar Journal,* was more alarmed: "Unless a more practical and realistic approach is made by the Courts and the peoples of other sections to this knotty problem, we are sore afraid of the consequences. . . . The pendulum, swinging, has swung too far. Liberalism, so welcomed by many of us, now becomes intolerance. . . . At the moment, the vista before our beloved Southland is clouded and lowering."[34]

Creating a black law school would not end Oklahoma's legal and practical difficulties. On the last day of the registration period in January 1948, six blacks applied for admission to various graduate programs. The regents, confronted with a new set of problems, appointed a committee of deans to advise it on creating graduate programs at Langston. The committee's report noted inequalities in the segregated system and, emphasizing the expense of establishing separate but equal graduate programs, recommended that blacks be admitted to graduate programs at the University of Oklahoma. The regents rejected the recommendation and decided not to create any graduate programs for blacks. George McLaurin, a black teacher in his sixties who wanted to pursue a doctoral program in education, sued the university. Given the university's complete failure to provide even a separate program, McLaurin easily secured an order directing the university to do something. The regents then authorized segregated classes in the graduate school and directed that McLaurin be admitted. McLaurin registered for four courses. All of them were rescheduled so that they could meet in a classroom that had a small anteroom or alcove on the side. McLaurin was required to sit in the anteroom. McLaurin and the NAACP continued to pursue his case, claiming that the university's response failed to meet constitutional requirements. Over the next year, five more applications for admission to graduate programs in engineering, social work, sociology, and pharmacy were received. Soon forty-three blacks were enrolled in the university's summer session. Some legislators objected to the "desegregation" of the university and preferred to restore complete segregation. It seems clear that the university could not long sustain its position: it would have to desegregate completely or create a host of separate programs.[35]

Even as *Sipuel* was being litigated, the Texas law school case had moved to the center of the NAACP's attention. The usual difficulties in locating potential plaintiffs led Marshall in early 1946 to prod A. Maceo Smith, secretary of the Conference of NAACP Branches in Texas, with the information that Oklahoma was about to get ahead of Texas in suing. Some potential applicants changed their minds or decided not to act in the face of family resistance; another was unacceptable to Marshall because the applicant was an associate in Smith's law firm. At the end of January 1946, local NAACP officials had located Heman Sweatt, a letter carrier whose desire to attend law school was fueled by his effort to challenge the failure of his employer to give him a clerical position. Although Sweatt had graduated from an unaccredited school, Marshall decided that it was worth proceeding on the chance that the authorities would deny Sweatt's application on the ground of race rather than qualifications. Theophilus Painter, the president of the University of Texas, did just that, and the lawsuit was filed in May, one month after Sipuel's case had been filed.[36]

The development of the NAACP's litigation strategy in *Sweatt v. Painter* can be understood only in light of the complex procedural history of the case.[37] Painter's letter denying admission to the white law school in Austin informed Sweatt that he could demand that a black law school be established. The trial judge agreed. Although he held that the existing situation, in which blacks had no separate law school and could not attend the white one, violated the Constitution, he gave the state six months to establish a black law school. Just before that period expired, the state moved to dismiss Sweatt's complaint, presenting a resolution by the state's board of regents vowing to set up a school in Houston. The trial judge held that the resolution satisfied the Constitution, even though the school consisted at that time of two rooms and one part-time instructor. The NAACP appealed, and the state recognized how weak its position was. Instead of continuing to rely on the obviously inadequate Houston school, the state shifted the school's location and organization, and adopted a version of the "sharing of facilities" strategy. Pending the creation of a full law school in Houston, the black law school would be located in Austin. Three rooms, sufficient to accommodate an expected enrollment of ten blacks, were rented in a building across the street from the state capitol. The students, like other citizens of Texas, would have access to the state law library in the capitol. Several members of the faculty of the white law school were to be the faculty of the black school, teaching there while continuing their work uptown. The state and the NAACP agreed that these changes, instituted in February and March 1947, altered the facts on which the decision about substantial equality was to be based. On March 26 the appeals court therefore reversed the judgment of the trial court and sent the case down to be tried fully.[38]

The NAACP had six weeks to prepare for the trial. This time constraint and the new factual posture of the case affected Marshall's strategic decisions. At the outset the case seemed almost as straightforward as Sipuel's, and even the creation of the Houston makeshift school injected only a simple element of proving the obvious physical inequality between the black and white schools. The move to Austin complicated the factual case and provided a real opportunity to use the case for the broader purpose of attacking "separate but equal."

Conceptually, there were two stages in the NAACP's decisions. First,

Marshall had to decide how much to focus on the physical aspects of inequality. As he developed the record, an honest but, fairly speaking, rather weak case of physical inequality could be presented. The black school was small, but on a per capita basis it provided equivalent floor space to that given in the white school. Of course, the comparisons were based on the assumption that ten blacks would enroll, and because of deep opposition in the black community to the state's strategy, only one black actually enrolled. But that could hardly be attributed to the state's failure to provide adequate physical facilities.[39] The state law library was not designed to accommodate use by students, but it had essentially the same contents as the library at the white school. The instructors in the black school did not teach full time there, but they were not part-time teachers. The undeniable differences between the schools lay in their extracurricular, intangible aspects. These included the absence of a law review and a moot court program at the black school, and the inability of a school with a projected enrollment of ten to support such activities. But once the attention shifted from physical facilities and the formal program, it was easy to broaden the argument to include all sorts of noncurricular differences between the schools: reputation, opportunity for developing professional contacts, and the like. And once those differences became relevant, the sociological argument could be deployed fully. Thus, the manner in which *Sweatt* developed made it seem easy and indeed perhaps necessary to attack *Plessy*. The flaws the Supreme Court had found in the attempt to do so in *Sipuel* were eliminated because *Sweatt* was in some ways a harder case, in which all relevant arguments seemed appropriate and possibly essential.

The second stage in *Sweatt* followed almost inexorably once the case had been broadened. If "separate but equal" was to be attacked using the sociological argument, it made sense to attack it across the board, not just for law schools or graduate education. Here the points about reputation and professional contacts would serve only as specific examples of the general harms that segregation imposed. Thus, Marshall's approach in *Sweatt* would give the Supreme Court a choice. It could follow the physical inequality route, for which there was some evidence. If it did so, the NAACP would have lost nothing and gained a little. But if the Court faced the record more honestly, and wanted to rule in Sweatt's favor, it would have to recognize the significance of the intangible aspects of education. Having done so, Marshall hoped, the Court would be committed to moving farther down the path that the sociological argument provided.

But six weeks was an extremely short period in which to develop all this. Marshall was not entirely happy about the prospects of a "wide open" trial, although he understood the opportunity he had been given. On April 3, 1947, he wrote William Hastie and several other members of an informal group of advisers seeking their help "in view of the fact that all the Negroes in the State of Texas, with the exception of Carter Wesley, are determined to hit segregation . . ."

So, whether we want it or not, we are now faced with the proposition of going into the question of segregation as such. I think we should do so because even if we don't take the case far, we at least should experiment on the type of evidence which we may be able to produce on this question. For example, we want to produce experts such as Charlie Thompson to testify as to the inevitable effects of segregation in per capita expenditures, etc. We are also contemplating putting up Otto Kleinberg to testify as to the racial characteristics not being present and other evils of segregation. We are also contemplating putting on anthropologists to show that there is no difference between folks.[40]

Hastie urged Marshall to be cautious. He apparently believed that the issue of substantial equality would turn on physical and curricular matters, where the NAACP's case was weakest. He thought that Marshall could preserve "at least an infinitesimal chance of winning the law suit" by emphasizing that "at the graduate and professional level limited demand for training and high per capita cost make discrimination in fact inevitable." Without "argu[ing]" that segregation at the lower levels is permissible," this approach would "give the court a basis for distinguishing the general public school situation from the case at hand." He also agreed that the NAACP might not take *Sweatt* to the Supreme Court, but noted that "public pressure to carry the case as far as possible will be tremendous. You might warn NAACP speakers against uncautious predictions of what will be done in this litigation."[41]

But, consistent with his preference for the direct attack on segregation, Marshall's enthusiasm was not to be dampened. After the 1948 trial on substantial equality in *Sipuel*, for example, he wrote Erwin Griswold, dean of Harvard Law School and a witness for the NAACP at that trial, "Frankly, I am seriously worried that the Judge will go off on the point of physical inequality and will completely dodge the segregation issue." Griswold replied, "Of course I understand your great desire to carry on the legal battle and to win a complete victory in very short order." But, Griswold said, *Sipuel* was a good case on inequality and a bad one on segregation, and he hoped that the judge would indeed do what Marshall feared. "The thing to do with this case, as I see it, is to win it. That will be a very great step forward. It will, indeed, be one of the most important steps yet taken on the segregation problem."[42]

The time limitations in *Sweatt* led Marshall to pursue a dual strategy. Because it was a law school case, he relied on experts in legal education to testify in court about what substantial equality would be and how it could not be reached in separate schools. The more general points were made by presenting one witness, Robert Redfield, an anthropologist, and by invoking social science research like Gunnar Myrdal's *American Dilemma,* surveys published in the *Journal of Negro Education,* and the report of the President's Committee on Civil Rights. This made it possible to press the specifics on the court through direct testimony and, perhaps more important, to coordinate the presentation of the sociological argument in the limited time available.

While these cases were pending, the white community responded to the changes that seemed near. At the University of Texas, an all-white branch of the NAACP was formed, and a large crowd rallied to demonstrate support for Sweatt. A black was admitted to the law school of the University of Arkansas, though it was said that he would be "given instruction apart from white students" in the law school building. The *Charlotte News* saw "Segregation under Fire" in the NAACP's cases. It said:

> It is almost impossible at this stage to forecast the great upheaval, the turmoil and the bitterness which would result from a judicial ruling that separate facilities do not satisfy the Constitution, even though they are identical. Although the court is supposed to consider only the legality of the question, it cannot but be aware of the explosive forces a reversal would set in motion.
>
> Even if the court upholds the constitutionality of the system of separate facilities, the handwriting is on the wall for states of the South and elsewhere where segregation is the rule. There will be an increasing demand from minority groups that facilities be equal, if they are to be separate.
>
> They are not equal today. . . .
>
> Hence, no matter which way the Supreme Court rules, the South is going to have to bestir itself in the next decade. It had best get busy and adjust its thinking accordingly, for there's a deal of adjusting to be done.

Arthur Krock, the influential Washington correspondent for the *New York Times,* wrote a column that presented Texas's position sympathetically, and concluded: "[The justices might be] seeking some basis for overturning what has long been held to be a constitutional exercise of state power on the ground that interpretation of law must change with economic and social change and the change of ideas. This attitude has been assumed by some current justices. However, the Texas brief suggests that it would be very difficult for any so minded to find legal reasoning wherewith to reverse the 'separate and equal' doctrine."[43]

The NAACP strategy succeeded, not in the Texas courts, which to no one's surprise rejected Sweatt's claim, but in the United States Supreme Court. *Sweatt* and *McLaurin* were accompanied by another case. *Henderson* v. *United States* involved segregated dining car service on a railroad regulated by the Interstate Commerce Commission.[44] In *Sweatt* and *McLaurin* the NAACP coupled the attack on "separate but equal" with straightforward inequality arguments. By this time the sociological argument had been worked over repeatedly, and the NAACP brief, though quite polished, contained little that was new. *Henderson* was a different matter. In the lower courts the government had argued that segregated service was not illegal under the relevant statutes and was not unconstitutional either. When the case reached the Supreme Court, responsibility for representing the United States shifted to Philip Perlman, the solicitor general. Perlman had signed the *amicus* brief in the restrictive covenant cases, and now concluded that the government's position in *Henderson* was wrong. His brief confessed error on the statutory issue and then urged that *Plessy* be overruled. The arguments were the familiar ones, not significantly different from those made by the NAACP. But they carried added weight when the solicitor general made them. Attorney General Howard McGrath presented the government's argument in *Henderson*. He told the Court, "Segregation signifies and is intended to signify that a member of the colored race is not equal to a member of the white race." The doctrine of "separate but equal," he said, was an "anachronism which a half-century of history and experience has shown to be a departure from the basic constitutional principle that all Americans, regardless of their race or color or religion or national origin, stand equal and alike in the sight of the law."[45]

Benjamin Fine, the education reporter for the *New York Times,* summarized the view from outside the Court:

> Not only educators, but politicians, lawyers and many citizens are aware of the significant issues involved. Many Southerners have warned that a reversal of the segregation policy would be disastrous and lead to riots and bloodshed. On the other hand, it has been argued that this would be a tremendous affirmation of American democracy, a triumphant answer to the Communists, both here and abroad, who say that the United States talks but does not practice democracy. . . .
> It is felt in some quarters that since the education cases now before the court

do not concern either elementary or secondary schools the decision may not encompass them. . . .

Those who favor the one-school system maintain that if the Supreme Court reverses past rulings, public education will improve in the South. On the other hand, advocates of the dual program warn of dire consequences in any court decision that might upset local tradition.[46]

The Supreme Court was receptive to the attack on *Plessy,* though outsiders other than Marshall would have been surprised to see what the justices were thinking about while the three cases were under consideration. Justice Harold Burton's law clerks sent him a long memorandum, with a cover note saying, "We think this is a good time and a good case for reconsidering *Plessy* v. *Ferguson.*" A later memorandum to him in *Sweatt* relied centrally on the sociological argument and referred to the solicitor general's brief in *Henderson* rather than the NAACP's briefs. Tom Clark, a Texan who had only recently taken a seat on the Court, circulated a memorandum to the entire Court in which he outlined his position. He thought that *Plessy* had to be confronted, and would hold it inapplicable to graduate schools. Established white schools had intangible assets like reputation, alumni to provide professional contacts, better professors, and "a cross section of the entire State . . . and, in the combat of ideas, . . . a greater variety of minds, backgrounds and opinions." Chief Justice Fred Vinson was skeptical about the Court's ability to draw a constitutional line between graduate and elementary schools.[47]

Ultimately Vinson wrote the opinions in *Sweatt* and *McLaurin.* Both held that the actual conditions in Texas and Oklahoma did not provide blacks with an education substantially equivalent to that available to whites. Thus the Court did not directly face the questions of overruling *Plessy* or openly denying its applicability to graduate education. In *Sweatt,* Chief Justice Vinson began by disclaiming any need to reach the "broader issues" that had been raised by the parties' "excellent research and detailed arguments." But, after reciting the facts, he emphasized the intangible factors in legal education. The black school was inferior "in terms of number of the faculty, variety of courses, . . . size of the student body, [and] scope of the library." More important, the white law school "possesses to a far greater degree those qualities which are incapable of objective measurement but which make for greatness in a law school," such as "reputation of the faculty, experience of the administration, position and influence of the alumni, standing in the community, traditions and prestige." He found it "difficult to believe that one who had a free choice between these law schools would consider the question close." Further, practical learning in law school required "the interplay of ideas and the exchange of views with which the law is concerned." By admitting blacks to a segregated law school, the state denied them contact with "most of the lawyers, witnesses, jurors, judges and other officials with whom petitioner will inevitably be dealing" as a lawyer. No education under those conditions could be "substantially equal" to that in the University of Texas Law School. It "overlook[ed] realities" to contend that just as blacks were excluded from the white school, whites were excluded from the black one. "It is unlikely that a member of a group so decisively in the majority, attending a school with rich traditions and prestige . . . , would claim that the opportunities afforded him for legal education were unequal to those held open to petitioner."[48]

The opinion in *McLaurin* was similar in its attention to intangibles. By setting McLaurin apart, the state imposed a handicap on him. "Such restrictions impair and inhibit his ability to study, to engage in discussion and exchange views with other students, and, in general, to learn his profession." It was irrelevant that the white students might choose to avoid McLaurin. "The removal of the state restrictions will not necessarily abate individual and group predilections, prejudices and choices. But at the very least, the state will not be depriving appellant of the opportunity to secure acceptance by his fellow students on his own merits."[49]

The justices were acutely aware that the opinions laid the ground for future developments. In describing the inequalities in *Sweatt*, the Court's opinion listed both the physical aspects and the intangibles on which Clark and the NAACP had so heavily relied. Given the discussions within the Court, invoking the intangibles committed the justices as much as any doctrine could to the position that equality could not be achieved in separate graduate and professional schools. And recognition of the relevance of intangibles opened the way to adoption of the sociological argument. Judges concerned about precedent could have drawn distinctions had they wanted to, but as the nine men who made the decisions grappled with *Sweatt* and *McLaurin*, they became convinced as individuals that, once they decided or were forced to face the issue, they would overrule *Plessy*. As Clark had concluded in his memorandum, "If some say this undermines *Plessy* then let it fall, as have many Nineteenth Century oracles."[50]

Once again observers in the North welcomed the hints of the demise of segregation in *Sweatt* and *McLaurin,* and those in the South anxiously suggested ways to confine the impact of the cases. An editorial in the *New York Times* asked for "continued cooperation by the enlightened leaders of both races," because, even though the "republic cannot recognize degrees of citizenship," blacks and whites would need to reconcile their concerns: "The situation calls for a period of education—how long a period no one can say." Arthur Krock thought that the decisions left *Plessy* "a mass of tatters. . . . It still exists in the realm of judicial theory. . . . But the net of the decisions was that 'equal' must be as definitely proved as 'separate,' by tests which obviously will be difficult if not impossible for the states to meet." Krock went on to say:

> From now on a community must be able to prove beyond question that a segregated complainant receives educational services equivalent to those rendered the racial majority. And to do that will impose crushing financial burdens on the community.
>
> Hence, while Mr. Perlman did not get the *Plessy* doctrine specifically overruled, he got the Supreme Court to put a price-tag on it which may have the same effect in numerous localities. . . .
>
> The facts . . . were so minutely inspected that litigation inevitably will follow, based on conditions in segregated primary and secondary schools and colleges. The Court made it crystal clear today that it will sympathetically entertain any plea of inequality.
>
> In the field of lower education, especially in the secondary public schools, the social bases of segregation are much broader and deeper than in the colleges. If and when the Supreme court applies today's formula and solution to these, where it finds segregated facilities "unequal," the real test of community acceptance will come.

Commonweal called the decisions "a milestone," and also emphasized the burdensome cost of providing equal facilities. It thought that "the decision would have been infinitely more clear-cut" had the Court rejected segregation per se, for "a certain comparison and a certain proof are still required. . . . [B]ut the way is now open." According to the *New Republic,* segregation was now "clearly doomed" because of the cost element. The decisions, it said, bore "directly on segregated primary and secondary schools, since it is impossible for them adequately to prepare the Negro for life in a predominantly white society." Among those who approved the decisions, the only reservation was that, in order to secure unanimity, the Court had "opened the doors to a flood of new cases calling for decision on the *fact* of equality." But, it was said in response, "this kind of piecemeal readjustment is often better than a frontal attack on long-standing traditions."[51]

Southern members of Congress attacked the decisions. One report indicated that the decisions had assured the election of Herman Talmadge as governor of Georgia, enhancing his "white supremacy" appeals. Southern educators "were plainly worried" that segregation "was on the way out." They saw that the issue was "rapidly heading for a showdown," even though they insisted that elementary and secondary schools would never be desegregated. Any attempt to do so, they said, "would lead to a dangerous situation." Even liberals "agreed that grave problems were posed," and that "the decisions had added to the difficulty and danger of issues which enlightened Southern leaders are earnestly trying to meet with justice for all concerned."[52] Whatever their point of view, most observers agreed that the decisions were unlikely to remain confined to the area of graduate and professional education.

Comments in the law reviews sounded similar themes. They agreed in general that *Sweatt* strongly suggested that segregation in elementary and secondary schools was unconstitutional in view of the Court's apparent insistence on strict equality in fact. Many also noted that litigating equality in fact would be time-consuming, which might allow time for gradual adaptation in the South. Perhaps the most delicate assessment was that in the *Virginia Law Review,* which first noted that the Court's arguments were applicable to undergraduate education: "[T]here is only a thin line which can be drawn between the importance of ideas at the post-graduate and at the collegiate level, and political and social factors would seem to be the controlling criteria as to whether or not equality demands intellectual commingling in colleges and lower grades." The author called the decisions "far reaching," and praised the Court for being "most politic in leaving the 'separate but equal' doctrine existent but the door open for gradual change."[53]

Two liberal legal scholars reached identical conclusions. Bernard Schwartz, writing for a British audience about "The Negro and the Law in the United States," ended by discussing *Sweatt*. He "hope[d] that the strict enforcement of the requirement of equality in facilities will ultimately force an abandonment of most legally required segregation." The expense of providing duplicate facilities would make segregation "impracticable," for "segregation is tolerable financially only if equality between the races is not required. Decisions such as *Sweatt* v. *Painter* should thus ultimately lead to the ending of most forms of segregation." Another author concluded that the cases now required "actual . . . equality of opportunity. . . . If commingling with his fellow students was essential for McLaurin, it can be cogently argued that it is of even greater importance to students of all races in American primary and secondary schools in order that both the individuals primarily concerned and society at large may secure the greatest possible advantage from the public educational program." [54]

Writers for the black press were more restrained, perhaps because they were more aware of the limited impact that previous decisions had had. The *Boston Chronicle* noted how few blacks would benefit directly from the decisions. Others criticized the Court for failing to address and repudiate the "separate but equal" doctrine. [55]

Marshall had a different view of the cases. He had lived with the attack on segregated education all his professional life. When he read the opinions in *Sweatt* and *McLaurin,* he understood what the justices had done when they chose to rely on intangibles. One week after the decisions were announced, he wrote one of his law school expert witnesses, "All three of the decisions [including *Henderson*] are replete with road markings telling us where to go next." He believed that the law had reached a turn in the road. [56]

It was time, Marshall concluded, to begin the direct attack on segregation. The NAACP's decision was influenced by more than the Court's action in *Sweatt* and *McLaurin,* however. By the end of World War II the NAACP had become a mass organization. In 1930 its budget was $54,300, financed by a mix of contributions and memberships. Throughout the 1930s contributions gradually declined from one-third to one-fifth of the NAACP's income. By 1947 the NAACP's budget was over $319,000, almost none of which came from contributions. Between 1940 and 1946 the number of branches tripled, and membership grew from 50,500 to 450,000. In South Carolina, membership grew from 800 in 1939 to over 14,000 in 1948. [57] The formal separation of the NAACP and the "Inc Fund" did not divorce the lawyers from concern for the larger organization. It thus made sense to design the litigation program to satisfy the NAACP membership, as well as liberal supporters of the NAACP's general goals. [58] The prior litigation was important in developing helpful precedents and in symbolizing the possibility of change, but it seems likely that only an attack on elementary and secondary education would have appealed to the full membership. [59]

Further, the Court's decisions in *Sweatt* and *McLaurin* were widely regarded as having direct implications for elementary and secondary education. Partisans on both sides had, of course, an interest in reading the decisions for all that they were worth, and even *Gaines,* eleven years before, had been treated by some as a sign of imminent change in all schools. Yet the expectations generated in 1950 seem to have been both well enough grounded and widely enough shared to create a problem in public relations if less than a direct attack were begun. In addition, the lawyers were committed to the elimination of segregation everywhere. The only possible dispute concerned the timing of efforts to attack segregation. But by drafting complaints to challenge inequality as well as segregation, the lawyers could defer the crucial decisions until they were faced with a judge who upheld segregation in a case where the record could not support a claim of inequalities in material endowments. Finally, the NAACP legal staff had become an organization able to deploy its forces easily. Previous constraints engendered by limited resources were relaxed when, by 1950, the legal staff could be formed into five teams, each headed by a staff lawyer and supported by local attorneys, to handle five major cases.

Three weeks after *Sweatt* and *McLaurin* were decided, Marshall convened a conference of lawyers to "map . . . the legal machinery" for an "all-out attack" on segregation. At its conclusion, Marshall announced, "we are going to insist on nonsegregation in American public education from top to bottom—from law school to kindergarten." The conference developed a resolution, adopted in July 1950 by the NAACP Board of Directors, stating that all future education cases would seek "education on a non-segregated basis and that no relief other than that will be acceptable." [60]

Recently some have suggested that Marshall remained cautious even in 1950. There is no documentary evidence for that suggestion. Marshall's caution ran from 1945 to June 5, 1950, when *Sweatt* and *McLaurin* were decided. [61] Marshall's position was based not simply on his assessment of what changes in the law could reasonably be expected during that period, but also on his assessment of the needs of the NAACP and its various constituencies. Marshall had preferred the direct attack from the start, and between 1945 and 1950 there were essentially no legal developments making it more sensible to begin the attack in 1950 than it would have been in 1945. But Marshall deferred the decision from a time when it would have seriously split the NAACP to a time when the external environment, in politics and legal doctrine, and the internal politics of the organization made it easier for others to agree that what Marshall wanted was in their interest too. Marshall's strength had always resided in his superb judgments about life and law, rather than in his ability to construct a legal argument. The way in which the direct attack decision was made shows him at his best.

8. Conclusion:
Some Lessons from
the Campaign

The decision to attack segregation in elementary and secondary schools closed one era in the NAACP's attack on segregation. The NAACP's lawyers had learned how to organize complex litigation, and how to maintain central control while encouraging local support during the inevitably extended period before visible results were forthcoming. But their decision opened another era of litigation, during which the problems the NAACP had earlier faced presented themselves in different forms.

Because litigation is a social process, all litigation campaigns have elements in common. Before we consider several of the broader implications of the litigation effort from 1925 to 1950, it may be useful to highlight some of those elements by describing a few of the difficulties that attended the ligitation that culminated in *Brown* v. *Board of Education*.[1]

Two of the cases decided in *Brown* faced serious initial difficulties. In June 1947, James Hinton, the president of the South Carolina Conference of NAACP Branches, addressed the students at Allen University, a black institution. He said that the schools for blacks in the state were a disgrace, and mentioned the NAACP's desire to challenge policies that deprived black children of bus transportation equivalent to that provided white children. One member of the audience, J. A. DeLaine, returned to Clarendon County, where he was a schoolteacher and minister, and began to organize his neighbors on the bus issue. They presented a petition to the school board in July 1947. When this accomplished nothing, they filed a lawsuit in March 1948. The suit was dismissed in June on the ground that the plaintiff, whose formal justification for the suit was that his taxes were being used improperly, did not in fact pay taxes to the school board whose policies he attacked. Almost a year later, DeLaine met with Marshall, who persuaded DeLaine that a full-scale attack on material inequalities

138

made more sense than a lawsuit limited to the bus issue. DeLaine organized a series of meetings at black churches to persuade the community to act. Ultimately, provoked by actions of a new black principal whom they regarded as incompetent and high-handed, a substantial portion of the black community urged DeLaine to take the lead in beginning a lawsuit. He did so only on the condition that a comprehensive lawsuit would be the goal. DeLaine was soon fired by the school board. Then, in September 1949, the board fired the black principal who had provoked the community. The job was first offered to DeLaine and then was given to his wife. These efforts to buy off opposition failed, and a comprehensive lawsuit was filed in November 1949, more than two years after the first petition had been sent to the school board.[2]

The situation in Kansas was more confused. In late 1947 Esther Brown, a thirty-year-old white woman, became concerned about the state of the schools for blacks in South Park, outside of Kansas City. After efforts to persuade the school board to improve the grade school proved futile, Brown consulted Elisha Scott of Topeka, a black attorney. The legal issue was clear, for Kansas law authorized segregation only in school districts larger than South Park. For three weeks at the beginning of the 1948 school year, the parents and children of South Park boycotted the schools, ending the boycott only after testimony was taken in the lawsuit Scott filed. During that same month, Z. Wetmore, a member of the Wichita branch of the NAACP, renewed his efforts to generate a lawsuit there. He had previously found that "a considerable number of colored people, including some of the colored teachers . . . [feared] that if these changes were made, some of the colored teachers would lose their positions in the schools." But by September 1948, Wetmore thought that the branch, though "weak in numbers, in workers, and in finances," was eager to pursue a desegregation case. The executive committee of the Kansas State Conference of NAACP Branches voted 7–2 to support a desegregation suit in Wichita rather than Topeka, largely because the committee expected to rely on three Wichita attorneys. But the Wichita teachers mobilized in opposition to the proposed lawsuit. The Wichita branch elected a new board in December. It was opposed to desegregation litigation and included one member who, during the controversy, had praised the Wichita schools in a letter to the local newspaper. Although Franklin Williams of the national legal staff urged the new board to "press . . . this proposed suit," it did not. Instead, Esther Brown joined Elisha Scott and his sons, also lawyers, in persuading the Topeka branch to support a lawsuit. The

Topeka black community had gradually come to support challenges to the administration of the schools, beginning with a petition in the autumn of 1948. In August 1950, the Topeka branch was ready to initiate litigation. Coordinating the effort between the Scotts and the national office was particularly difficult, but eventually a complaint was drafted and filed at the end of February 1951.[3]

Similar interactions between clients' desires and lawyers' concerns occurred in Virginia, Delaware, and the District of Columbia, where other desegregation suits began at around the same time.[4] In Virginia, local activists were led by a minister who had, among other things, supported Henry Wallace for president in 1948 and helped organize the local branch of the NAACP. They pressed the school board of Prince Edward County to construct a new high school for blacks to replace the old, overcrowded building that had been supplemented by some "temporary" wood outbuildings. The school board's temporizing provoked a student strike. The students met with Oliver Hill and Spottswood Robinson, who told them that the NAACP would support a desegregation case but not a suit aimed solely at forcing the construction of a new high school. A week later a mass meeting of the black community authorized the lawyers to proceed.

The NAACP's local legal contact in Delaware was Louis Redding, a black attorney who had graduated from Harvard Law School and then had pursued a number of NAACP cases in Delaware. One group of potential plaintiffs requested Redding's assistance for a desegregation lawsuit. Another plaintiff initially wanted no more than that the school bus for white children stop to pick up her daughter as well. Redding told her that he would not help in that effort, but that he would support a desegregation suit, to which she immediately agreed to be a party.

During the 1940s the black community in the District of Columbia sued to force the school board to permit blacks from an overcrowded junior high school to attend white schools with vacant seats. When the school board designated two white schools as "annexes," black parents pointed out that students in shop classes had to travel between the junior high and the annexes, and so did not receive an adequate or "equal" education. Their children began a student strike that lasted over a month. The parents turned to the possibility of litigation, and approached Charles Hamilton Houston, then in private practice. The parents were uncertain about the wisdom of a direct attack on segregation, and agreed with Houston's suggestion that they sue for equalization of facilities. The parents had no organized connection to the NAACP. Houston conducted the lawsuit independently of the NAACP legal staff, and the suit was supported by fund-raising within the black community. Over a powerful dissent by Judge Henry Edgerton, the District of Columbia court rejected the parents' lawsuit. Houston died a few months later, and the parents asked James L. Nabrit, a law professor at Howard, to continue the litigation effort. Nabrit refused to assist in equalization litigation, but offered to bring a direct challenge to segregation. That lawsuit, which like the Kansas one was supported by the NAACP national office, was filed in early 1951.[5]

By that time the NAACP lawyers had gained substantial experience in conducting complex desegregation litigation. The national office could coordinate four major lawsuits in South Carolina, Virginia, Kansas, and Delaware, essentially simultaneously. Different lawyers from the national staff could supervise one of the lawsuits—Marshall in South Carolina, Carter in Kansas and South Carolina, Jack Greenberg in Delaware. Talented local counsel such as Robinson in Virginia, Redding in Delaware, and Nabrit in the District of Columbia could handle substantial parts of the litigation. Further, the framework of the sociological argument had already been constructed for the law school cases. The lawyers understood that expert testimony on the social and psychological effects of segregation was useful, and they had developed a network of academic experts who could provide that testimony. They had only to substitute a few experts in child psychology for a few experts in the legal profession, and the structure of the desegregation cases would be complete.

Thus, once the initial difficulties in mobilizing communities to support a direct attack on segregation had been overcome, the desegregation cases flowed relatively smoothly. A few minor tactical issues remained to be worked out. For example, Marshall believed that Judge J. Waties Waring of South Carolina would be sympathetic to the direct attack, for Waring had ruled in favor of black plaintiffs in some earlier cases, including a challenge to South Carolina's failure to provide a law school for blacks. Other federal judges who might hear a South Carolina case were likely to be much less sympathetic. Federal statutes allowed a single judge to decide certain constitutional claims, but required that a panel of three judges hear suits seeking to enjoin the operation of state statutes. Marshall therefore attempted to persuade Judge Waring that the South Carolina lawsuit was not really an attempt to enjoin segregation. When that failed, as Marshall surely expected it would, he tried the case before a three-judge court.

The direct attack lawsuits shared two characteristics. First, they included substantial amounts of testimony from social psychologists. Perhaps because of the uncertain scientific status of social psychology, or because its conclusions are frequently at odds with common sense, the testimony of these witnesses was more controversial than the expert testimony in the previous cases had been. This testimony attracted a great deal of attention after *Brown*, which cited some of its foundations—though none of the testimony itself—in a celebrated footnote. Yet the Court's internal discussions in *Sweatt* strongly suggest that the testimony of the social psychologists had little direct impact on the outcome in *Brown*. Instead, it provided part of a general climate of opinion sympathetic to the claims made by the NAACP.

Second, the facts in the cases undermined efforts to leave open the issue of equalization versus desegregation. In South Carolina and Virginia the facilities were conceded to be unequal, but the states claimed that their legislatures had started substantial programs to upgrade black schools; they argued that an injunction was therefore unnecessary to guarantee equality. In Kansas the facilities were nearly enough equal to make it futile to focus the litigation on material inequality. As lawyers the NAACP's attorneys would have preferred to leave the question of material inequality open, because that would have expanded their tactical options. But as activists they were content with the lawsuits as they had been framed.

Each lawsuit proceeded at its own pace. Not unexpectedly the cases in Kansas, Virginia, and South Carolina went against the NAACP; in Delaware the court held that the facilities were substantially unequal and ordered desegregation rather than equalization. In November 1951 the NAACP asked the Supreme Court to review the Kansas case. The Court refrained from acting on the request until June 1952. In the meantime the Court asked the trial court in South Carolina to consider the implications of a reported equalization effort. After the trial court adhered to its original position, the Supreme Court accepted the appeal of that case on the same day that it agreed to review the Kansas case.

The justices plainly knew of the scope of the NAACP's attack. In October 1952, shortly before the Kansas and South Carolina cases were to be argued in the Supreme Court, the Court accepted the Virginia case for review and postponed the other arguments until all three could be heard together. Then the justices directed the clerk of the Supreme Court to contact the lawyers in the District of Columbia case, and asked that they seek immediate review in the Supreme Court, bypassing the court of appeals. After the petition for review before judgment in the court of appeals was filed, the Court granted it in early November and added the Washington case to those already set for argument. Three days later the Delaware attorney general sought review of his case. The four other desegregation cases were scheduled to be argued in early December. The Court's clerk asked the Delaware authorities to accelerate their appeal, but the state's attorney general wanted to follow the normal timetable, which would have given him more time to prepare. Nonetheless, the Court did accelerate the process. When it accepted the Delaware case for review on November 24, 1952, the Court scheduled argument for December 11, immediately after the other four cases would be argued. It allowed the parties in the Delaware case to file their formal briefs after the argument.

The Court's extraordinary actions in the Washington and Delaware cases signaled its determination to dispose of the segregation issue as it was then framed. Discussions among the justices in the 1950 cases had shown that they were ready to abandon the "separate but equal" doctrine. They still needed time to figure out what remedy should be used: immediate desegregation nationwide, prompt desegregation with minor adjustments for peculiar local conditions, or gradual desegregation to take account of anticipated resistance. When the Court rejected the "separate but equal" doctrine in its first decision in *Brown* v. *Board of Education* on May 17, 1954, it rescheduled the cases for argument the following fall, on the issue of remedy. By deferring the question that it found most difficult, the Court opened up a different phase in the litigation campaign and in the nation's experience with the issue of race.[6]

The NAACP's litigation effort illustrates the dimensions of litigation as a social process. A group of people discover that they agree that something is wrong. They formulate their grievance in light of what they have learned over the course of their lives. They discuss matters with their lawyers, and the grievance may be reshaped. They present their claims, and discover that a remedy will not be immediately forthcoming, and that the remedy may provide some of them with what they want while depriving others of what they already have. Their opponents respond, sometimes by settling the dispute, sometimes by changing their behavior to make it harder for the plaintiffs to win. However the courts respond to a lawsuit, the problem is not resolved. Settlements and decrees must be enforced. Often the locus of controversy shifts from the courts to the legislatures, as prevailing plaintiffs seek more effective relief, or as losing plaintiffs seek to get some relief from someone. Thus the social process of litigation begins well before a lawsuit is filed and ends well after a judgment is entered.[7]

By seeing litigation as a social process, we may consider whether the analysis of the NAACP's litigation activities from 1925 to 1950 supports broader conclusions. These conclusions can be grouped under three headings: the meaningfulness of characterizing the litigation as the execution of a previously developed plan, the implications of the issue of planning for a more general view of public interest litigation, and the relative importance of internal and external influences on the events. The discussion of the third topic will lead to some speculations about the larger consequences of the litigation effort.

Most commentators on the NAACP's litigation have seen the campaign as a combination of strategic planning and successful implementation.[8] Because the NAACP's litigation ended so spectacularly with the decision in *Brown*, it has been hard to resist two temptations: the first is to see the outcome as the obvious product of plans that had been laid many years before, and the other is to take the campaign as a model for public interest law generally. Thus, viewing the campaign in the light cast by its results, Richard Kluger tends to tell a story of unproblematic success: that the campaign was rationally and without fundamental error designed to maximize the chance that the NAACP would win.[9] In a more analytical study, which explicitly treats the NAACP campaign as a "forerunner . . . to the public interest firms" of today, Prof. Robert Rabin similarly presents it as a process guided by rational planning.[10] He describes it as originating in "a strategic plan for cumulative litigation efforts aimed at achieving specified social objectives."[11] A final example can be drawn from a report by the Council for Public Interest Law on financing public interest law. Its brief historical section summarizes the NAACP's "institutional model" as one that used a full-time salaried staff that would not handle routine or defensive cases but would take "an active role in the strategic accomplishment of goals," and that relied on membership for financial support, and its plan as one that developed incremental victories that could be followed up by a network of affiliated local attorneys.[12]

These approaches seriously overestimate deliberate design as a characteristic of the NAACP campaign.[13] The campaign was animated by a continuing and always self-conscious dedication to the destruction of the constitutional support for segregation. Further, participants repeatedly characterized their efforts as the execution of a plan. But the contents of that "plan" changed with some frequency. Only between *Alston* in 1940 and the initiation of the university lawsuits in 1945 was there an extended period of relatively consistent strategic activity, and even during that period the nature of the salary equalization suits changed dramatically as the NAACP lawyers had to develop responses to newly instituted merit pay systems.

The NAACP and the lawyers associated with it identified several targets. Racial subordination was enforced in part by lynch law and other forms of terror, so the NAACP devoted major efforts to securing the enactment of a federal antilynching law.[14] Lynch law sometimes took the form of kangaroo courts, so the NAACP sought to hold the states to constitutional requirements, well established by 1909, according to which the process of selecting jurors could not discriminate against blacks. Jim Crow laws in transportation and residential segregation by ordinance and private agreement were other elements in the system of racial subordination, and the NAACP acted against them, too.[15] In addition, the NAACP tried to enforce the right to vote by attacking systems of primary elections from which blacks were excluded.[16] Thus, the attack on school segregation was only part of a much broader effort. The NAACP was never committed to destroying school segregation because it was central to the system of racial subordination. Rather, school segregation was just one of many targets, and it became an increasingly attractive one as precedents dealing with schools accumulated precisely because the NAACP had been litigating school cases for nonstrategic reasons. But destroying any of the various targets would help undermine the system that the NAACP wanted to eliminate.

The NAACP thus identified not a single target but a group of generically described evils—school segregation, lynch law, Jim Crow laws—and directed its efforts at those broadly defined evils. The areas narrowed the NAACP's concerns somewhat by specifying where to look for opportunities to attack the legal basis of racial subordination. Within the general areas, though, the NAACP's efforts were not systematic or strategic. Instead, the organization attacked what might be called targets of opportunity. The history of the NAACP's litigation strategy repeatedly discloses, within the broad commitment to a legal attack on racial subordination, proposals made by planners who were removed from implementation of the plans, the abandonment of those plans in favor of others that reflected the NAACP's internal organizational constraints, decisions altered because of preferences of the staff, and negotiations over plans with constituencies having diverse interests.

If the military metaphor referring to a litigation campaign is helpful, the campaign was conducted on a terrain that repeatedly required changes in maneuvers. Sometimes changes were required because the planners had relied on a stability in their environment that proved to be lacking, and sometimes because those implementing the plans had their own needs and priorities, which became clear only after some actions had begun. Thus, salary equalization litigation became transformed in part because southern school boards responded to attacks on salary schedules that explicitly discriminated against black teachers by developing equally discriminatory merit systems that did not refer expressly to race. Needs internal to the NAACP led to the shift from the Garland Fund proposal to the Margold Report to Houston's approach, and may have played a decisive role in the abandonment of equalization litigation in favor of a direct attack on segregation.[17]

These adaptations, particularly to the extent that they resulted from internal organizational influences, raise questions about the practice of public interest law in general. One question frequently raised in discussions of public interest law is, to what extent are litigation campaigns independent of the wishes of a defined group of clients? The professional relationship between lawyer and client has its basis in the fact that the lawyer acts on behalf of a client. Lawyers who use litigation only to advance their personal goals, rather then the goals of their clients, are usually thought to act unethically. Answering the question about the independence of the NAACP lawyers requires that a couple of careful distinctions be drawn. First, one must distinguish potential clients who desired to attack segregation through litigation from those who did not, either because they preferred other modes of attack or because they preferred to avoid disrupting a set of accommodations on the issue of race that they found satisfactory. Second, in regard to the group preferring litigation, one must separate those who desired the direct attack on segregation from those who preferred to continue the effort to equalize facilities.

It distorts the inquiry in important ways to frame the first distinction as involving a broad choice between litigation and other modes of attack. The NAACP was not the only organization in the black community, and the obvious resolution of the question of how to attack segregation was the one that was finally reached. Different types of organizations would engage in different types of activities.[18] Because of their varied histories and ideological commitments, organizations in the black community had what might be called comparative advantages in different spheres. The NAACP could carry out litigation, the National Negro Congress could engage in direct political action, and the Urban League could concentrate on generating jobs for blacks by persuading leading white employers to provide them. If each type of activity could contribute to the advancement of black interests, allocating efforts on the basis of comparative advantage was an entirely sensible way to maximize the chance that the black community as a whole would benefit. Reaching this outcome was, of course, not easy. The leaders of each organization undoubtedly wanted personal recognition as leaders of the black community. It was hard for a person like Walter White to be generous to his competitors, and Roy Wilkins engaged in a running feud through the early 1940s with Lester Granger, the executive director of the Urban League.[19] These difficulties, though, would have had little significance for the black effort unless one organization came to dominate the competition and thus eliminated the popular basis on which other groups drew for support. Such domination may have occurred briefly in the late 1940s, when the NAACP's litigation campaign appears to have pushed other forms of mobilization aside. Yet that was a time when it may have been proper to devote more resources to a single activity for a short period.

The NAACP's litigation effort raises a second issue about its basis in the black community. Some blacks, usually called accommodationists, opposed nonevolutionary changes in the system of race relations in the South.[20] They therefore opposed any active efforts to alter that system. Clearly the NAACP's litigation could not satisfy those elements in the black community. Two factors diminish the significance of accommodationist opposition in an assessment of the NAACP's activities as a form of public interest law. First, with few exceptions state defendants presented as effectively as they could be presented the arguments that accommodationists had. Even where the nominal defendants, such as the presidents of some segregated universities, may have tacitly supported desegregation, their lawyers had close ties to the dominant segregationist elements in the white community. In an era when few were embarrassed when whites made assertions about what was good for blacks, defendants may have represented accommodationist interests fully. Second, as we have seen, successful litigation required strong support from the community. University desegregation was thwarted in North Carolina by the strength of the accommodationist elements there, and the opposition of Wichita teachers to the direct attack forced the NAACP to shift its attention to Topeka. It overstates the matter only slightly to say that the NAACP lawyers simply could not win their lawsuits unless they represented the majority of the black community.[21]

Principles of comparative advantage, and the impact of community division on the prospects for success, thus seem sufficient to alleviate whatever concern there might be about the representativeness of the NAACP in its choice of litigation as against other activities. In 1935 that was the only issue. Du Bois had asked whether blacks should try to use the courts at all. Once that question was answered, primarily by the principle of comparative advantage, there was at that time nothing else to discuss. By the late 1940s the issues became more complicated, as plausible alternative strategies of litigation became available. In pursuing the direct attack, how free were the NAACP lawyers of control by clients?[22]

Every case had a real client with whom the NAACP lawyers had personal contact. These clients were volunteers in the sense that they usually initiated the contact with the lawyers. Of course, the NAACP and its lawyers made it widely known, through speeches to community organizations, through *The Crisis,* and through general publicity, that the lawyers were available to assist people who wanted to challenge segregation. In this sense they were looking for clients. But the available evidence includes many instances of clients such as Walter Mills and Lucile Bluford stepping forward in response to general invitations, and no instances of an NAACP lawyer approaching a potential client on an individual basis uninvited. For internal organizational purposes, perhaps to bolster their own sense of being in control of things, the NAACP lawyers often said that they were trying to find plaintiffs. Their activities were far more efforts to educate the community than attempts to solicit clients.

Just as they did not solicit clients, the NAACP lawyers did not dominate their clients' decisions except by educating them. In part, this occurred because the lawyers had little to offer clients.[23] Formally speaking, they offered clients chances to increase their salaries or to attend better graduate schools. But those rewards were attended by so much difficulty that, on balance, the material incentives for becoming a plaintiff were extremely small. Teachers would be harassed by their employers and, especially as settlement negotiations advanced, might find themselves in conflict with other teachers over the terms of the settlement; applicants to graduate schools would have their life plans disrupted by the delays of litigation and would occasionally have difficulty in finding work during the indefinite interval between suing and attending school. In addition, to the extent that a person wanted material gains from litigation, a serious "free rider" problem intervened. Why should a teacher volunteer for an equalization suit when the benefits would accrue to all teachers? Why not wait until someone else assumed the obvious burdens? Thus, as Melvin Alston said, it made little sense to become a plaintiff in the hope of securing material gains. Rather, clients had to be in the fight as a matter of principle, and people who undergo serious strains for matters of principle are likely to be rather aggressive sorts, both in initiating contacts with lawyers and in dealing with their attorneys once litigation begins. Lucile Bluford and Ada Sipuel are only the most dramatic examples among the NAACP's plaintiffs; they were women who knew what they wanted and surely would not have acquiesced in legal maneuvers with which they disagreed.

Because material incentives to sue were slight, ideological incentives had to be available. But precisely because the plaintiffs' incentives were ideological, the NAACP lawyers could not dominate their choices. The plaintiffs came forward because they saw the congruence between their views and those publicized by the NAACP lawyers. The fact that ideological congruence was needed at the start served to screen out potential plaintiffs with whom the lawyers would disagree, and, as the South Carolina law school case suggests, when disparities in views became apparent, the plaintiff tended to abandon the lawsuit. The lawyers therefore could not have imposed, and did not need to impose, decisions on their clients.

In addition, the initial phases of the litigation campaign involved suits on behalf of well-educated blacks, who could be expected to, and usually did, take great interest in their lawsuits. When decisions had to be made, the lawyers could easily present their clients with the options and explain their significance. By educating the clients in the law, the lawyers could persuade them to do what the lawyers thought best. In situations where the educators have no power to make their students worse off if the students reject the lessons, persuasion by education is not usefully thought of as domination. This sort of education occurred repeatedly, even on such technical issues as the choice between injunctive and mandamus relief, as some of the activities after the *Alston* decision indicate.[24]

The best examples come from later stages in salary suits, when Marshall frequently had to explain why proposed settlements were not as good as those the teachers could secure if they held firm. I have sometimes spoken of this process as "keeping the teachers in line," but it was one of persuasion by a respected and informed attorney. Most of the disputes were over the period during which equalization was to be accomplished; Marshall persuaded teachers to insist on shorter rather than longer periods; and settlements that were more favorable along the only relevant dimension were in fact routinely reached. Here once again the extraordinary character of Thurgood Marshall played a crucial part. Though no adequate biography of Marshall has yet been written, there is enough information available to tell us that Marshall was a charismatic figure in the black community. He loved its institutions, and his deep commitment to the community was evident in his manner of dealing with black people as well as in his more public actions.

There is, of course, a sense in which Marshall and the legal staff had and exercised power on these issues.[25] The staff had expertise in the area of segregation litigation and occasionally discouraged potential litigants who wanted to assert claims other than those favored by the staff. Even though the staff did not have a monopoly on the relevant areas of the law, such threats obviously reduced, and in some instances may have eliminated, the range of possibilities open to potential litigants. In addition, Marshall had built up a fund of respect in the community, on which he could draw to overcome hesitancy among possible dissidents. To say this is to say only that the NAACP lawyers participated in the political life of their community. What matters is not the inevitable, that lawyers have a kind of power with respect to their clients, but the variable, what disciplines them in the exercise of the power they have. Marshall's educational efforts show that he was indeed subject to the discipline of his constituency.[26]

The argument as to facilities suits and the direct attack on segregation elaborates these points by introducing the fundamental importance of community organization. The NAACP had always been an organization whose black membership was drawn from the middle class.[27] In facilities suits, the lawyers were not dealing with a clientele composed exclusively of well-educated blacks, but with entire communities. However, within each community, the leadership was likely to be relatively sophisticated, and the process of generating support for the lawyers' decisions through community education would occur in two steps, from the lawyers to the leadership to the community as a whole. The problem of representativeness is linked to the existence of community organization, too. There always existed a range of views within the black community on questions involving litigation to end segregation. In that sense, the NAACP could not fairly purport to articulate the views of a united community. But until the lawyers had to face the direct attack decision, they could fairly say that what they did in fact exhausted the community demand for litigation. For those in the community who thought that a litigation strategy was desirable, the NAACP's strategy was uncontroversial; thus, no one fell outside the range of what the NAACP lawyers did.

Thurgood Marshall's exchanges with Carter Wesley show that by the late 1940s the NAACP legal staff could no longer identify their views with those of all in the black community who were interested in litigation. The staff therefore had to choose which segments of the community to represent, and the form that the choice took is significant. The lawyers did not go into communities where they would have faced substantial internal dissent; that is, they regarded black communities, more than individual blacks, as arrayed along a continuum measured by the degree of support for their preferred direct attack strategy, and they sued only in those communities where the degree of support was high. For organizational reasons, the legal staff always pressed the branches to support the litigation, and frequently would not pursue a case unless the local branch joined it. Although there was no guarantee that even a local branch represented the views of the community as a whole, certainly there was no better evidence then available.

There were two important aspects of their situation that made it likely that the NAACP lawyers represented a majority of the black community. Despite the way it may seem in retrospect, the national NAACP staff and the lawyers on the NAACP's Legal Committee were not the only lawyers available to the black community, although they probably were the best ones. Other lawyers could represent black communities desiring services the NAACP lawyers might refuse to supply. In addition, the NAACP lawyers were members of the black community and as a result were sensitive to its wishes. The evidence, summarized in what follows, strongly suggests that the NAACP lawyers did in fact represent the larger portion of the black community.

Before *Brown* v. *Board of Education* was filed in 1951, at least eleven lawsuits challenging unequal physical facilities at elementary and secondary schools were brought in Arkansas, Texas, North Carolina, Virginia, and Missouri.[28] This figure compares favorably with the number of reported decisions in salary equalization cases. The national NAACP staff became involved in four additional facilities suits, in Texas, North Carolina, Kansas, and Tennessee.[29] Further, as we have seen, the legal staff offered to review pleadings and briefs in equalization cases that might be brought in North Carolina, consistently the most conservative constituency that the NAACP had,[30] though one cannot be too confident that the staff would have welcomed a request even for that limited assistance. Even the lawsuits in which the NAACP national staff did not participate were influenced by the NAACP experience. The lawyers in seven of the eleven non-NAACP lawsuits had significant past contact with the NAACP legal campaign.[31] Unaffiliated lawyers may not have been as able as the NAACP lawyers, and could not draw on the staff's resources. Indeed, the lawyers without NAACP experience were less successful in these equalization cases than those with it. But apart from the difficulties involved in investigating at the site (which local lawyers could do more easily than NAACP staff could), facilities equalization cases were relatively straightforward. Even more dramatic, Carter Wesley, the most vocal advocate of facilities litigation, was a lawyer with significant experience in constitutional litigation from the white primary cases. He presumably was available for those communities in Texas which were less convinced of the desirability of a direct attack on segregation than were the NAACP's staff and Legal Committee. The fact that Wesley did not mobilize any communities for facilities cases suggests that he did not speak for a significant portion of the black community anywhere in the country. That is, because the NAACP lawyers knew that there were at least a few lawyers who were available for facilities suits, they could be reasonably confident that, when no such suits were brought, the black community taken as a whole did in fact prefer the direct attack to equalization litigation.

The fact that the present study was written primarily on the basis of evidence in the papers of the national office of the NAACP reduces, though it does not eliminate, the significance of the absence of requests for assistance in facilities equalization cases. Yet when the available items of evidence are considered together, it seems significantly more likely than not that the NAACP's legal staff, in pursuing the direct attack, was acting in accordance with the desires of a broad segment, and perhaps more, of the affected class.

Probably more important, the NAACP lawyers were themselves part of the community they sought to represent. They could not, of course, identify their personal preferences with those of their constituents. But the lawyers were part of a relatively dense network of community organizations—churches, newspapers, social fraternities—that rather effectively exerted discipline on them.[32] For example, when political differences broke out between the teachers in New Orleans and the NAACP branch, a prominent black newspaper editor served as the intermediary between the disputing elements and communicated the political problems to the national staff, thus informing the lawyers of what had to be done if the suits were to continue. The editor, Donald Jones, later became a member of the NAACP staff. Similarly, Roy Wilkins had been the managing editor of the *Kansas City Call* before he joined the NAACP staff; Lucile Bluford was one of his successors. That the NAACP was only one of many organizations in the black community therefore not only supported the use of comparative advantage in allocating activities to different groups; it also contributed to that same comparative advantage by bolstering the lawyers' sense that they were indeed in tune with the community's values.

The network of community groups played another equally important part in the litigation campaign. The pattern of successes and failures provides support for the hypothesis that community support was not just ethically desirable but an essential condition of success. If the hypothesis is correct, it also makes less pressing the questions about the lawyers' domination of the clients' choices; if they wished to succeed, the lawyers could not afford to strong-arm the clients into supporting the lawyers' decisions. Even if the lawyers individually did not care about the community's wishes, which, of course, they did, they had to persuade, not coerce, their clients if they were to win. The arrangements for paying the fees of affiliated attorneys also made it important for the staff to persuade their clientele, at least so long as the staff thought it important for both practical and ideological reasons to retain the ability to farm cases out to local lawyers. It is a nice example of real world constraints on behavior supporting ethical action.

Aside from the pattern of results, there are reasons that make plausible the hypothesis that success depended on community support. The teachers' associations, for example, provided the names of potential plaintiffs, some emotional support when individual plaintiffs were harassed, and material support by promising a year's salary to plaintiffs, like Aline Black, who were fired. Similarly, black fraternities provided money for plaintiffs in the graduate school cases to pursue their educations while awaiting the outcomes. And, of course, Lucile Bluford was employed by a black newspaper. In contrast, several plaintiffs in graduate school cases lost interest when they found that local groups did not support them. In this light, perhaps Lloyd Gaines's disappearance can be attributed to the relative isolation of the Missouri litigation from community groups in 1938.[33] Another set of examples of the importance of community support is provided by North Carolina, where divisions within the black community aborted both graduate school and salary cases whenever the NAACP tried to get them started.

Community organizations, then, were useful, though perhaps not absolutely essential, in generating plaintiffs and keeping them satisfied while the litigation proceeded. They also performed important tasks directly related to the litigation. Parents in the Baltimore County case collected information about their children's performance on entrance examinations; the teachers' associations compiled data on salary disparities and counseled members on ways to deal with their employers that would not prejudice the litigation. Occasionally, as in several law school cases, the NAACP lawyers could take the time to investigate the conditions of the separate graduate programs, drawing in those cases on their own knowledge of what mattered in a law school. But in general they lacked the resources to do the detailed investigation that was necessary to litigate any lawsuit well. The "outline of procedures" sent to the branches quite rightly emphasized the importance of preliminary investigation, which had to be done in the field and which could not be done by the national staff or by affiliated attorneys, who had their fee-generating practices to take care of. A dedicated individual might have done the work, but it was precisely such an individual who was likely to be a community leader; indeed, investigating some incident could serve as an activity that would itself foster organizational growth. For example, in Atlanta and Baltimore the branches used surveys comparing the quality of facilities at black and white schools as tools for stimulating interest in the organization.[34]

The investigating group might have been a fringe element in a broader community opposed to litigation, but the NAACP did not face that problem during the period covered by the present study. In fact, the national staff had reasons to try to guarantee that the groups on which they relied for work in the field were broadly representative. A case could be litigated well, to a favorable judgment, with only some community support. But litigation does not end with the judgment. A decree must be written, which calls for extensive negotiation over details like timing, and, once the decree is entered, compliance must be monitored. Divisions within the local community seriously impeded negotiations over the terms of decrees and settlements in salary cases throughout the South, for school boards knew how to treat such divisions for what they were—indications of weakness in the negotiating position of the NAACP lawyers. Where differences over compliance arose, defendants who had lost could play on the divisions to gather support for the claim that they had fully complied with the decree.

Thus, at every stage of the NAACP's litigation, from the time that a plaintiff appeared until the time during which compliance with the terms of a victory had to be secured, support from a substantially unified local community was important in the lawyers' efforts. Under the circumstances, the lawyers' wishes and those of the community were blended so thoroughly that they cannot be distinguished. From a slightly different, more sociological point of view, the association between community support and success in litigation can be seen to have resulted from the prerequisites to successful litigation. If the NAACP lawyers were to serve the black community, the realities of litigation compelled them to act ethically, that is, on behalf of their clients.

The argument about legal ethics can now be summarized. The NAACP lawyers, in all three kinds of cases, had flesh-and-blood clients who wanted equal salaries, admission to professional schools, or desegregated elementary and secondary schools. The clients' desires were shaped by their personal ideological views and by interactions with the NAACP staff. The staff had good reason to litigate cases only in localities where a substantially united community backed the litigation. In localities where the black community desired to pursue a course of litigation different from that which the NAACP staff preferred, it was occasionally possible to do so. There is no evidence that the staff's position deprived any such community of legal assistance, though such deprivations may have occurred.

Many of the issues just addressed are not peculiar to the area of public interest law. Attention has focused on that area because it is closely connected to the policy-making processes of government and because information is available about the practice of public interest law that is in general not available about the practice of law on behalf of corporations and individuals.[35] Lawyers who represent entities rather than individuals always have to decide to whom within the entity they are primarily responsible. Observers of the legal system must consider the adequacy of the courtroom as a forum for resolving differences over social policy whenever the outcome of a lawsuit will have an effect on others not directly represented in it. A brief comparison of public interest law with three other types of legal practice suggests that there is no reason to reject the "null hypothesis" that the problems and available solutions are no different in the area of public interest law than in other areas. The areas to be considered are representation of corporations, of governments, and of victims injured by defective products.

Tensions might have arisen between the NAACP lawyers and some clients and potential clients because the lawyers were ideologically committed to a broader challenge to segregation than the potential clients were. Similar divergences of interest between lawyers and clients are common. For example, corporations seeking to expand by selling stock must disclose certain information about their financial condition. Disclosing more than is necessary may impair the corporation's competitive position and may make it harder to sell the stock. Yet under some circumstances the corporation's lawyers may be required to pay damages out of their own pockets, not the corporation's, if the disclosure is inadequate. The lawyers therefore have an interest in urging maximum disclosure, which may not be in the corporation's interest. Attorneys for government agencies, like many bureaucrats, must sometimes decide whether their career interests will be better served by representing the agency's point of view or by representing the program of the current administration. And even at the core of the system of legal representation, where a lawyer represents an individual injured by a defective product, the lawyer's interest in generating publicity that can attract additional clients may put the lawyer at odds with the present client, as for example, where the publicity attaches to pretrial activities while the ultimate result goes unnoticed.

Representation of entities also involves choosing the people in the entity to whom one should be responsible. Should the lawyer for the corporation represent the board of directors, the management, the shareholders, or the public interest? Should the government attorney represent the head of the agency, who may have political ambitions that shape his or her perceptions of the agency's interests, or the administration, or the public interest?[36] These questions are not different in principle from those raised by the activities of the NAACP's lawyers.

Recent discussions of such issues have focused on two solutions to the supposed difficulties. The first is to stipulate by some formal rule whom the lawyer is to represent. The attorney general represents the public even though, as in the South during the period examined here, a substantial portion of the public could not influence the positions taken by the attorney general. Corporate lawyers might represent the board of directors even in situations in which their interests and those of stockholders or the public may conflict. The NAACP lawyers, according to this approach, would be taken to represent those included in the class formally identified in the lawsuit, such as "black teachers," or those affected by the operation of rules of law in a precedent system, such as "black applicants to segregated universities." The formal solution is unsatisfying precisely because it may lead litigators and judges to ignore the real interests of some who are actually affected by the outcome. For example, a successful direct attack on segregation almost certainly would cause problems for black teachers; and, as it turned out, resistance to desegregation substantially delayed improvements in the education of black children that might have been attained earlier in equalization suits. The second solution is to develop procedures that allow those who disagree with the positions asserted by their nominal representatives to present their own views to the courts. These procedures are sometimes inadequate, though. Dissidents may lack resources. Defendants such as school boards may present dissenting views, and yet the force of dissent may be weakened when it is presented through those who, judges may think, wish only to obstruct all change.[37]

The NAACP's experiences suggest that there is a third solution possible, which can be called political.[38] The formal solution relies on legal rules to designate representatives of the affected community, and the procedural one accepts as a fact of life division within that community. The political solution relies on informal processes to produce community leaders who are able to reconcile the initially divided segments of their community and then to develop a unified position. In this connection, the crucial decision in the litigation campaign may have been the one to create a central staff concerned with litigation, not any of the particular decisions the staff made. Once the staff existed, a number of strategic decisions—to use federal rather than state courts in salary cases, for example—followed easily.

But it was not just "a" staff that was created. By the 1950s the NAACP lawyers had included Charles Hamilton Houston and Thurgood Marshall. Both had achieved positions of leadership in the black community because of their visible efforts to advance the interests of the race, and they had the skills that enabled them to unify the community behind their efforts. Among those skills were narrowly legal ones. In a situation where adverse precedents abounded, they maneuvered between them, and sometimes by doing the legally unthinkable they made it thinkable. But the immense dedication of Houston and Marshall to their work may have done more to foster success than any strategic decisions they made. Both Houston and Marshall had enormous ability at the essential, and fundamentally political, task of coordinating the conflicting interests of the various constituencies that the NAACP's litigation had to satisfy. Charles Lindblom has written that societies have developed only two ways, politics and markets, to coordinate human activity.[39] If that is true in the small as well as the large, the success of public interest law, which is by definition not subject to ordinary market discipline,[40] may depend on the appropriation of political skills, a resource that is rarely as concentrated as it was in Houston and Marshall.

Although the preceding discussion has touched on the general social, political, and economic climate in which the NAACP's decisions were made, it has emphasized internal aspects of the litigation effort as the primary elements of its explanations of those decisions—to pursue litigation, to challenge unequal salaries in the 1930s, to delay the direct attack on segregation until 1950, and the like. In general, social and political developments provided the framework within which the NAACP acted. But that framework could have accommodated rather wide variations in the legal status of segregation, and ultimately it contributes rather less than do the internal elements to an explanation of the events with which this book is concerned.

The southern economy began to be transformed between 1925 and 1950. Mechanization of agriculture increased, as did the penetration of large-scale manufacturing. Migration from the South altered the composition of the work force. Race policy in the South was placed under some pressure from these changes. A sensible response would be to increase investment in education and human capital, and to rationalize the work force. Both of these goals could be accomplished by reducing the disparities in education based on race.

Further, the continued existence of a rigid system of racial discrimination was inconsistent with what came to be seen as the requirements of the nation's commitment to equality. The tension between ideal and reality was exacerbated by international and national politics. After 1945 competition with the Soviet Union for world leadership involved ideological differences as well as other sociopolitical factors. Yet the persistence of racial discrimination supported by law constituted a continuing embarrassment to the United States. In addition, black votes, especially in the North, had become an important element in the Democratic coalition in national politics. Preserving the gains of the New Deal in the face of increasing conservative opposition required liberal Democrats to consolidate their support among blacks. Political mobilization of the black community, in such activities as the NAACP's antilynching campaign and the threatened 1941 March on Washington for a fair employment commission,[41] meant that the liberal Democratic coalition had to satisfy directly some specific demands of the black community.

Finally, once the litigation began, variations within the South affected the outcomes. In particular, once it became clear that blatantly discriminatory systems could no longer survive legal challenge, decision makers in the upper South found it more sensible to abandon discrimination than to engage in expensive litigation aimed at preserving sophisticated systems of discrimination, the outcome of which would be uncertain. Thus, Maryland, North Carolina, and Tennessee, finding salary discrimination under attack, yielded completely and legislated equalization.

Changes in the economic and political environment thus supported changes in racial policy. But they did not strongly determine what those changes would be. Consider the possibility of a serious effort to equalize facilities at all educational levels, by supposing that Marshall had been more cautious than he was, and had decided to press for equalization rather than the direct attack. On the economic level, increased investment in education, and its attendant rationalization of production, could obviously have been provided by enforcing a requirement of material equality in facilities. In the political arena, it is not overly cynical to suggest that sympathetic whites would have accepted the leadership of the NAACP on this issue, particularly because equalization would be less disruptive of existing patterns of racial accommodation.[42] As press comments after the Court's decisions in *Sweatt* and *McLaurin* suggest, unsympathetic whites would have found equalization easier to accept than desegregation, thus making success more likely. The equalization strategy would have reduced tensions within the Democratic party, and would have provided the opportunity for rebuilding the New Deal coalition—for example, by uniting it in support of a program of federal aid to education. It has been argued that blacks were drawn into the New Deal coalition less by Roosevelt's racial policies than by his economic ones.[43] Democratic support for material equalization could have satisfied black demands for specific programs while preserving the coalition's ability to advance its economic policies, themselves the primary reason why blacks were part of the coalition. Internationally, and more generally on the level of ideology, repudiating "separate but equal" served important propaganda goals, which an equalization program would not. Yet a Cold War administration, and other publicists concerned with ideology, could have gotten some mileage out of a stated commitment to an equalization program. All things considered, though the direct attack on segregation made sense in light of the wider social and political environment, a decision to pursue an equalization strategy would also have made sense.

It might even have been possible to persuade the black community, mobilized and made more militant by its experiences during and after World War II, to support equalization. Du Bois in the 1930s and Wesley a decade later had stressed the burdens a direct attack would place on black children. Black teachers were an important constituency with justifiable concerns over the implications of desegregation for their careers. Further, as we have seen, parents were regularly provoked by material inequalities, and only after they discussed their problems with NAACP lawyers did they reconceptualize their complaints into a challenge to segregation. Of course, there were other important black constituencies impatient with litigation and pressing for a direct attack. A powerful leader such as Marshall might well have been able to satisfy even those constituencies by repeating the point made throughout the litigation effort, that equalization would be so costly that desegregation was inevitable even without a direct attack, and by appealing to the black nationalist impulses that recurrently affected the black community.

Finally, we should consider the possibility that an equalization strategy might have produced, by 1970, a distribution of investment in the education of black children not very different from the one that actually prevailed at that time. In the upper South, the costs of maintaining a dual system, coupled with a relatively weaker commitment to strict segregation, might have led to relatively rapid desegregation. In the Deep South, little desegregation occurred before 1970 anyway, and an equalization strategy might have yielded some material benefits to black children before then.

Yet two things stand out about the actual course of events: Marshall in fact wanted to pursue the direct attack, and an equalization strategy would have placed enormous strains on the resources available for litigation. These are respectively a choice and an internal element, and they seem to provide a better explanation for what happened than more direct reference to economics and politics could.

An equalization strategy would not have been compatible with the idea of equality that was successfully invoked in *Brown*. Yet there was no relatively fixed ideal of equality with which racial discrimination was incompatible. The crucial cases in the litigation campaign show that the courts chose to enforce one of a number of plausible theories of equality. Indeed, without suggesting that alternative choices would have been less arbitrary, one can readily identify arbitrariness at key points in each opinion. Perhaps the most obvious is the Supreme Court's rejection in *Gaines* of out-of-state scholarships after it had assumed that the quality of out-of-state education was equal to that within the state. This disposition was said to be required because the state had to provide equality. But, of course, it was the state that provided the scholarships. On the assumptions used to decide *Gaines*, the geographical line dividing one state from another became crucial, for reasons the Court did not adequately explain.

The decisions in the university cases of 1950 were similarly innovative in rejecting a requirement of material equality by emphasizing the intangible elements of education. First, accepting the NAACP's sociological argument was an innovation. Previously such arguments had been used to demonstrate that, because reasonable decision makers could have believed that their actions promoted the public good, their decisions should be upheld. Now the argument was used to challenge legislative decisions, not on the ground that no reasonable decision maker could believe that the legislative action in question promoted the public good, but on the ground that sociological evidence showed that the policy espoused was inconsistent with a higher norm of equality. Plainly that innovation could have been resisted. Second, more mundanely, the intangibles the NAACP emphasized—law reviews, making contact with potential sources of business thoughout the state, social interaction with people of different backgrounds—could have been seen as the result of economies of scale in education. On this view, the states were providing equal education at equal levels of demand; the apparent inequality resulted from different levels of demand by blacks and whites, coupled with economies of scale.[44] Seen in that light, the university cases might have had few implications for elementary and secondary education, where economies of scale might well be smaller, and where demand-based "separate but equal" schools could have resulted from the use of techniques like consolidating rural schools rather than by desegregating. In short, there was no conception of equality waiting to be enforced. Rather, the courts and the NAACP were engaged in a process of constructing one out of many possible conceptions of equality.

This is not to say that economic, social, and political developments were irrelevant to the NAACP's decisions. The NAACP's lawyers interpreted those developments to themselves, and their interpretations affected what they did. For example, the ideology of the NAACP's leadership had a pervasive effect on strategy, and at an important point in the litigation campaign the federal government relied on concern about the adverse international consequences of segregation to justify its position. But the degree to which the larger developments strongly affected behavior can easily be overestimated.[45] The NAACP's national staff was quite small, and individual members of the staff understood the external elements in different ways, as the discussion in chapter 7 of the impatience of the younger members of the legal staff suggests. In addition, the staff consisted of political and legal activists, not systematic ideologues or social theorists. They tended to use whatever was available in the environment that seemed likely to help with the problem at hand, without worrying too much about whether their actions over the long run could be fit into some rationalized pattern.[46] The existence of debates over appropriate strategies, not the details of the competing positions, created the atmosphere that affected the staff's actions. Finally, at its inception and for perhaps a decade thereafter, the litigation effort was one relatively small part of a broad range of actions by a variety of dissidents, radicals, and other black activists aimed at changing the American social system. During this period few people outside the circle of those actually involved would have found it sensible to devote much time to considering exactly what should be done in the litigation campaign; by the time the campaign became a major effort, it had developed its own dynamic. For all these reasons, economic and political developments had no more than a rough connection to what occurred during the litigation campaign.

The role of organizational factors seems significantly more important than that of variations in the general social environment. With minor exceptions the NAACP lawyers won all of their early lawsuits challenging discriminatory teachers' salaries, and again with minor exceptions lost all the lawsuits they brought in state courts to challenge the exclusion of blacks from state-supported graduate and professional schools. Organizational constraints such as the paucity of lawyers in the Deep South to assist them, and the sheer convenience of litigating in Maryland and Virginia rather than in South Carolina or Georgia, meant that the litigation was concentrated in the upper South, just as, due to the same constraints, it was concentrated in urban areas. School boards in both parts of the region responded to the salary lawsuits by developing methods of discriminating that were more difficult to challenge. The various planning documents do not show the NAACP strategists deliberately selecting the upper South as a site for litigation on the ground that success would be more likely, or opposition less heated, there. But after the litigation had been under way for some time, common intuitions about the differences within the region came into play as NAACP officials tried to reconstruct what had happened and to present it as the implementation of a properly designed plan.

Similarly, the changes in strategy that occurred after 1945 were primarily the result of factors internal to the legal staff. The increased difficulty of winning lawsuits coincided with an apparently more favorable political climate, thus making a change in strategy seem sensible. But it is important to emphasize that from 1935 to 1945 the lawyers were pursuing a strategy that was new in their experience. Given their limited resources, their desire to see how effective the initial strategy would be, and the pace of change on the national scene, it would have been surprising had they altered the strategy much earlier than they did. Given the demands they faced from various constituencies, it would also have been surprising had they altered the strategy much later. Thus, the concerns that bear on the story of the litigation campaign appear to be primarily organizational.

Perhaps the best metaphor for the litigation effort is that it was one piece of the larger mosaic of the transformation of the country's race relations. It can be seen fully only as a part of a larger pattern, yet had the litigation effort been different so too would the pattern have been different.

Kluger treats the litigation campaign as an unqualified triumph for the strategy of challenging segregation in the courts, and for the liberal ideal of equality on which it rested. Those sympathetic to Du Bois's skepticism about the ability of blacks to wrest permanent concessions from whites may be more ambivalent. They might prefer to leave open the question of whether the interests of the black community could have been better served by an alternative course. Skepticism like Du Bois's raises questions about the political significance of the decisions taken during the litigation effort.

Given the military metaphors that have pervaded the discussion, it is useful to begin by focusing more precisely on the distinction between strategy and tactics.[47] In all the debates over the use of the courts, the participants agreed that courts and litigation could on occasion be used to gain tactical advantage; even the instrumentalists agreed that in specific situations litigation could be used to mobilize a group whose efforts could then be directed to other forms of political and economic action. Indeed, the differences in principle between the NAACP and the Communist party took shape around exactly this issue. To the Communists, legal action was explicitly and exclusively a tactic, to be used in some circumstances, when political conditions, as they analyzed them, were favorable. But it was to be abandoned in other settings, which Communist political analysis showed to be different even though strangers to the political analysis might think the settings were the same.

This tactical flexibility infuriated the NAACP's leadership, who thought the Communists totally unprincipled and purely opportunistic, as, for example, in the party's support of the Scottsboro defendants and its use of political criteria as the basis for refusing to support other blacks falsely accused of rape. Flexibility did have its costs, especially in creating the appearance that those who used legal action solely as a tactic were manipulating both their nominal clients and those who supported the cases on legalistic grounds. After all, from the tactical point of view, it was useless to generate supporters in individual cases who would disappear once the cases ended; the point was to convert them from legalists to political and economic activists. But tactical flexibility made that point all too apparent to those whose views were to be transformed. To put it as a paradox: if a group was to use law effectively as a tactic, it had to be committed to it as a strategy.

Once legal action became a strategy, though, the flexibility that made legal action an attractive tactic necessarily disappeared. Here again, this would be relatively unimportant so long as the principle of comparative advantage that allowed for a range of activities to be conducted by a number of community groups was itself an essential ingredient in the success of the legal strategy. But the success of the NAACP's legal strategy may have weakened the institutions that provided the preconditions for that very success. In part the successes were so substantial as to make support for institutions that specialized in activities other than legal action much less attractive, possibly depriving those institutions of the resources to maintain themselves. But, more significantly, as the NAACP's litigation proceeded to the decision to attack segregation directly, the organization's goal of equity between black and white became defined as the joint participation by both races in all institutions of the organized community. Principled lines could have been drawn to defend some kinds of autonomy for black institutions, but the ideal of joint participation was powerful enough to induce some discomfort with the separate institutions of black community life.

The paradox then has a more complex version: for legal action to be an effective tactic, it had to be a strategy, but if it was a strategy, it placed limits on its own effectiveness, by undermining some of the institutions within the black community that provided essential support for sustained litigation. The paradox should not be overstated; although some institutions in the black community, such as separate newspapers, have lost their importance, others, such as black churches, remain significant. Surely it is important, though, that *Brown* v. *Board of Education* meant that associations of black teachers, the progenitors of *Brown,* no longer had any obvious institutional basis.[48]

By emphasizing that a useful and flexible tactical commitment to litigation may have produced a less useful and more rigid strategic one, I have returned to Du Bois's arguments. But one final speculation is needed to complete the picture. Perhaps the paradoxes did not result from the choice of litigation as a tactic or strategy per se. They may have resulted from the particular strategy that the NAACP chose. The motor of that strategy was a vision of American society founded on competitive individualism, most dramatically expressed in Thurgood Marshall's statement in the argument on the remedy in *Brown:* "Put the dumb colored children in with the dumb white children, and put the smart colored children with the smart white children."[49] Yet competitive individualism almost by definition denies the importance of collective action for mutual aid. As a social movement the NAACP certainly saw its role as using collective power to establish the framework within which competitive individualism could operate fairly. Yet it has always been difficult to accommodate that pragmatic approach within the confines of legal doctrine, which pushes toward categories that have a more coherent, albeit less realistic, internal logic.[50] Further, a social movement is constituted by people who come to see that their daily struggles are somehow similar to those of other people, that is, by the development of a shared worldview. But it is not easy to share the view of competitive individualism, though one may notice that others happen to hold it as well. Given the individualist character of American law, it would have been inordinately difficult to develop what might be called a communitarian legal strategy. It would be unfair and anachronistic to tax the NAACP's lawyers for working within a framework of legal ideas that held some promise for relief from the massive insults that white society gave every day to black people; their job was hard enough as it was. But, fifty years later, it may be worth wondering whether Du Bois was right.

On May 17, 1954, the Supreme Court held in *Brown* v. *Board of Education* that "in the field of public education the doctrine of 'separate but equal' has no place. Separate educational facilities are inherently unequal." The Court then ordered reargument, which was held in April

1955, on the question of the appropriate remedy. It wanted discussion of whether desegregation should be immediate or gradual.[51] Shortly before the reargument, Marshall and the other NAACP attorneys engaged in a wide-ranging discussion of the question of remedy. Marshall's notes indicate that the lawyers wanted to cite instances of unjustified delay, of retaliation against black teachers, and of other forms of southern recalcitrance. At one point in the discussion, the lawyers mentioned the claim by Maryland's attorney general that "thoughtful leaders in Maryland of both races [were] for gradual [desegregation]." Marshall noted that it had taken Maryland until 1954—"16 years after Gaines case and nineteen (18) [sic] years after Pearson v. Murray"—to abolish its system of out-of-state scholarships. He then scrawled, "Now after all of this shit—no valid reason for delay—no hope that time would help."[52]

Notes

Introduction

1. 163 U.S. 537 (1896).
2. For the history of the early years of the NAACP, see Kellogg, *NAACP*.
3. 347 U.S. 483 (1954).
4. Kluger, *Simple Justice*.
5. The narrative omits many of the details of the proceedings in court, which, if presented, would frequently degenerate into lists of docket entries. Where a published opinion is available, I have cited it. I have sometimes omitted citation to the docket sheets of cases for procedural details referred to in the text; those docket sheets are contained in the files holding the letters discussing the proceedings, which *are* cited. In addition, the preliminaries to litigation in many communities differed only in the names of the participants from the preliminaries elsewhere. Because the patterns of activity repeated themselves, I have presented only the examples that are most productive in terms of the interpretation I offer; I do not believe that the omissions distort the overall picture.
6. Recent studies that describe the "resource mobilization" theory are McAdam, *Political Process;* Morris, *Origins of Civil Rights Movement;* Jenkins, *Politics of Insurgency;* Killian, "Organization, Rationality and Spontaneity." The authors differ, sometimes sharply, among themselves, but all provide helpful insights into the role of rational decision making in social movements.
7. See, e.g., McAdam, *Political Process,* p. 133 (figure presenting a "model of factors contributing to the development of a favorable context for black insurgency, 1900–1954").
8. For examples of the role of chance events, see Jenkins, *Politics of Insurgency,* pp. 145–46, 173–76.
9. Most of the lawsuits discussed here involved one or two primary plaintiffs, a local attorney or two, and one or two members of the national staff of the

NAACP. At the national level, perhaps six or seven people played important parts in the litigation effort for extended periods during the overall time from 1925 to 1950.

10. See, e.g., Chayes, "Role of the Judge"; Fiss, *Civil Rights Injunction;* Rhode, "Class Conflicts in Class Actions."

11. One limitation occurs because the social process of litigation is usually rather dull. If the military metaphor of a litigation "campaign" is appropriate, then the image should be of trench warfare over long periods in which nothing dramatic happens. During the NAACP's litigation effort, there were few trials, and none of the cases appears to have been resolved on the basis of facts or impressions that could only have emerged at a trial. The reality of the southern system of racial oppression provides another reason for emphasizing the routine of investigating complaints and drafting documents. In that system what mattered was the day-to-day grind of living in a segregated society, not the insults or courtesies offered to black litigants or lawyers once they managed to bring a case to court. The few dramatic incidents in the litigation campaign have been recounted by Kluger. See, e.g., Kluger, *Simple Justice,* pp. 203–4.

12. See Felstiner, Abel, and Sarat, "Emergence and Transformation," for a theoretical analysis of this stage of the process.

13. Macaulay, "Lawyers and Consumer Protection Laws," provides an overview of this stage of the process.

14. I depart from this approach in chapter 7, where I do not follow through on the story of university desegregation in Texas and Oklahoma. I do so because, as I argue there, by the time the cases were decided, the NAACP staff had decided that, if they won those cases, the decisions would become only way stations for the attack on segregation in elementary and secondary schools.

15. Three less important reasons for ending in 1950 should be mentioned. First, the post-1950 papers of the NAACP's lawyers, which are likely to reveal much about the litigation process, were not readily available when I conducted my research. When I began the research, the papers were stored, floor to ceiling, in a closet at the overcrowded offices of the NAACP Legal Defense and Educational Fund. They were in unlabeled boxes, and there was no apparent order to the location of the boxes. (One file, labeled "*Brown* v. *Board of Education,*" had been extracted from this group, and was available. It did not contain the sort of information that a study of the early stages of *Brown* required.) It was physically impossible to examine the boxes on the bottom of each stack; the weight of those above made the lower ones inaccessible, and there was no room in the offices to which I could move the upper ones without interfering with the office's ongoing operations. In the middle of the research, the papers were transferred to the Library of Congress. The processing of the acquisition, and restrictions on access apparently imposed out of

concern for lawyer-client confidentiality and for then-active litigation between the Legal Defense Fund and the NAACP, made the papers inaccessible at that point. Second, ending with *Brown* may suggest that the Supreme Court's decision is the triumphal capstone of the NAACP's activities, a suggestion that I question in the concluding chapter. Third, ending with a Supreme Court decision may suggest that the justices of the Supreme Court were the central actors in these events. I believe, instead, that the litigants and their attorneys were.

Chapter 1

1. The history of the NAACP's early years is recounted in Kellogg, *NAACP*. Its founders' views are discussed on pp. 9–19; its legal activities on pp. 57–64 (initial efforts), pp. 183–87 (residential segregation), pp. 205–8 (disfranchisement), pp. 241–45 (mob violence), and passim. The Supreme Court cases mentioned in the text are *Buchanan* v. *Warley*, 245 U.S. 60 (1917), and *Moore* v. *Dempsey*, 261 U.S. 86 (1926).

2. NAACP Annual Report for 1926, p. 3.

3. *New York World*, July 19, 1922 (clipping in NAACP Papers, Box I-C-196); Lamson, *Roger Baldwin*, p. 148. See also Curti, "Subsidizing Radicalism."

4. In 1921, Garland brought a young woman to live in his household, to form a ménage à trois. Shortly thereafter, both his wife and his friend left Garland, who continued to farm on Cape Cod. *New York World*, July 24, 1922 (clipping in NAACP Papers, Box I-C-196).

5. In 1943 Congress enacted a statute to bar Lovett from receiving a salary as government secretary for the Virgin Islands because of his left-wing associations. See *United States* v. *Lovett*, 328 U.S. 303 (1946) (holding statute unconstitutional).

6. *New York Call*, April 13, 1923 (clipping in NAACP Papers, Box I-C-196).

7. See Lamson, *Roger Baldwin*, pp. 27–83, for Baldwin's early career. For background on the formation of the American Civil Liberties Union, see Murphy, "Communities in Conflict," pp. 23–30.

8. Lamson, *Roger Baldwin*, pp. 110, 124, 191–92. For an expression of Baldwin's views in 1924, see Baldwin, "Challenge to Social Work."

9. Lamson, *Roger Baldwin*, p. 193. See Daniel, *ACLU and Wagner Act*.

10. Moorfield Storey to James Weldon Johnson, Sept. 15, 1925, NAACP Papers, Box I-C-76; Storey to Elizabeth Gurley Flynn, Oct. 23, 1925, ibid., Box I-C-196.

11. Storey to Flynn, Jan. 5, 1926, NAACP Papers, Box I-C-196; Flynn to Storey, Jan. 20, 1926, ibid. See also Du Bois, "Nation Wide Defense Fund a Success."

12. Report of the American Fund for Public Service for 1925–28 (Feb. 1929),

p. 10, in NAACP Papers, Box I-C-196; Roger Baldwin to Johnson, Aug. 27, 1926, Board of Directors Correspondence, 1923–1933, American Fund for Public Service Papers.

13. Menchan, "Florida Public Schools"; "The Negro Common School in Georgia," *The Crisis* 32 (Sept. 1926): 248; "The Negro Common School in Mississippi," *The Crisis* 33 (Dec. 1926): 90; "The Negro Common School in North Carolina," *The Crisis* 34 (May 1927): 79, and (June 1927): 117; "South Carolina Negro Common Schools," *The Crisis* 34 (Dec. 1927): 330; Bond, "Negro Common School in Oklahoma."

14. "The Sterling Discrimination Bill," *The Crisis* 27 (Mar. 1924): 199; "Education," *The Crisis* 36 (Apr. 1929) : 132. See also "To Your Tents, O Nordics!" *The Crisis* 28 (July 1924): 103; "Education," *The Crisis* 29 (Nov. 1924): 8; "The Sterling Discrimination Bill," *The Crisis* 29 (Dec. 1924): 106; "Education," *The Crisis* 37 (Feb. 1930): 65; "Education," *The Crisis* 38 [misprinted "40" on title page] (Oct. 1931): 330.

15. The Committee on Negro Work was part of a general reorganization of the fund, designed to process applications more effectively by channeling them to specialized committees.

16. Committee on Negro Work, draft proposal, Sept. 1929, NAACP Papers, Box I-C-196; Minutes, May 14, 1929, American Fund for Public Service Papers, Miscellaneous Reports, vol. 3.

17. Committee on Negro Work, proposal as submitted, Oct. 18, 1929, NAACP Papers, Box I-C-196; Walter White to Johnson, Sept. 16, 1929, ibid.

18. Committee on Negro Work, proposal as submitted, Oct. 18, 1929, NAACP Papers, Box I-C-196.

19. Roger Baldwin to L. Hollingsworth Wood, Oct. 21, 1929, quoted in Vose, *Caucasians Only,* p. 42; Lamson, *Roger Baldwin,* p. 128. On the division of labor between the NAACP and the Urban League, see Weiss, *National Urban League,* pp. 64–70, 174, 223. The widow of one of Roger Baldwin's uncles was a founder of the Urban League, and Baldwin served on the League board (ibid., pp. 21, 249n.). Baldwin recalled that he felt closer to the " 'conservative' Urban League" than to the NAACP because of his "accustomed old role as social worker" (ibid., p. 57).

20. Du Bois, "The Right to Work."

21. Du Bois, "Segregation."

22. The best short treatment of the controversy is Ross, *J. E. Spingarn,* pp. 186–98. See also Rudwick, *W. E. B. Du Bois,* pp. 176–85; Wolters, *Negroes and the Great Depression,* pp. 217–352.

23. De Bois, "A Free Forum."

24. Du Bois, "Separation and Self-Respect." Du Bois reiterated the argument in Du Bois, "Does the Negro Need Separate Schools?"

25. Du Bois, "Segregation in the North"; Du Bois, "The Board of Directors on Segregation"; Du Bois, "Dr. Du Bois Resigns."

26. See Ross, *J. E. Spingarn*, pp. 159–69.
27. See ibid., pp. 218–41; the quotation is from a letter by William Hastie quoted on p. 228. The NAACP did undertake a more limited expansion of its concern for economic issues.
28. Kirby, *Black Americans in the Roosevelt Era*, p. 181.
29. Bunche, "A Critical Analysis."
30. Thompson, "Court Action."
31. Hubbard and Alexander, "Types of Potentially Favorable Court Cases."
32. Minutes, Nov. 8, 1929, American Fund for Public Service Papers, Miscellaneous Reports, vol. 3; Walter White to Morris Ernst, Nov. 6, 1929, NAACP Papers, Box I-C-196; White to Johnson, Jan. 9, 1930, ibid.; Ernst to White, Jan. 17, 1930, ibid.; Ernst to White, Mar. 8, 1930, ibid.; White to Johnson, Mar. 10, 1930, ibid.
33. Ernst to White, Mar. 14, 1930, NAACP Papers, Box I-C-196; Draft report by Committee to Fund, pre-May 1930 (prepared by Ernst and White), ibid. On the growth of the staff, see chapter 7 below—in particular, the discussion accompanying note 11.
34. Minutes, May 28, 1930, American Fund for Public Service Papers, Miscellaneous Reports, vol. 4; Charles Garland to Board, Nov. 30, 1931, Johnson Papers, Series I, Folder 14; Walter White to Will Alexander, Aug. 16, 1932, Johnson Papers, Series I, Folder 541.
35. Committee Report, May 28, 1930, NAACP Papers, Box I-C-196; Memorandum from Committee, Johnson Papers, Series I, Folder 14; NAACP Annual Report for 1930, p. 17. The joint committee consisted of the members of the Committee on Negro Work (Johnson being counted as an NAACP representative), Arthur Spingarn, and Roger Baldwin.
36. White to many addressees, Sept. 1930, Spingarn Papers, Box 29; Arthur B. Spingarn to Nathan Margold, July 14, 1930, ibid., Box 9; Minutes of Joint Committee, Sept. 3, 1930, Johnson Papers, Series I, Folder 542; Charles Hamilton Houston to White, Sept. 3, 1930, NAACP Papers, Box I-C-196; White to Houston, Sept. 4, 1930, ibid. On Frankfurter's relation to Hastie, see Ware, *William Hastie*, pp. 31, 81, 98.
37. Nathan Margold to White, Sept. 4, 1930, NAACP Papers, Box I-C-196; contract with Margold, Oct. 4, 1930, ibid.; White to Johnson, Sept. 19, 1930, Johnson Papers, Series I, Folder 540. See Meier and Rudwick, *Along the Color Line*, p. 132. (Frankfurter had persuaded the faculty at Harvard to offer Margold a permanent position, but the appointment was blocked by the university administration. Parrish, *Felix Frankfurter*, pp. 157–58.)
38. White to Spingarn, Sept. 29, 1930, Spingarn Papers, Box 9; Minutes of Joint Committee, Oct. 2, 1930, ibid.; A. Philip Randolph to White (copy), Oct. 6, 1930, ibid.; White to Randolph (copy), Oct. 7, 1930, ibid.; Baldwin to White (copy), Oct. 9, 1930, ibid.; White to Spingarn, Oct. 10, 1930, ibid.
39. White to Anna Marnitz, Aug. 14, 1930, NAACP Papers, Box I-C-196; Robert

Dunn to White, May 7, 1931, ibid.; Dunn to White, May 23, 1931, ibid.; Marnitz to White, June 12, 1931, ibid.; White to Margold, June 13, 1931, ibid.

40. *New York Herald-Tribune,* May 18, 1931 (clipping in NAACP Papers, Box I-C-196); Secretary's Report, Nov. 9, 1931, NAACP Papers, Box I-A-17; Marnitz to White, June 6, 1932, ibid., Box I-C-196; Lewis Gannett to White, June 13, 1932, ibid.; White to Spingarn, Sept. 2, 1932, Spingarn Papers, Box 11; White to Spingarn, Feb. 3, 1933, ibid., Box 11; Dunn to White, June 15, 1932, NAACP Papers, Box I-C-196; White to Marnitz, June 22, 1932, ibid.; Roger Baldwin to White, Nov. 10, 1932, ibid.; White to Margold, Mar. 20, 1933, ibid.

41. Baldwin to White, July 7, 1933, NAACP Papers, Box I-C-196; Secretary's Report, July 10, 1933, ibid., Box I-A-16.

42. White, Report to Joint Committee, Mar. 21, 1935, Spingarn Papers, Box 29; White, Report to Joint Committee, July 29, 1935, ibid.; Houston, Report to Joint Committee, Nov. 14, 1935, ibid.

43. White to Baldwin, June 24, 1937, NAACP Papers, Box II-L-14; Baldwin to White, June 24, 1937, ibid.; Charles Hamilton Houston to Baldwin, June 28, 1937, ibid.; Baldwin to Houston, July 7, 1937, ibid.

44. Houston to Secretary, Joint Committee, Sept. 25, 1937, NAACP Papers, Box II-L-14; Baldwin to White, May 26, 1938, ibid.

45. NAACP Annual Report for 1934, p. 22.

46. In 1934, Leon Ransom and Houston prepared a procedural outline for grand jury challenges. Ransom to Spingarn, July 5, 1934, Spingarn Papers, Box 12.

Chapter 2

1. For general background on the adoption of segregation statutes, see Woodward, *Strange Career.* On *Plessy* v. *Ferguson,* see Woodward, "The Case of the Louisiana Traveler."

2. *Plessy* v. *Ferguson,* 163 U.S. 537 (1896). For a discussion of the Boston case, see Levy, *The Law of the Commonwealth,* pp. 109−17.

3. *Cumming* v. *Board of Education,* 175 U.S. 528 (1899). For background, see Kousser, "Separate but Not Equal."

4. *McCabe* v. *Atchison, Topeka & Santa Fe R. Co.,* 235 U.S. 151 (1914). For a more complete discussion, see Schmidt, "Principle and Prejudice," pp. 485−94. The railroad was failing to honor black demands for Pullman service as late as 1930, when it refused to provide such service to George Washington Carver. McMurry, *George Washington Carver.*

5. 118 U.S. 356 (1886).

6. Margold to White, Oct. 14, 1930, NAACP Papers, Box I-C-196.

7. Margold to White, Mar. 31, 1931, NAACP Papers, Box I-C-196.

8. Johnson, Synopsis for Program, June 27, 1930, NAACP Papers, Box I-C-196.
9. Margold Report, pp. 30–38, NAACP Papers, Box I-C-200. For the latter proposition, he cited *Barney v. New York,* 193 U.S. 430 (1904), but not *Home Telephone Co. v. Los Angeles,* 227 U.S. 278 (1913). This approach probably derived from Frankfurter, who later articulated it in *Snowden v. Hughes,* 321 U.S. 1, 15–17 (1944) (Frankfurter, J., concurring). Frankfurter had taught courses in the law of federal jurisdiction at Harvard Law School while Margold was his student, and it seems likely that he had developed this interpretation of *Barney* and *Home Telephone* then. The first edition of the leading casebook on federal jurisdiction was dedicated to Frankfurter, "who first opened our minds to these problems," and included Frankfurter's concurrence in its notes on the *Barney–Home Telephone* problem. Hart and Wechsler, *Federal Courts and Federal System,* pp. ix, 820–33.
10. Margold Report, pp. 93–95, NAACP Papers, Box I-C-200. Equalization would lead to desegregation because, by maintaining dual systems, school boards would be unable to realize economies of scale, most obviously those available in connection with expenditures on laboratories, auditoriums, and gymnasiums. Similar concerns led to rural school consolidations after 1950.
11. Margold to White, May 2, 1932, NAACP Papers, Box I-C-196.
12. White to Margold, May 22, 1932, NAACP Papers, Box I-C-196; Houston to White, Oct. 26, 1934, ibid.
13. White to Margold, May 22, 1934, NAACP Papers, Box I-C-196.
14. Meier and Rudwick, "Attorneys Black and White," in *Along the Color Line,* pp. 128 –73.
15. Woodson, *Negro Professional Man,* pp. 184–249.
16. Meier and Rudwick, "Attorneys Black and White," in *Along the Color Line,* pp. 144–45; McNeil, "To Meet the Group Needs," especially pp. 158–59; Accreditation Report, Nov. 24, 1933 (copy), Spingarn Papers, Box 29; *Howard University Law Bulletin,* undated (after 1939), in Law School Files, Moorland-Spingarn Research Center, Howard University.
17. White to James A. Cobb, June 1, 1932, NAACP Papers, Box I-A-27; White to Spingarn, Oct. 25, 1933, ibid.; Spingarn to White, June 15, 1932, ibid.; Spingarn to White, Oct. 27, 1933, ibid.
18. See generally Meier and Rudwick, "Attorneys Black and White," in *Along the Color Line;* William T. Andrews file, NAACP Papers, Box I-C-62; Spingarn Papers, Boxes 9 and 10.
19. White to Baldwin, July 8, 1933 (copy), Spingarn Papers, Box 11; White to Spingarn, July 8, 1933, ibid.; White to Spingarn, July 17, 1933, ibid. (quoting Baldwin).
20. White to Spingarn, Sept. 23, 1933, Spingarn Papers, Box 11; White to Spingarn, Oct. 30, 1933, Spingarn Papers, ibid.; White to Spingarn, Apr. 13, 1934, ibid.; White to Spingarn, May 14, 1934, ibid.; White to Spingarn, May

22, 1934, ibid.; White to NAACP Board of Directors, Oct. 6, 1934, ibid. Houston was born in Washington in 1895. He graduated from Amherst College, and after wartime experiences brought home to him the realities of American racism, he then went to Harvard Law School. There, in addition to sponsoring a luncheon for Marcus Garvey, the black nationalist, Houston became the first black elected, on the basis of his grades, to the *Harvard Law Review.* He took a postgraduate fellowship in Spain and then joined his father's law practice in 1924. He also began teaching at Howard Law School, and gradually his teaching activities replaced his law practice as his primary career. An account of Houston's life appears in McNeil, *Groundwork.*

Chapter 3

1. Houston, "Tentative Statement Concerning Policy of N.A.A.C.P. in Its Program of Attacks on Educational Discrimination," July 12, 1935, NAACP Papers, Box I-C-197; Houston, "[Uncorrected] Summary of Speech . . . to National Bar Association Convention," Aug. 1, 1935, ibid., Box I-C-420. I have been unable to discover any indication that the "Tentative Statement" was issued to the public. The National Bar Association speech reiterates the themes of the "Tentative Statement," and includes additional technical details of the sort discussed above in chapter 2.
2. Houston to William Houston, Apr. 14, 1938, NAACP Papers, Box I-C-82; Houston to Leon A. Ransom et al., Sept. 17, 1936, ibid., Box I-C-84.
3. In 1934, Woodson, *Negro Professional Man,* p. 188, reported that 30 percent of all black lawyers had been graduated from Howard. The next largest group, 4.7 percent, had been graduated from Harvard Law School. W. E. B. Du Bois described the leadership class of the black community as its "talented tenth." See Meier, *American Negro Thought,* pp. 196–97.
4. On Houston's work on behalf of railway laborers in the late 1930s and early 1940s, see McNeil, *Groundwork,* pp. 157–71.
5. See Houston, "Cracking Closed University Doors"; Houston, "Enrollment in Negro Colleges"; Houston, "The Negro's Educational Advantages." See also Johnson, *Negro College Graduate;* Wesley, "Graduate Education for Negroes" (as of 1940, graduate education for blacks unavailable in seventeen states, of which seven border and upper South states had programs of out-of-state scholarships).
6. See, e.g., Report to Secretary, Mar. 9, 1939, NAACP Papers, Box I-A-18.
7. Hastie to J. M. Tinsley, May 31, 1933, Hastie Papers, Box 105, file 13. See also Houston to Fred Wilkinson, Nov. 8, 1937, NAACP Papers, Box I-C-199 ("We should not take any cases except those of students whose qualifications are beyond question"); Ware, *William Hastie,* p. 52 (in North Carolina,

Hastie wanted an "outstanding" applicant because he or she would be a center of community attention).

8. See Zangrando, NAACP *Crusade against Lynching*, pp. 88ff., 108.

9. Thurgood Marshall to Charles Todd, Aug. 30, 1937, NAACP Papers, Box I-C-198; Marshall to J. M. Tinsley, Aug. 30, 1937, ibid., Box I-D-91.

10. On Houston's relations with Communists during the 1930s, see McNeil, *Groundwork*, pp. 101–8.

11. Carter, *Scottsboro*. The details of the dispute between the Communists and the NAACP appear thoughout Carter's book; for a sustained analysis, see pp. 51–103; see also pp. 247–52. On the aims of the International Labor Defense in general, see Martin, "International Labor Defense."

12. Quoted in Wolters, *Negroes and the Great Depression*, p. 221.

13. Wilkins to Spingarn, Jan. 16, 1933, Spingarn Papers, Box 11; White to Bidwell Adam, Dec. 15, 1932, NAACP Papers, Box I-D-49. Adam rejected the offer of publicity because it might prejudice Carraway's case (Adam to White, Jan. 10, 1933, ibid.). In 1935 Carraway's sentence was commuted to life imprisonment.

14. See Carter, *Scottsboro*, pp. 129–35.

15. White to Board of Directors, Feb. 23, 1932, NAACP Papers, Box I-D-65; White to Roderick Beddow, Feb. 24, 1932, ibid.; White to C. F. McPherson, Mar. 4, 1932, ibid.; Houston to R. R. Moton, July 29, 1932, ibid.; Houston, Report on Peterson Investigation, Sept. 2, 1933, ibid., Box I-D-66.

16. White to Butler Wilson, Jan. 24, 1933, NAACP Papers, Box I-D-51; White to John Collins, Feb. 17, 1933, ibid.; White to Spingarn, Mar. 8, 1933, ibid.

17. Houston to White, Mar. 12, 1933, NAACP Papers, Box I-D-51; White to Wilson, Mar. 22, 1933, ibid.; White to J. Weston Allen, Apr. 17, 1933, ibid., Box I-D-52.

18. *Hale v. Crawford*, 65 F. 2d 739 (1st Cir.), cert. den., 290 U.S. 674 (1933). After the reversal, Felix Frankfurter wrote a short note to White, saying that the reversal could have been expected because Judge Lowell had been wrong. Frankfurter to White, June 23, 1933, NAACP Papers, Box I-D-52.

19. Meier and Rudwick, *Along the Color Line*, pp. 149–50; White to Roy Wilkins, Nov. 15, 1933, NAACP Papers, Box I-D-52; White to A. E. O. Munsell, Dec. 18, 1933, ibid.; William Pickens to C. A. Barnett, Dec. 18, 1933, ibid. Pickens, commenting at a time when the outcome of the Scottsboro case was yet to be determined, exaggerated the differences between the Crawford case and Scottsboro. He was correct in suggesting that the innocent Scottsboro defendants were unfairly serving prison sentences, though they, like Crawford, had been saved from execution.

20. White, "George Crawford—Symbol;" White, "The George Crawford Case, Part I"; White, "The George Crawford Case, Part II"; Du Bois, "The Crawford Case"; "Betrayal by the N.A.A.C.P." *New Masses* 14 (Jan 8, 1935): 6; Gruen-

ing, "The Truth about the Crawford Case"; Boardman and Gruening, "Is the NAACP Retreating?"; Boardman and Gruening, "The Crawford Case," in NAACP Papers, Box I-D-53; Houston to *Norfolk Journal and Guide*, Feb. 12, 1934, NAACP Papers, Box I-D-53. Gruening had a long-standing connection with the NAACP, beginning in 1912 as a staff member involved in organizing, and later as a researcher on race riots and lynching. See Kellogg, *NAACP*, pp. 92, 224, 261; Zangrando, *NAACP Crusade against Lynching*, p. 37; Lewis, "Parallels and Divergences," p. 553.

21. Houston to Douglas Freeman, Sept. 19, 1934, NAACP Papers, Box I-C-64; Houston to White, Jan. 1, 1935, ibid.; Houston to White, Jan. 23, 1935, ibid.; Wolters, *Negroes and the Great Depression*, p. 46.

22. The hope that the litigation effort would quickly strengthen the NAACP in the South was disappointed, but disillusionment did not set in until Houston's organizational concerns had given shape to the campaign. After a successful salary suit in Norfolk, Virginia, had failed to increase NAACP membership there, Walter White wrote to Hastie and Marshall that the teachers were a group of ingrates, and recounted one teacher's refusal to give a contribution for a celebration to honor the plaintiffs: "Why should I have to give anything else now that we have won?" Disturbed by this classic free-rider response, the NAACP Board of Directors asked that prelitigation agreements be signed in which the local teachers would agree to join the NAACP and work to expand membership. Marshall replied that such agreements were far too close to solicitation of clients, a violation of professional ethics. White to William Hastie and Marshall, March 3, 1941, NAACP Papers, Series II-B, Teachers' Salaries—Virginia—Norfolk file; Minutes, June 9, 1941, Board Meeting, ibid.; Marshall to White, July 23, 1941, ibid. An editorial in the *Charleston Lighthouse and Informer* on Nov. 8, 1941, criticized teachers for their apathy: "This lack of support, this lack of appreciation, this lack of gratitude is so shameful as to be scandalous."

23. See McNeil, *Groundwork*, pp. 87–88.

24. In retrospect it may appear that graduate and professional school challenges, and salary equalization suits, had such obvious merit that the likelihood of success, rather than ease of conducting litigation or the other factors discussed in the text, made them clearly preferable to other kinds of litigation. But although southern states did not maintain separate graduate schools, several provided scholarships to allow blacks to attend out-of-state schools. In salary cases, school boards might have defended salary differentials by claiming that black teachers, many of whom were graduates of unaccredited or low-ranking colleges, were less qualified than white teachers, and that the cost of living in the black community was lower than the cost of living in the white one. These complexities reduce, though they probably do not eliminate, the differences in likelihood of success between the types of cases that Houston brought and other types.

25. Woodson, *Negro Professional Man*, p. 43.
26. See Houston, "Educational Inequalities Must Go!"; Houston, "How to Fight for Better Schools"; Houston, "Don't Shout Too Soon."
27. There is no adequate biography of Marshall. For the background recounted here, see Flynn, *Negroes of Achievement*, pp. 66–70. On Marshall's organizational activities, see, e.g., Marshall to Houston, Sept. 12, 1935, NAACP Papers, Box I-C-84.
28. Houston to Marshall, Sept. 21, 1935, NAACP Papers, Box I-C-84; Marshall to Houston, Aug. 21, 1935, ibid. (describing his plans for preparing a brief); Marshall to Houston, May 25, 1936, ibid.
29. Marshall to Houston, Apr. 23, 1936, NAACP Papers, Box I-C-84; Marshall to Houston (copy), Sept. 14, 1936, Springarn Papers, Box 13; Houston to Marshall, Sept. 17, 1936, NAACP Papers, Box I-C-84; Marshall to Houston, Sept. 19, 1936, ibid. Hastie wrote to the president of Howard suggesting that Marshall be appointed to the faculty (Hastie to Mordecai Johnson, May 29, 1936, Hastie Papers, Box 79, file 7).
30. Houston to White (copy), Sept. 17, 1936, Spingarn Papers, Box 13; White to Houston (copy), Sept. 18, 1936, ibid.; Houston to Marshall, Sept. 28, 1936, NAACP Papers, Box I-C-84; Spingarn to White, May 15, 1935, ibid., Box I-C-74; Houston to Marshall (draft), Sept. 28, 1936, ibid., Box I-C-84; Houston's note on Lillie Jackson to White, Oct. 19, 1936, ibid., Box I-D-45.
31. See McNeil, *Groundwork*, pp. 145–49, for a discussion of Houston's private life.
32. See, e.g., Leon A. Ransom to Marshall, Oct. 24, 1935, NAACP Papers, Box I-C-84 ("Nogood"); "Eddie" [Lovett?] to Marshall, Oct. 26, 1935, ibid. ("Turkie").

Chapter 4

1. Fiss, *Civil Rights Injunction*.
2. Houston to Roger Baldwin, Mar. 9, 1938, NAACP Papers, Box II-L-14.
3. For some hints at these points, see Ware, *"Hocutt,"* pp. 231–32 (the state trial judge in North Carolina university case of 1933 "had a reputation of being a decent man as southerners went"); interview, Constance Baker Motley, Columbia Oral History Collection, Columbia University, New York, N.Y., 1978, p. 254 (federal judges in the 1950s were "a little better" than state judges, but many were hostile to blacks).
4. White to C. O. Pearson and Cecil McCoy, Feb. 8, 1933, NAACP Papers, Box I-D-96; McCoy to White, Feb. 11, 1933, ibid.; White to McCoy, Feb. 17, 1933, ibid.; McCoy to White, Mar. 19, 1933, ibid.; McCoy to White, Mar. 21, 1933, ibid. McNeil, *Groundwork*, p. 66, calls Hastie a "distant cousin by marriage" of Houston's.

5. Shepard opposed the application in part because he favored the use of out-of-state tuition grants, and in part because he desired to have departments of law, medicine, and pharmacy created at his college. See Ware, *"Hocutt,"* p. 228.

6. Edward Lovett to White, Dec. 6, 1933, NAACP Papers, Box I-D-96; Houston to White, July 31, 1935, ibid. See Kluger, *Simple Justice*, pp. 155–58; Ware, *"Hocutt,"* pp. 232–33, where it is said that Hocutt moved to New York and became a subway worker.

7. J. Reuben Sheeler to Houston, Aug. 31, 1935, NAACP Papers, Box I-D-96; Houston to Sheeler, Sept. 6, 1935, ibid.; Sheeler to Houston, Oct. 14, 1935, ibid.; Houston to Sheeler, Oct. 18, 1935, ibid.; Carl Cowan to Houston, Apr. 6, 1936, ibid.

8. William Redmond to Houston, Jan. 23, 1936, NAACP Papers, Box I-D-96; Charles Johnson to Houston, Feb. 17, 1936, ibid.; Houston to Redmond, Feb. 7, 1936, ibid.; Houston to file, June 16, 1936, ibid.; Houston to Redmond, Sept. 24, 1936, ibid.; Elmer Imes to Walter White, Dec. 7, 1936, ibid.; White to Imes, Dec. 10, 1936, ibid.; White to Houston, Dec. 10, 1936, ibid.; Houston to Roy Wilkins, Apr. 22, 1937, ibid., Box I-D-97; Houston to Cowan et al., May 6, 1937, ibid.; Leon A. Ransom to Houston, May 7, 1937, ibid.; Houston to Cowan, May 11, 1937, ibid.; Houston to Z. Alexander Looby and Ransom, May 16, 1937, ibid.; Houston to Looby, June 19, 1937, ibid.

9. Wilkins to Lewis Swingler, Mar. 13, 1937, NAACP Papers, Box I-D-96.

10. Cowan to Houston, July 12, 1939, NAACP Papers, Box I-D-97; Houston to White et al., Aug. 22, 1939, ibid.; Cowan to Looby, Feb. 28, 1940, NAACP Papers, Series II-B, University Cases—Tennessee file; Ransom to Looby, Mar. 7, 1940, ibid. The procedural history is outlined on the docket sheet in this file. It should be noted that the technical issue on which the case turned is the sort of issue that an unsympathetic judge could have resolved against plaintiffs no matter which set of defendants they had chosen to serve.

11. Juanita Jackson to Houston, Sept. 24, 1934, NAACP Papers, Box I-C-85; William Gosnell to Houston, Dec. 18, 1934, ibid.; Marshall to Houston, Jan. 25, 1935, ibid.; Marshall to Houston, Mar. 18, 1935, ibid., Box I-D-93; *Baltimore Evening Sun*, Apr. 22, 1935 (clipping in NAACP Papers, Box I-D-93).

12. Marshall to Houston, Sept. 17, 1935, NAACP Papers, Box I-D-93; Houston to Marshall, Sept. 21, 1935, ibid.; Marshall to Houston, Jan. 1, 1936, ibid.; Marshall to Houston, Jan. 9, 1936, ibid.; Marshall to Houston, Aug. 21, 1935, ibid., Box I-C-84; Houston to Marshall, Sept. 23, 1935, ibid.; Houston to Charles Wesley, Dec. 7, 1935, ibid. See also Houston, Report to National Conference, June 24, 1935, ibid., Box I-C-85 (using *Murray* to formulate a model procedure).

13. *Pearson v. Murray*, 169 Md. 478, 182 A. 590 (1936).

14. "The Admission of Negroes to the University of Maryland," *School and So-*

ciety 46 (Sept. 11, 1937): 335; White to Murray, Sept. 20, 1935, NAACP Papers, Box I-D-93; Marshall to Ransom, Jan. 8, 1936, ibid., Box I-C-85; White to Murphy, Jan. 24, 1936, ibid., Box I-D-93.

15. Cecil McCoy to White, Aug. 22, 1933, NAACP Papers, Box I-C-281; Conrad Pearson to White, Sept. 7, 1933, ibid.; White to Hastie, Sept. 8, 1933, ibid.; White to Hastie, Sept. 14, 1933, ibid.; Hastie to White, Sept. 19, 1933, ibid.; memorandum, Sept. 20, 1933, ibid.; Hastie to White, Sept. 22, 1933, ibid.; Marshall to Ralph Harlow, Jan. 8, 1938, ibid., Box I-D-89; George Streator to White, Sept. 24, 1933, ibid., Box I-C-281; Streator memorandum, Sept. 28, 1933, ibid.; White to J. N. Mills, Oct. 3, 1933, ibid. Hastie reported that there was "nothing to the I.L.D. scare." Hastie to White, Sept. 22, 1933, ibid. See also Ware, *William Hastie*, pp. 56–60. From 1939 on, North Carolina school boards, whether fearing litigation or for other reasons, gradually equalized salaries without the direct pressure of court orders. In 1942, the legislature appropriated $242,000 to narrow the differential, and the N.C. School Commission indicated its desire to eliminate all differences within two or three years. Burns, "North Carolina and the Negro Dilemma," pp. 77–80; *Greensboro Daily News*, June 12, 1942, sec. 1, p. 12.

16. Marshall to office, Oct. 9, 1936, NAACP Papers, Box I-D-88.

17. There was one exception. One plaintiff, a principal, was reassigned to another school; the effect was to place him on probationary status as a principal, and he lost his position after one year but retained tenure as a teacher. See Marshall to Executive Staff, June 23, 1938, NAACP Papers, Box I-D-89.

18. See Fenton, *Politics in the Border States*, p. 8; Walsh and Fox, *Maryland*, pp. 720, 767 (quoting *Afro-American*), 780.

19. Marshall to office, Oct. 9, 1936, NAACP Papers, Box I-D-88; Marshall to White, Dec. 5, 1936, ibid.; Murphy to Marshall, Nov. 6, 1936, ibid.; Pettigen to Marshall, Nov. 6, 1936, ibid.; Pettigen to Marshall, Nov. 8, 1936, ibid.; Pettigen to Marshall, Nov. 16, 1936, ibid.; Marshall memorandum, Nov. 13, 1936, ibid.; Marshall memorandum, Oct. 12, 1936, ibid.

20. Gibbs to Marshall, Oct. 22, 1936, NAACP Papers, Box I-D-88; Marshall to Houston, Oct. 20, 1936, ibid.; Marshall to White et al., Nov. 21, 1936, ibid.

21. William Prettyman to Marshall, Feb. 2, 1937, NAACP Papers, Box I-D-88; Marshall to Gibbs, Jan. 29, 1937, ibid.; Marshall to Lillie Jackson, Mar. 20, 1937, ibid., Box I-D-89; Marshall to Gibbs, Apr. 5, 1937, ibid.; Marshall to Murphy, Apr. 24, 1937, ibid.; Marshall to Charles Woodward, Mar. 25, 1937, ibid.; Leon Ransom to Edward Lovett, May 1, 1937, ibid.; Wolters, *Negroes and the Great Depression*, pp. 98–106.

22. Prettyman to Marshall, June 29, 1937, NAACP Papers, Box I-D-89; Marshall to Houston et al., July 19, 1937, ibid.; Gladys C. Boston to White, Aug. 24, 1937, ibid.

23. Enolia [Pettigen] McMillan to Marshall, Aug. 27, 1937, NAACP Papers, Box

II-L-41; Elizabeth Brown to Marshall, Aug. 31, 1937, ibid.; Marshall to McMillan, Jan. 17, 1938, ibid., Box I-D-89; Marshall to Thompson, Feb. 25, 1938, ibid.; Marshall to Executive Staff, June 23, 1938, ibid.; Marshall to Murphy, Apr. 19, 1938, ibid., Box I-D-90; undated memorandum re Calvert County, ibid.; Marshall to Harry Nice, June 23, 1938, ibid.; Murphy to Marshall, Sept. 29, 1938, ibid.; *Baltimore Evening Sun,* Dec. 29, 1937 (quoting Gov. Nice).

24. Marshall to Joint Committee, May 13, 1938, NAACP Papers, Box I-D-89; Houston to Marshall, Jan. 18, 1938, ibid., Box I-D-90; Marshall to file, Jan. 25, 1938, ibid.; Lovett to Marshall, Feb. 22, 1938, ibid.; Marshall to Lovett, Feb. 23, 1938, ibid.; press release, Apr. 22, 1938, ibid.; press release, May 27, 1938, ibid.; Houston to White, June 18, 1938, ibid.; Marshall to White and Houston, June 21, 1938, ibid.; Marshall to Executive Staff, June 23, 1938, ibid.; Marshall to file, June 6, 1938, ibid.; Lovett to Marshall, June 6, 1938, ibid.

25. Marshall to Joint Committee, June 10, 1938, NAACP Papers, Box I-D-90; Houston to file, Oct. 5, 1938, ibid.; Marshall to McMillan, Oct. 6, 1938, ibid.; Marshall to Houston, Oct. 6, 1938, ibid.; Lovett to Marshall, Oct. 10, 1938, ibid.; Marshall to Board of Education, Jan. 13, 1940, ibid.; Adrian Fisher to Marshall, Jan. 25, 1940, ibid.; Marshall to Fisher, Feb. 1, 1940, ibid.; Houston to Roy Wilkins, May 22, 1940, ibid.

26. McMillan to Marshall, Mar. 7, 1938, NAACP Papers, Box I-D-89; Noah Hillman to Marshall, May 12, 1938, ibid.; George Fox to Marshall, June 10, 1938, ibid.

27. *Mills* v. *Lowndes,* 26 F. Supp. 792 (D. Md. 1939).

28. Benjamin Kaplan to Marshall, May 10, 1939, NAACP Papers, Box I-D-89; Marshall to McMillan, Oct. 4, 1939, ibid.; *Mills* v. *Board of Education,* 30 F. Supp. 245 (D. Md. 1939).

29. Marshall to Hastie and Ransom, Dec. 14, 1939, NAACP Papers, Box I-D-89; Kaplan to Marshall, Dec. 15, 1939, ibid.; Marshall to Hillman, Dec. 18, 1939, ibid.; Marshall to Joint Committee, Dec. 22, 1939, ibid.; Marshall to Hastie and Ransom, Jan. 12, 1940, ibid.

30. "Recent Cases," *Harvard Law Review* 53 (Feb. 1940): 669–71; George Murphy to Marshall, Apr. 3, 1941, NAACP Papers, Series II-B, Teachers' Salaries—Maryland—Recommendation file.

31. Carl Murphy to Marshall, Aug. 5, 1935, NAACP Papers, Box I-C-84; Marshall to Houston, Sept. 12, 1935, ibid.; Houston to Marshall, Sept. 14, 1935, ibid.; Houston to White, Oct. 8, 1935, ibid., Box I-D-45; Marshall to White, Oct. 8, 1935, ibid., Box I-C-84; Marshall to Houston, Sept. 16, 1935, ibid.

32. Marshall to Houston, Aug. 24, 1935, NAACP Papers, Box I-C-84; Marshall to Houston, Feb. 5, 1936, ibid., Box I-D-45; Houston to Marshall, Mar. 30, 1936, ibid.

33. *Williams* v. *Zimmerman*, 172 Md. 563, 192 A.353 (1937).
34. Marshall to J. M. Tinsley, Aug. 30, 1937, NAACP Papers, Box I-D-91.
35. Marshall to Martin Martin, Aug. 12, 1940, NAACP Papers, Series II-B, Schools—Virginia—Pittsylvania file.
36. Outline of Procedure for Legal Defense, Education, and Voting Cases, NAACP Papers, Series II-B, Outline of Procedure file. The outline was revised, with little change in substance, in 1943, and was distributed to the branches in April 1944.

Chapter 5

1. Houston to Sidney Redmond, July 15, 1935, NAACP Papers, Box I-D-94; Redmond to Houston, Aug. 27, 1935, ibid.; Houston to Redmond, Oct. 4, 1935, ibid.; Houston to Redmond, Dec. 26, 1935, ibid.; Marshall to Houston, Dec. 10, 1936, ibid., Box I-D-88; Marshall to Ridgely Melvin, Mar. 15, 1937, ibid. In 1949, after he had served on the St. Louis Board of Aldermen, Redmond became the first black member of the St. Louis Bar Association. On Gaines, see Bluford, "The Lloyd Gaines Story."
2. See Grothaus, "'The Inevitable Mr. Gaines,'" pp. 22–24. Three other blacks applied to the engineering, medical, and graduate schools, but the university did not act on their applications (Sawyer, "The Gaines Case," p. 159).
3. Houston to file, July 10, 1936, NAACP Papers, Box I-D-94; Gaines to Houston, Aug. 5, 1936, ibid.; Houston to White and Arthur Spingarn, Sept. 4, 1936, ibid. For a report of the oral argument, see "Decision of the Missouri Supreme Court . . . ," *School and Society* 48 (Dec. 3, 1938): 726.
4. *Missouri ex rel. Gaines* v. *Canada*, 305 U.S. 337 (1938). Justice McReynolds, joined by Justice Butler, dissented in a brief opinion that called the scholarship system "far from unmistakable disregard of [Gaines's] rights and in the circumstances . . . enough to satisfy any reasonable demand for specialized training." The system, he said, was "a fair effort to solve" a "difficult and highly practical" problem. He also cast some doubt on Gaines's good faith in seeking admission by saying that the system offered Gaines the "opportunity for study of the law—if perchance that is the thing really desired."
5. Press release, May 12, 1939, NAACP Papers, Box I-D-95; Bluford, "Missouri 'Shows' the Supreme Court"; *State* v. *Canada*, 131 Sw. 2d 217 (Mo. 1939); Redmond to Houston, Aug. 7, 1939, NAACP Papers, Box I-D-95; "The Establishment of School of Law by Lincoln University," *School and Society* 50 (Sept. 9, 1939): 339; Grothaus, "The 'Inevitable Mr. Gaines,'" p. 27; "'Jim Crow' Law School," *Newsweek*, Oct. 2, 1939, p. 32; "The Gaines Case and Its Effect on Negro Education in Missouri," *School and Society* 51 (Mar. 9, 1940): 309–13.

6. White to Redmond, May 26, 1939, NAACP Papers, Box I-D-95; Houston to White (copy), May 22, 1938, Spingarn Papers, Box 14; Houston to White, May 22, 1939, NAACP Papers, Box I-D-95; Houston to Marshall, Aug. 8, 1939, ibid.; White to Houston, Aug. 11, 1939, ibid.

7. Houston to Marshall, Aug. 3, 1939, NAACP Papers, Box I-D-95; Redmond to Houston, Aug. 7, 1939, ibid.; Houston to White et al., Aug. 22, 1939, ibid., Box I-D-97; Houston to Marshall, Oct. 10, 1939, ibid., Box II-L-41; Houston to Redmond, Dec. 27, 1939, ibid., Box I-D-95; Sawyer, "The Gaines Case," pp. 192–95.

8. Virginius Dabney, "South Put in Quandary," *New York Times,* Dec. 18, 1938, p. 10E. An editorial in *Commonweal* praised the decision as "just in principle" but foresaw problems. It urged Missouri to open the state university to blacks and thereby "tak[e] the lead for the South in a direction in which sooner or later it will have to go." Segregation was inconsistent with the "interior obligations" of higher education. The more likely alternative, though, was the costly program of separate black schools. The editorial regretted, as did Dabney, that *Gaines* foreclosed the alternative, talked about in the past but never acted upon, of creating a first-rate regional university for blacks ("The Gaines Decision," *Commonweal* 29 [Jan. 6, 1939]: 282). Other editorial comments are summarized in Sawyer, "The Gaines Case," pp. 241–54.

9. "Case Comment," *University of Chicago Law Review* 6 (Feb. 1939): 301–5; "Decision," *Brooklyn Law Review* 8 (May 1939): 442–44; "Recent Case," *George Washington Law Review* 7 (May 1939): 900–902.

10. "Case Comment," *Kentucky Law Journal* 27 (Mar. 1939): 335–38 (on state court's initial decision); "Recent Decision," *Kansas City Law Review* 6 (Feb. 1938): 154–57 (on state court's initial decision); "Note," *Tulane Law Review* 13 (April 1939): 465–66.

11. "Recent Decision," *Fordham Law Review* 8 (May 1939): 260–63. Other comments on *Gaines* are Baker, "Trend of United States Supreme Court Decisions," p. 34 ("sound and realistic"); "Recent Case," *Temple Law Quarterly* 13 (Feb. 1939): 255–56 (skeptical); "The Negro Citizen in the Supreme Court," *Harvard Law Review* 52 (Mar. 1939): 823–32 (pp. 830–31: "serves [a] useful purpose"); "Recent Decision," *Michigan Law Review* 37 (Feb. 1939): 649–51 ("not only logical but commendable as well"); "Comment," *Cornell Law Quarterly* 24 (Apr. 1939): 419–22 (neutral); "Recent Case," *University of Pennsylvania Law Review* 87 (Feb. 1939): 478–80 (neutral); "Recent Case," *Georgetown Law Journal* 27 (Jan. 1939): 331–32 (neutral); "Recent Case," *St. John's Law Review* 13 (Apr. 1939): 420 (neutral); "Comment," *Iowa Law Review* 24 (Mar. 1939): 604–5 (skeptical, benefit "is questionable, for the underlying social problem remains"); "Note and Comment," *North Carolina Law Review* 17 (Apr. 1939): 280–85 (mildly hostile); "Case Note," *Georgia Bar Journal* 1 (May 1939): 54–55 (dissent has "the better view").

12. Weaver and Page, "The Black Press," pp. 17–18. See also Sawyer, "The Gaines Case," pp. 252–54.

13. Buni, *Negro in Virginia Politics,* pp. 119–26; Key, *Southern Politics,* pp. 19–35. Key notes that blacks voted in the highest proportions in the state in cities where they were allied with the dominant Byrd machine, "which in turn has protected their right to suffrage" (p. 32 n. 11). The Virginia white primary had been held unconstitutional by a district court in Virginia, whose decision was affirmed in *West* v. *Bliley,* 42 F. 2d 101 (4th Cir. 1930). The case had been initiated by the Richmond NAACP branch, but the branch was relatively apathetic. Even after the lawsuit succeeded, black participation in elections did not increase dramatically. See Hine, *Black Victory,* pp. 92–96. Hine argues that this resulted from the fact that the litigation in Virginia was seen by many blacks as a middle-class effort, unlike that in Texas, where the litigation was part of a broader effort to mobilize the entire black community (pp. 102–4, 235–36).

14. Marshall to White, Nov. 26, 1937, NAACP Papers, Box I-D-91; Marshall to J. M. Tinsley, Oct. 4, 1937, ibid.; Marshall to W. P. Milner, Oct. 22, 1937, ibid.; Houston to L. F. Palmer, Oct. 15, 1937, ibid.; James A. Jones to Marshall, Dec. 5, 1937, ibid.

15. Marshall to Ransom, Apr. 15, 1938, NAACP Papers, Box I-D-91; Tinsley to Marshall, Oct. 7, 1938, ibid.; Tinsley to Marshall, Oct. 19, 1938, ibid.; Marshall to P. B. Young, Mar. 29, 1938, ibid.; Marshall to Joint Committee, May 13, 1938, ibid.; Minutes, Legal Committee, Aug. 18, 1939, ibid., Box I-A-28; Marshall to Chauncey Harmon, June 16, 1938, ibid., Box I-D-91; John Walker to White, June 23, 1938, ibid.; J. Thomas Hewin to Marshall, Oct. 12, 1938, ibid.

16. Young to Marshall, Nov. 4, 1938, NAACP Papers, Box I-D-91; Ransom, notes on school board minutes, May 15, 1939, ibid.; Marshall to White, May 31, 1939, ibid.; Marshall to Joint Committee, June 17, 1939, ibid.; Norfolk *Virginian-Pilot,* Mar. 4, 1939 (clipping in NAACP Papers, Box I-D-91); Suggs, "Black Strategy and Ideology," pp. 183–84.

17. Melvin Alston to Marshall, Oct. 6, 1938, NAACP Papers, Box I-D-91; Marshall to Young, Oct. 31, 1938, ibid.; Marshall to Austin [*sic;* sent to Alston], Oct. 31, 1938, ibid.; Marshall to Alston, July 27, 1939, ibid.; Alston to Marshall, Aug. 21, 1939, ibid.; Marshall to Young, Aug. 25, 1939, ibid.; press release, Sept. 28, 1939, ibid.

18. William Cooper to White, Oct. 23, 1939, NAACP Papers, Box I-D-91; White to Cooper, Oct. 25, 1939, ibid.; Alston to Marshall, Oct. 8, 1939, ibid.; Marshall to White and Wilkins, Oct. 18, 1939, ibid.; Marshall to Aline Black, Oct. 27, 1939, ibid.; Marshall to Joint Committee, Oct. 30, 1939, ibid.; Young to Marshall, Oct. 13, 1939, ibid.

19. Sidney Redmond to Houston, July 22, 1936, NAACP Papers, Box I-D-94; *Alston* v. *School Board of Norfolk,* 112 F. 2d 992 (4th Cir.), cert. denied, 311

U.S. 693 (1940). The law review comments were confined to speculation about the application of the court's decision to nonprofessional employees. "Notes and Cases," *Bill of Rights Review* 1 (Winter 1941): 142–44; "Recent Case," *Minnesota Law Review* 25 (Jan. 1941): 236–38; "Decision," *Virginia Law Review* 27 (Dec. 1940): 245–46; "Note," *Louisiana Law Review* 3 (Nov. 1940): 232–35.

20. Marshall to Wilkins, Nov. 12, 1940, NAACP Papers, Series II-B, Teachers' Salaries—Virginia—Norfolk file; Marshall to Hastie et. al., Nov. 28, 1940, ibid.; Marshall to White, Dec. 8, 1940, ibid.; Jerry Gilliam to White, Mar. 8, 1941, NAACP Papers, Series II-B, Teachers' Salaries—Virginia—Norfolk—Gilliam file.

21. White to Alston, Mar. 3, 1941, NAACP Papers, Series II-B, Teachers' Salaries—Virginia—Norfolk file; Alston to White, Mar. 16, 1941, ibid.

22. *Teachers' Salaries in Black and White* (New York: NAACP, 1941); this publication is available in NAACP Papers, Series II-B, Teachers' Salaries—Maryland—Anne Arundel County file.

Chapter 6

1. For a range of views on the implementation of judicial decrees, see sources cited in Rebell and Block, *Educational Policy-Making*, pp. 301–3.

2. Marshall to J. M. Tinsley, Aug. 17, 1938, NAACP Papers, Box I-D-91; Leon A. Ransom to Houston, Sept. 20, 1936, ibid., Box I-D-96; Houston to Walter Goldston, Sept. 26, 1936, ibid. Goldston, the potential plaintiff, went to Meharry Medical School instead (Goldston to Houston, Sept. 13, 1936, ibid.).

3. Houston to Bluford, Jan. 27, 1939, NAACP Papers, Box I-L-41. On Bluford, see Sawyer, "The Gaines Case," pp. 198–201.

4. Houston to Bluford and Redmond, Sept. 12, 1939, NAACP Papers, Box I-L-41.

5. Sawyer, "The Gaines Case," pp. 201–8, 210, 235–39.

6. *Bluford* v. *Canada*, 32 F. Supp. 707 (W. D. Mo. 1940).

7. *State* v. *Canada*, 153 S. W. 2d 12 (Mo. 1941).

8. Bluford to Marshall, July 10, 1941, NAACP Papers, Series II-B, Universities—Missouri file; Sidney Redmond to White, Aug. 12, 1941, ibid.; Bluford to White, Mar. 4, 1941, ibid.; Grothaus, "'The Inevitable Mr. Gaines'," p. 30; Sawyer, "The Gaines Case," pp. 301–2, 306.

9. Houston to Frank Reeves, Mar. 26, 1942, NAACP Papers, Series II-B, Universities—Missouri file; Houston to files, Apr. 26, 1942, ibid.; Houston to Edith Massey, Dec. 16, 1943, ibid.; Houston to Wilkins, Dec. 16, 1943, ibid.; Lincoln University press release, Jan. 29, 1944, ibid.; Grothaus, "The 'Inevitable Mr. Gaines'," pp. 31–32. Sawyer, "The Gaines Case," pp. 288–315, details

the University of Missouri's maneuvers. In 1950 the university itself sought a judicial declaration that its continued segregation was unconstitutional (ibid., pp. 328–32).

10. Houston to Prentice Thomas, Jan. 22, 1940, NAACP Papers, Series II-B, Universities—Kentucky file; Thomas to Houston, June 23, 1941, ibid.; Thomas to Ransom, Sept. 10, 1941, ibid.; Thomas to Marshall, Oct. 2, 1941, ibid.; Marshall to Thomas, Oct. 9, 1941, ibid.; press release, Oct. 17, 1942, ibid.

11. Memorandum, Nov. 17, 1941, NAACP Papers, Series II-B, Universities—Kentucky file; Godfrey Cabot to White, Oct. 20, 1941, ibid.; Thomas to Marshall, Apr. 1, 1942, ibid.; J. W. Jones to Thomas, Apr. 15, 1942, ibid.; Thomas to Marshall, May 4, 1942, ibid.; Thomas to Marshall, Apr. 15, 1942, ibid.; Thomas to Houston, Mar. 17, 1943, ibid.; Thomas to S. A. Burnley, Mar. 24, 1943, ibid.; Thomas to Burnley, Apr. 19, 1943, ibid.; Thomas to Lewis Downing, Aug. 20, 1943, ibid.; Eubanks affidavit, Jan. 18, 1945, ibid.

12. Robert Carter to Harold Boulware, Sept. 10, 1946, NAACP Papers, Series II-B, Universities—South Carolina file; James Hinton to Marshall, Nov. 29, 1946, ibid.; Carter to Hinton, Dec. 2, 1946, ibid.; Boulware to Marshall, Oct. 1, 1947, ibid.; John Wrighten to Marshall, Sept. 29, 1947, ibid.; Marshall to Hinton and Boulware, Sept. 30, 1947, ibid.; Wrighten to Hinton, Oct. 6, 1947, ibid.; Boulware to Edward Dudley, Oct. 13, 1947, ibid.; Marshall to Boulware, Mar. 3, 1948, ibid. A typescript of the court's decision is stored with the foregoing correspondence.

13. NAACP Annual Report for 1941, pp. 15–19; memorandum, Jan. 18, 1947, NAACP Papers, Series II-B, Teachers' Salaries—General 1947 file. A more accessible list is published in Editorial Note, "Constitutionality of Educational Segregation," *George Washington Law Review* 17 (Feb. 1949): 208, 215–16 n. 37. The author lists twenty-two cases settled or decided favorably, four unfavorably, and twelve pending. Of the latter, the seven from Louisiana should be counted in the "favorable" category because of legislation equalizing salaries.

14. On the role of race in the politics of Florida and Louisiana, see Key, *Southern Politics,* pp. 82–105 (Florida), 156–82 (Louisiana). Under the heading "Florida Is Different," Key discusses the state's size, uneven distribution of population, tradition of highly localized politics, and relative urbanization, to the last of which he attributes "Florida's relative unconcern about the Negro" (pp. 83–87, 84). Key's discussion of Louisiana emphasizes the dominance of the Longs in reducing the salience of racial politics.

15. Houston to Walker S. Walker et al., Jan. 4 1935, NAACP Papers, Box I-D-96; White to Milman Mitchell, Sept. 16, 1940, NAACP Papers, Series II-B, Teachers' Salaries—Tennessee—Nashville file; *Thomas v. Hibbetts,* 46 F. Supp. 368 (M. D. Tenn. 1942).

16. W. Henry Elmore to Marshall, Mar. 5, 1941, NAACP Papers, Series II-B, Teachers' Salaries—Tennessee—Chattanooga file; Elmore to Marshall, July 14, 1941, ibid.; Marshall to Elmore, July 22, 1941, ibid.; NAACP Annual Report for 1941, p. 17.

17. Victor Perry to Marshall, Jan. 21, 1938, NAACP Papers, Box I-L-41; Marshall to P. O. Sweeney, June 10, 1939, NAACP Papers, Series II-B, Teachers' Salaries—Kentucky—Louisville file; Marshall to Prentice Thomas, Jan. 31, 1940, ibid.; Charles Anderson to Marshall, Dec. 18, 1939, NAACP Papers, Box I-L-41; Anderson to Marshall, Dec. 22, 1939, ibid.; Marshall to Sweeney, Dec. 26, 1939, NAACP Papers, Series II-B, Teachers' Salaries—Kentucky—Louisville file; Yolanda Barnett to Marshall, Jan. 4, 1940, ibid.; Marshall to Barnett, Sept. 11, 1940, ibid.; Barnett to Marshall, Sept. 16, 1940, ibid.

18. Thomas to Marshall, Oct. 18, 1940, NAACP Papers, Series II-B, Teachers' Salaries—Kentucky—Louisville file; Thomas to Marshall, Dec. 14, 1940, ibid.; press release, Jan. 17, 1941, ibid.; Thomas to Marshall, Apr. 5, 1941, ibid.; Marshall to Thomas, Feb. 24, 1941, ibid.; NAACP Annual Report for 1941, p. 16.

19. Solar Carrethers to Melvin Austin [*sic;* sent to Alston], Feb. 20, 1941, NAACP Papers, Series II-B, Teachers' Salaries—Arkansas—Little Rock file; Carrethers to White, Feb. 22, 1941, ibid.; Marshall to Carrethers, Feb. 28, 1941, ibid.; J. L. Wilson to Marshall, Dec. 9, 1941, ibid.; Marshall to Roy Wilkins, Feb. 28, 1942, ibid.; *Morris* v. *Williams,* 59 F. Supp. 508 (E. D. Ark. 1944).

20. Milton Konvitz to J. R. Booker, Jan. 11, 1944, NAACP Papers, Series II-B, Teachers' Salaries—Arkansas—Little Rock file; Booker to Marshall, May 13, 1946, ibid.; *Little Rock Gazette,* June 1, 1944 (clipping in this file).

21. *Morris* v. *Williams,* 149 F. 2d 703 (8th Cir. 1945).

22. See Marshall to White, Sept. 22, 1942, NAACP Papers, Series II-B, Teachers' Salaries—Arkansas—Little Rock file.

23. L. Raymond Bailey to Marshall, Nov. 28, 1940, NAACP Papers, Series II-B, Teachers' Salaries—South Carolina file; James M. Hinton to Marshall, Mar. 24, 1941, ibid.; O. E. McKaine to Marshall, Feb. 10, 1943, ibid.; Hinton to Marshall, Oct. 11, 1943, ibid.; Hinton to Marshall, Oct. 16, 1943, ibid.; Hinton to Marshall, Nov. 2, 1943, ibid.; Edward Dudley to Harold Boulware, Feb. 18, 1944, ibid.

24. See *United States* v. *South Carolina,* 445 F. Supp. 1094, 1102 (D.S.C. 1977).

25. Marshall to A. Heningburg, May 21, 1938, NAACP Papers, Box I-C-82; Marshall to Joseph Nicholson, Apr. 1, 1940, NAACP Papers, Series II-B, Teachers' Salaries—Alabama file; J. C. LeFlore to Marshall, Oct. 30, 1940, ibid.; Marshall to Emory Jackson, Dec. 12, 1940, ibid.; LeFlore to Marshall, Dec. 11, 1940, ibid.; Marshall to LeFlore, Dec. 12, 1940, ibid.; Arthur Shores to Marshall, May 30, 1941, ibid.; Marshall to Shores, June 6, 1941, ibid.; Shores to Marshall, Oct. 29, 1941, ibid.; Shores to Marshall, Dec. 30,

1941, ibid.; Shores to Marshall, Jan. 31, 1942, ibid.; press release, Mar. 27, 1942, ibid.; Shores to Marshall, May 30, 1942, ibid.; Shores to Marshall, Oct. 9, 1944, ibid.; press release, Apr. 27, 1945, ibid. See also Autrey, "The NAACP in Alabama," pp. 138–39, 208–10.

26. Houston, Report to National Conference, June 24, 1935, NAACP Papers, Box I-C-84; Houston to White, May 22, 1939, ibid., Box I-D-95.

27. Harry Moore to White, Aug. 2, 1937, NAACP Papers, Box I-D-88; Marshall to Houston, Aug. 9, 1937, ibid.; Houston to Marshall, Aug. 13, 1937, ibid.; S. D. McGill to Marshall, Nov. 5, 1937, ibid.; McGill to Marshall, Nov. 27, 1937, ibid.; Marshall to McGill, Mar. 4, 1938, ibid. On McGill's background, see Meier and Rudwick, *Along the Color Line,* p. 159 n. 21 and sources cited there.

28. Press release, June 28, 1939, NAACP Papers, Box I-D-88; Marshall to McGill, Sept. 9, 1939, ibid. As discussed in chapter 4, there seems to be no reason as a matter of law to attribute the difficulties to the use of mandamus.

29. S. D. McGill to Marshall, May 6, 1940, NAACP Papers, Series II-B, Teachers' Salaries—Florida—Escambia County file; Marshall to Harry Moore, July 25, 1940, ibid.; Marshall to Vernon McDaniel, Aug. 20, 1941, ibid.; L. E. Thomas to White et al., Sept. 28, 1942, NAACP Papers, Series II-B, Teachers' Salaries—Florida—Duval County file.

30. L. E. Thomas to Marshall, Feb. 20, 1942, NAACP Papers, Series II-B, Teachers' Salaries—Florida—Marion County file; Marshall to Leon Ransom, July 8, 1942, ibid.; Thomas to Marshall, July 29, 1942, ibid.

31. Clarinda Speed McCambridge to Marshall, Feb. 27, 1943, NAACP Papers, Series II-B, Teachers' Salaries—Florida—Palm Beach County file; Ransom to Milton Konvitz, July 8, 1943, ibid.

32. *Turner* v. *Keefe,* 50 F. Supp. 647 (S. D. Fla. 1943).

33. Marshall to Edward Graham, Nov. 8, 1945, NAACP Papers, Series II-B, Teachers' Salaries—General 1941–45 file; Marshall to office, April 30, 1945, ibid.; *Reynolds* v. *Board of Public Instruction,* 148 F. 2d 754 (5th Cir. 1945). See also Marshall to files, Jan. 23, 1945, NAACP Papers, Series II-B, Teachers' Salaries—Louisiana—Baton Rouge file (Baton Rouge rating system).

34. J. E. Perkins to White, May 10, 1939, NAACP Papers, Box I-D-88; Marshall to Perkins, May 20, 1939, ibid.; White to H. Horne Higgins, June 16, 1939, ibid.; Archie LeCesne to Marshall, Nov. 27, 1939, ibid.; Donald Jones to Marshall, Aug. 10, 1940, NAACP Papers, Series II-B, Teachers' Salaries—Louisiana—New Orleans file; Jones to Marshall, Sept. 30, 1940, ibid.; Jones to Marshall, Feb. 20, 1941, ibid.; Jones to Marshall, May 2, 1941, ibid.; Jones to Marshall, June 15, 1941, ibid.

35. Jones to Marshall, July 15, 1941, NAACP Papers, Series II-B, Teachers' Salaries—Louisiana—New Orleans file; Marshall to Jones, July 21, 1941, ibid.; A. P. Tureaud to Marshall, Feb. 2, 1942, ibid.; Tureaud to Marshall, June 14,

1942, ibid.; Marshall to Tureaud, June 19, 1942, ibid.; Marshall to White and Wilkins, June 27, 1942, ibid.; Tureaud to Marshall, July 3, 1942, ibid.; Marshall to Tureaud, July 6, 1942, ibid.; Tureaud to Marshall, July 22, 1942, ibid.; Tureaud to Marshall, July 29, 1942, ibid.; Marshall to Tureaud, July 30, 1942, ibid.; press release, Aug. 21, 1942, ibid. See also Worthy, "Travail and Triumph," pp. 37–46.

36. Jones to Marshall, Sept. 7, 1942, NAACP Papers, Series II-B, Teachers' Salaries—Louisiana—New Orleans file; Tureaud to Jones, Oct. 17, 1942, ibid.; Tureaud to Marshall, Oct. 17, 1942, ibid.; Jones to Marshall, Dec. 23, 1942, ibid.; Marshall to Jones, Sept. 9, 1942, ibid.; *New Orleans Sentinel*, Oct. 24, 1942 (clipping in this file). On Tureaud's career, see Worthy, "Triumph and Travail," pp. 3–22. From 1943 to 1946 Tureaud filed three additional equalization suits. A state statute equalized salaries in 1948 (ibid., pp. 50–56).

37. Secretary's Report, Nov. 11, 1935, NAACP Papers, Box I-A-18; Secretary's Report, Dec. 5, 1935, ibid. Compare Hastie to J. M. Tinsley, May 31, 1933, Box 105, file 13, Hastie Papers (applicant should be "unmistakably a Negro").

38. See interview, Arthur Spingarn, Columbia Oral History Collection, Columbia University, New York, N.Y., 1967, p. 84.

39. See Zangrando, NAACP *Crusade against Lynching*, pp. 139, 161–62; Kirby, *Black Americans in the Roosevelt Era*, p. 175. For a comment a decade later on personal tensions between White and Marshall, see Hastie to White, Nov. 20, 1950, Hastie Papers, Box 100, file 3.

40. D. H. Blair to NAACP, June 15, 1925 (copy), Spingarn Papers, Box 14; White to Spingarn, Sept. 30, 1938, ibid.; White to Spingarn, Nov. 28, 1939, ibid., Box 15; Marshall to White, Sept. 30, 1938 (copy), ibid., Box 14; NAACP v. NAACP *Legal Defense and Educational Fund*, Civ. No. 82-1424 (D.D.C.), Complaint, p. 3, May 25, 1982; ibid., "Supplement to Plaintiff's memorandum in opposition to defendant's motion for summary judgment," attachment (Marshall to Spingarn and White, July 27, 1939), October 1, 1982; ibid., "Plaintiff's memorandum in support of its motion for summary judgment," p. 5, Nov. 24, 1982; NAACP Legal Defense Fund, *Thirty Years of Building American Justice*, p. 39; White to Marion Stern, May 6, 1940, NAACP Papers, Series II-B, Incorporation—Legal Defense file.

41. NAACP v. NAACP *Legal Defense . . . Fund*, "Defendant's statement pursuant to Civil Rule 1-9(h)," p. 2, Aug. 4, 1982.

42. White to Committee on Administration, June 18, 1943, NAACP Papers, Box II-A-123; Study and Recommendations by Judge William H. Hastie, Aug. 1943, ibid., Box II-A-306; Hastie to Konvitz, July 13, 1943, ibid.; Marshall to White, Sept. 24, 1943, ibid., Box II-A-123; Minutes of Committee on Administration, Oct. 25, 1943, ibid. The available minutes of the NAACP Board of Directors do not indicate the extent to which Hastie's recom-

mendations were adopted. (The minutes for several months in 1943 and 1944 are missing from the NAACP Papers.) However, the recommendations and Marshall's acceptance indicate the existence of some psychological distance between the legal staff and the other staff.

43. Wilkins to White, Jan. 11, 1940, NAACP Papers, Series II-B, Universities—Missouri file; White to Wilkins, Jan. 13, 1940, ibid.; Houston to Marshall, Apr. 24, 1940, ibid.; Wilkins to Houston, Apr. 26, 1940, ibid.; Houston to White, Wilkins, and Marshall, May 8, 1940, ibid.; Marshall to Wilkins, Oct. 24, 1939, ibid., Box II-L-41.

44. Marshall to D. W. Perkins, Dec. 17, 1941, NAACP Papers, Series II-B, Teachers' Salaries—Florida—General file; N. W. Griffen to White, Feb. 28, 1941, NAACP Papers, Series II-B, Teachers' Salaries—Florida—Escambia County file; White to Marshall, Oct. 22, 1941, NAACP Papers, Series II-B, Teachers' Salaries—Florida—McGill file; Marshall to White, Oct. 23, 1941, ibid.

45. *Richmond News Leader,* Nov. 5, 1941, p. 8 (clipping in NAACP Papers, Series II-B, Teachers' Salaries—Virginia—Richmond file); Oliver Hill to Ransom and Marshall, Dec. 30, 1941, ibid.; Antoinette Bowler to White, Feb. 20, 1942, ibid.; Milton Randolph to White, Feb. 23, 1942, ibid.; Marshall to White and Wilkins, Feb. 17, 1942, ibid.

46. "The High Cost of Segregated Graduate Schools for Negroes," *School and Society* 63 (May 8, 1946): 358; *Charleston News and Courier,* Mar. 17, 1942. Sawyer, "The Gaines case," pp. 270–81, summarizes the minimal actions taken by southern state universities in response to *Gaines.*

47. Carter to White, Nov. 4, 1946, NAACP Papers, Series II-B, Teachers' Salaries—General 1946 file; Boykin, "Status and Trends;" Marshall, draft article, 1945, NAACP Papers, Series II-B, Teachers' Salaries—Arkansas—Little Rock file. See also Choper, "Consequences of Supreme Court Decisions," p. 24 (in 1945–46, black teachers' salaries as a percentage of salaries for white teachers equaled 61 percent in Alabama and Arkansas, 69 percent in Florida, 51 percent in Georgia, 53 percent in Louisiana, and 37 percent in Mississippi).

Chapter 7

1. Houston to Wilkins et al., Mar. 10, 1940, NAACP Papers, Series II-B, Schools—Virginia—Loudoun County file; Houston to White, Mar. 23, 1940, ibid.; Marshall to White, Mar. 18, 1940, ibid.

2. Herman Taylor to Marshall, Oct. 28, 1946, NAACP Papers, Series II-B, Schools—North Carolina—Lumberton file; Marshall to Taylor, Nov. 15, 1946, ibid.; Marshall to Ruby Hurley, Feb. 6, 1947, ibid.; Robert Carter to Curtiss Todd, July 28, 1947, ibid.; Taylor to Carter, Aug. 17, 1947, ibid.; Burns, "North Carolina and the Negro Dilemma," pp. 89–92.

3. A. Maceo Smith to Lulu White, Aug. 14, 1947, NAACP Papers, Series II-B, Schools—Texas file; Smith to Marshall, Sept. 12, 1947, ibid.; Report of Regional Special Counsel, Nov. 27, 1949, ibid.
4. Marian Wynn Perry to Marshall, Jan. 29, 1948, NAACP Papers, Series II-B, Schools—Texas file; Carter to Taylor, June 28, 1947, ibid.; Smith to Perry, Aug. 18, 1947, ibid.; Perry to Smith, Aug. 19, 1947, ibid.; Smith to Marshall, Sept. 12, 1947, ibid.; Carter to Louis McHenry, Sept. 5, 1950, NAACP Papers, Series II-B, Schools—Kansas—Merriam file.
5. See Hine, *Black Victory*, pp. 129ff. For a brief discussion of Wesley's background and views, see Smallwood, "Texas," pp. 364–65.
6. Marshall to Carter Wesley, Oct. 25, 1946, NAACP Papers, Series II-B, Wesley file; Wesley to Marshall, Dec. 23, 1946, ibid.
7. Wesley to Marshall, Oct. 8, 1947, NAACP Papers, Series II-B, Wesley file.
8. Marshall to Wesley, Oct. 16, 1947, NAACP Papers, Series II-B, Wesley file.
9. Greenberg, *Litigation for Social Change*, p. 19; Nabrit, "Resort to the Courts," p. 469; Marshall, Statement to Texas State Conference of Branches, Sept. 5, 1947, NAACP Papers, Series II-B, Marshall file.
10. Spottswood Robinson to J. M. Tinsley, Oct. 1, 1947, LDF Papers; Robinson to Marshall, Oct. 2, 1947, ibid.; Report of Legal Staff, Oct. 2, 1948, ibid.; Robinson, Report to Virginia Conference of Branches, Oct. 21, 1950, ibid.; Robinson to Marshall, Mar. 13, 1950, ibid.; Carter to Robinson, Apr. 5, 1951, ibid.; Marshall to A. C. Croft, Nov. 14, 1947, ibid. On Robinson's career, see Segal, *Blacks in the Law*, pp. 187–88.
11. Marshall to White, Nov. 14, 1945, NAACP Papers, Series II-B, Franklin Williams file. Carter was born in Caryville, Florida, received his initial law degree from Howard in 1940, and then moved to New York, where he received an advanced degree in law from Columbia University. Motley was born in New Haven, Connecticut, and received her legal education at Columbia University. She joined the NAACP staff immediately upon her graduation from Columbia in 1946. Dudley was born in South Boston, Virginia, was an undergraduate in North Carolina, and later moved to New York, where he received his law degree in 1941 from St. John's University. Konvitz, a white lawyer and political scientist, was older than the black lawyers. Williams received his law degree from Fordham University Law School in 1945. Each of these staff members was to have a distinguished career: Carter was general counsel for the NAACP and is now a federal district judge in New York, as is Motley. Dudley, after serving as ambassador to Liberia, was borough president of Manhattan, and is now a state judge in New York. Konvitz taught for many years at the Cornell School for Industrial and Labor Relations and the Cornell Law School. Williams served as assistant to the first director of the Peace Corps and as ambassador to Ghana; he is now president of the Phelps-Stokes Fund.

12. Robert L. Carter, interview with author, Feb. 25, 1980; Carter to Marshall, Apr. 28, 1948, NAACP Papers, Series II-B, Schools—Texas file.

13. Monahan and Monahan, "Some Characteristics of American Negro Leaders"; June Shagaloff to Marshall and Carter, Dec. 18, 1951, LDF Papers; Wendell Godwin to Darla Buchanan, March 13, 1953, ibid.; Earl T. Reynolds to Carter, Sept. 25, 1951, ibid.; McKinley Burnett to Carter, Sept. 30, 1951, ibid. See also Suggs, "Black Strategy and Ideology," pp. 187–88; Dudziak, "Limits of Good Faith," pp. 36–38.

14. Hudson, "History of Louisville Municipal College," pp. 27–105 passim.

15. Carter to George Wilson et al., Jan. 8, 1951, LDF Papers; Carter to Burnett, Oct. 1, 1951, ibid.; Notes on lawyers' conference, June 15, 1951, ibid.; Thompson, "Editorial Comment"; Greenberg, "Racial Integration of Teachers." See also Dewing, "Teacher Organizations and Desegregation," pp. 20–27.

16. For a hint of concern for black teachers, see Nabrit, "Resort to the Courts," p. 467 (noting "a considerable difference of opinion" about the merits of the decision to attack segregation directly).

17. Marshall to White, Oct. 24, 1945, NAACP Papers, Series II-B, Marshall file; Marshall to office, May 8, 1946, ibid., Schools—Atlanta Conference file; Digest of proceedings, ibid.; Marshall to Murphy, Dec. 20, 1946, ibid., Carl Murphy file. We should not make too much of Marshall's reference to the "present" Supreme Court. When the direct attack decision was made the Court's composition had changed slightly, with two more conservative justices (Minton and Clark) replacing two liberal ones (Murphy and Rutledge). If Marshall was concerned about the Court in 1946, he should have been more concerned in 1950. There is no evidence that he was, although, as argued below, he read the 1950 university decisions to support the decision to pursue a direct attack on segregation.

18. Marshall to Wilkins, Oct. 28, 1947, NAACP Papers, Series II-B, Marshall file.

19. Statement of Board of Directors, June 7, 1948, NAACP Papers, Series II-B, Marshall file; Resolution, 1948, ibid., Box II-A-40; Resume of N.A.A.C.P. Legal Conference, June 21, 1948, ibid., Box II-A-39; Report to 40th Annual Conference . . . of Conference of N.A.A.C.P. Lawyers held in New York City, June 23–25, 1949, ibid., Box II-A-42.

20. Franklin Williams to Marshall, Sept. 9, 1948, LDF Files; Perry to Benedict Wolf, Sept. 10, 1948, ibid.

21. Dudley to Kelly Alexander, Aug. 4, 1948, NAACP Papers, Series II-B, Schools—North Carolina file.

22. See Kellogg, "Civil Rights Consciousness"; President's Committee on Civil Rights, *To Secure These Rights*, pp. 166, 146–48; Kluger, *Simple Justice*, p. 253.

23. Clark and Perlman, *Prejudice and Property*, pp. 11–38 (reprinting the brief).

24. For introductions to Legal Realism, see Rumble, *American Legal Realism;* Purcell, *Crisis of Democratic Theory,* pp. 74–94; Schlegel, "American Legal Realism."

25. Hastie memorandum, Aug. 1, 1936, Hastie Papers, Box 79, file 7.

26. See Wollenberg, *All Deliberate Speed,* pp. 108–35; Hastie to Marshall, Oct. 25, 1946, NAACP Papers, Series II-B, Mendez file.

27. Roscoe Dunjee to Marshall, Jan. 15, 1946, NAACP Papers, Series II-B, Universities—Oklahoma file; Marshall to William R. Ming, Dec. 15, 1946, ibid.; Cross, *Blacks in White Colleges,* pp. 30–49 passim; *Oklahoma Daily,* Jan. 15, 1946. Cross was the president of the University of Oklahoma during this period. Throughout most of the litigation, Sipuel, though married, used her own name. This was sufficiently unusual in the 1940s to elicit comment, in the form of an approving letter, Jane Grant to Walter White, Jan. 18, 1948, NAACP Papers, Series II-B, Universities—Oklahoma file. The Supreme Court's final decision in her case, *Fisher* v. *Hurst,* 333 U.S. 147 (1948), uses her married name (Fisher). But she used her name only to make her application to the university conform with her undergraduate transcript (Cross, p. 37). See also Hubbell, "The Desegregation of the University of Oklahoma."

For Dunjee's background, see Hadley, "Roscoe Dunjee." In 1947, after arguing in an editorial for greater expenditures on Langston University, Oklahoma's state school for blacks, Dunjee wrote, "The *Black Dispatch* [his newspaper] is through with separate schools. We believe that separation is discrimination per se, but we are taking this occasion to point up our notion how the separate school proponents should arrive at something bordering on decency, if the state is going to continue maintenance of its shady separate school system" (Hadley, pp. 79–80).

28. White, *A Man Called White,* p. 145; *New York Herald-Tribune,* Nov. 12, 1947.

29. "Supreme Court Orders Oklahoma to Admit a Negro to Law School," *New York Times,* Jan. 13, 1948; *Sipuel* v. *Oklahoma State Regents,* 332 U.S. 631 (1948). The procedural history is taken from the record.

30. "Supreme Court Orders Oklahoma to Admit a Negro to Law School," *New York Times,* Jan. 13, 1948; *Oklahoma City Times,* Jan. 13, 1948; *Tulsa Tribune,* Jan. 13, 1948; Cross, *Blacks in White Colleges,* pp. 52–54; *Newsweek,* Feb. 2, 1948, p. 70; *Fisher* v. *Hurst,* 333 U.S. 147 (1948). See Stern and Gressman, *Supreme Court Practice,* pp. 630–32.

31. *Fisher* v. *Hurst,* 333 U.S. 147 (1948); Cross, *Blacks in White Colleges,* pp. 80–84, 113–14, 134. See Hutchinson, "Unanimity and Desegregation," pp. 7–9. After briefly practicing law, Sipuel became the director of public relations at the college from which she had been graduated, by then called Langston University. Later she returned to graduate school, received a degree in history, and taught at Langston.

32. "Equal Rights in Education," *New York Times,* Jan. 15, 1948; Cross, *Blacks in White Colleges,* p. 119; Weaver and Page, "The Black Press and the Drive for Integrated Schools," pp. 21–24.
33. "Note," *Boston University Law Review* 28 (Apr. 1948): 240–42; "Case Note," *Southern California Law Review* 21 (July 1948): 397–98; "Recent Decision," *Notre Dame Lawyer* 23 (Mar. 1948): 390–92; "Note," *New York University Law Quarterly Review* 23 (Apr. 1948): 298–303.
34. "Case Comment," *Washington and Lee Law Review* 5 (1948): 105–13; "Note," *Louisiana Law Review* 8 (Mar. 1948): 588–94; Harris, "The Fourteenth Amendment." Neutral summaries of the cases were "Case Comment," *University of Florida Law Review* 1 (Summer 1948): 296–98; "Note," *National Bar Journal* 6 (June 1948) : 159–60.
35. Cross, *Blacks in White Colleges,* pp. 65–66, 75–76, 89–115 passim; Hubbell, "The Desegregation of the University of Oklahoma," pp. 375–76, 379–81 (detailing difficulties of physical arrangements).
36. Marshall to A. Maceo Smith, Jan. 1, 1946, NAACP Papers, Series II-B, Universities—Texas file; Kenneth Lamkin to Marshall, July 13, 1945, ibid.; Smith to Marshall, Jan. 28, 1946, ibid.; Marshall to W. J. Durham, Jan. 30, 1946, ibid.; "Foe of Bias Awaits High Court Ruling," *New York Times,* Apr. 7, 1950.
37. The procedural history is drawn from the record in *Sweatt* v. *Painter,* 339 U.S. 629 (1950). See also Entin, *"Sweatt v. Painter,"* pp. 31–39.
38. Painter to Sweatt, Mar. 16, 1946, NAACP Papers, Series II-B, Universities—Texas file; Durham to Marshall, Nov. 30, 1946, ibid.; E. J. Mathews to Sweatt, Mar. 3, 1947, ibid. While the NAACP's appeal to the United States Supreme Court was pending, the black law school was moved back to Houston, where its facilities and program satisfied the preliminary accreditation standards of the American Association of Law Schools. The school was not accredited because of the pending litigation. See "Test Case," *Time,* Mar. 24, 1947, p. 52; "25 Years To Go," *Time,* Sept. 22, 1947, p. 60.
39. J. H. Morton to Marshall, Sept. 26, 1947, NAACP Papers, Series II-B, Universities—Texas file.
40. Marshall to Hastie, Apr. 3, 1947, NAACP Papers, Series II-B, Universities—Texas file.
41. Hastie to Marshall, Apr. 9, 1947, NAACP Papers, Series II-B, Universities—Texas file.
42. Marshall to Griswold, June 7, 1948, NAACP Papers, Series II-B, Universities—Oklahoma file; Griswold to Marshall, June 11, 1948, ibid.
43. Kluger, *Simple Justice,* p. 262; "Arkansas Offers Course for Negro," *New York Times,* Jan. 31, 1948; Leflar, *One Life in the Law,* pp. 82–85; "Segregation under Fire," *Charlotte News,* Apr. 11, 1950; Arthur Krock, "The Segregation Issue as Stated by Texas," *New York Times,* Apr. 18, 1950.
44. 339 U.S. 816 (1950). Although the NAACP's proposal to the Garland Fund

had included Jim Crow transportation among its targets, the limited staff and its concentration on education cases prevented any sustained attention by the national staff to discrimination in transportation. After Milton Konvitz was hired in 1943, he began to study the issue, and developed plans to challenge segregated transportation as a violation of the Interstate Commerce Act and as an unconstitutional burden imposed by state laws on interstate commerce. In Virginia, Oliver W. Hill, Martin A. Martin, and Spottswood Robinson, all closely affiliated with the NAACP, filed several suits, one of which was decided in their favor on commerce clause grounds in *Morgan v. Virginia*, 328 U.S. 373 (1946). However, the cases brought by the national staff before the Interstate Commerce Commission were unsuccessful. A planned appeal of one of these was abandoned in favor of participation as an amicus curiae in the independently brought *Henderson* case. (*Henderson* was financed by the black Alpha Phi Alpha fraternity.) For details on the transportation cases and the NAACP's activities in them, see Barnes, *Journey from Jim Crow*, pp. 41–48, 63–71.

45. "Bar Segregation, High Court Told," *New York Times*, Apr. 4, 1950.
46. Benjamin Fine, "Education in Review," *New York Times*, Apr. 9, 1950.
47. Hutchinson, "Unanimity and Segregation," pp. 19–24.
48. 339 U.S. 629, 634–35 (1950).
49. 339 U.S. 637, 641–42 (1950).
50. Hutchinson, "Unanimity and Segregation," p. 22.
51. " 'Separate but Equal,' " *New York Times*, June 6, 1950; Arthur Krock, "A Historic Day in the Supreme Court," *New York Times*, June 6, 1950; "A Milestone," *Commonweal*, June 16, 1950; "Jim Crow in Handcuffs," *New Republic*, June 19, 1950; Wilfred Parsons, "Washington Front," *America*, June 17, 1950; Editorial, *America*, June 17, 1950.
52. *Birmingham News*, June 9, 1950; "High Court Ruling Weighed in South," *New York Times*, June 11, 1950; Benjamin Fine, "Education in Review," *New York Times*, June 11, 1950.
53. "Recent Decision," *Georgetown Law Journal* 39 (Nov. 1950): 145–48; "Recent Decision," *Notre Dame Lawyer* 26 (Fall 1950) : 134–37; "Recent Case," *Wyoming Law Journal* 5 (Summer 1951): 211–14; "Note," *Boston University Law Review* 30 (Nov. 1950): 565–69; "Decision," *Brooklyn Law Review* 17 (Dec. 1950): 134–37; "Case Noted," *Miami Law Quarterly* 5 (Dec. 1950): 150–53; "Case Comment," *Washington and Lee Law Review* 8 (1951): 54–60; "Case Note," *Alabama Law Review* 3 (Fall 1950): 181–85; "Recent Decision," *Virginia Law Review* 36 (Oct. 1950): 797–800. Other comments are "Case Note," *Mercer Law Review* 2 (Fall 1950): 272–73 ("unlikely" to apply to elementary and secondary schools); Note, *University of Pittsburgh Law Review* 12 (Winter 1951): 261–69 (neutral summary); "Note," *Georgia Bar Journal* 13 (Aug. 1950): 88–89 (neutral summary).

54. Schwartz, "The Negro and the Law," p. 461; Ransmeier, "The Fourteenth Amendment," pp. 238–39.
55. Weaver and Page, "The Black Press and the Drive for Integrated Schools," pp. 27–28.
56. Marshall to Charles Bunn, June 12, 1950, NAACP Papers, Series II-B, Universities—Oklahoma file.
57. NAACP Annual Reports for 1930–49; Dalfiume, "The 'Forgotten Years' of the Negro Revolution"; Hoffman, "The Genesis of the Modern Movement for Equal Rights."
58. In 1953 Marshall wrote a memorandum stressing the close cooperation between the "Inc Fund" and NAACP branches. See *NAACP v. NAACP Legal Defense and Educational Fund,* Civ. No. 82-1424 (D.D.C.), plaintiff's memorandum in support of its motion for summary judgment, Nov. 24, 1982, p. 12.
59. Although most of the relevant papers are inaccessible at this time, I have found nothing to suggest that the lawyers were concerned that fears of interracial romance would impede desegregation of southern colleges. Kluger, *Simple Justice,* p. 266, quotes Marshall as saying that the NAACP "deliberately picked Professor McLaurin because he was sixty-eight years old and we didn't think he was going to marry or intermarry . . ." This appears to be incorrect—see text accompanying note 35 supra, and sources there cited—and suggests caution in imputing similar motives to the later decision. See also Ware, *William Hastie,* p. 46 (attributing similar concerns to later comments by Marshall).
60. "Association Hails Setbacks to Bias," *New York Times,* June 28, 1950; Marshall to Lem Graves, July 5, 1950, NAACP Papers, Series II-B, Universities—Texas and Oklahoma—Congratulatory Messages files; Resolution, July 1950, Board of Directors, NAACP Papers, Box II-A-132.
61. Kluger, *Simple Justice,* pp. 290–94.

Chapter 8

1. For a discussion of the elimination of the segregation of Mexican-Americans in Texas elementary schools, see San Miguel, "The Struggle against Separate and Unequal Schools." San Miguel describes the efforts of the League of United Latin American Citizens (LULAC), first through a lawsuit that failed, then through lobbying, to desegregate the Texas schools. After the California decision discussed in the preceding chapter, the Texas attorney general issued an opinion that segregation of Mexican-Americans was unconstitutional. LULAC secured an injunction against segregation in one district, but found it difficult to enforce the decree; the decision by the state superintendent of education to withhold accreditation from the district because it failed to comply

with the decree was reversed by the state board of education. San Miguel's discussion suggests that desegregation of Mexican-Americans was less contentious than that of blacks because schools could continue to separate children on the basis of language.

2. Kluger, *Simple Justice*, pp. 13–22.
3. Kluger, *Simple Justice*, pp. 388–95; Esther Brown to Franklin Williams, Sept. 29, 1948, NAACP Papers, Schools—Wichita, Kan., file; Z. Wetmore to NAACP, June 28, 1947, ibid.; Wetmore to Marshall, Sept. 7, 1948, ibid.; Minutes of Kansas State Conference of Branches, Sept. 3, 1948, ibid.; Williams to Marshall, Oct. 6, 1948, ibid.; Brown to Williams, Nov. 28, 1948, ibid.; Wetmore to Williams, Dec. 24, 1948, ibid.; *Wichita Star*, Nov. 5, 1948 (letter from Carrie L. Burney); Williams to Charles Bettis, Jan. 7, 1949, NAACP Papers, Schools—Wichita, Kan., file; Walter White to Bettis, May 2, 1949, ibid. The South Park case is reported as *Webb* v. *School District No. 90*, 206 P. 2d 1066, 167 Kan. 395 (1949).
4. The following paragraphs summarize Kluger, *Simple Justice*, pp. 433–35 (Delaware), 460–71 (Virginia).
5. See McNeil, "Community Initiative." Apparently relying on interviews with Nabrit, Kluger, *Simple Justice*, pp. 518–23, overestimates the degree to which Nabrit and Marshall disagreed on tactical issues.
6. The experience up to 1950 shows that the intra- and interorganizational problems that are the focus of this book tended to arise before litigation began or after a decree of some sort had been entered. The problems that arose after *Brown* were on such a different scale, especially in terms of their visibility to a national public, as to make their exclusion from this book almost a necessity. Two overviews of the period since *Brown*, from different ideological perspectives, are Wilkinson, *From Brown to Bakke*, and Metcalf, *From Little Rock to Boston*.
7. I have ended my discussion of the NAACP's campaign without considering the implementation of *Sweatt* v. *Painter*. Implementation occurred while the challenge to segregation in elementary and secondary education had fundamentally transformed the social setting. I believe that this transformation places the story of university desegregation with the social process of the *Brown* litigation.
8. Early expressions of this view, by participants in the litigation, are Hastie, "Charles Hamilton Houston," and Marshall, "The Supreme Court as Protector of Civil Rights." This view of the campaign is supported by the classical theory of organizational behavior, which treats organizations as rational decision makers, evaluating benefits and costs, estimating uncertainty in the environment, and choosing the course that would most probably lead to the preferred result. The theory recognizes that plans could misfire, through miscalculation or environmental limitations on what could reasonably be ex-

pected to occur, but it treats planning as a rational process. A useful summary of organization theory is Perrow, *Complex Organizations*. For a presentation and critique of the rational-decision-maker approach, see Allison, *Essence of Decision*.

9. Kluger, *Simple Justice*.
10. Rabin, "Lawyers for Social Change," p. 207.
11. Rabin, "Lawyers for Social Change," p. 216. See also Dreyfuss and Lawrence, *The Bakke Case*, p. 185.
12. Council for Public Interest Law, "Balancing the Scales of Justice," pp. 48–49.
13. Recent papers by Stephen Wasby present a more complex view of the realities of litigation, though I believe that he stresses too much the novelty of the problems he has found in his interviews with contemporary public interest lawyers. See Wasby, "Interest Groups in Court"; Wasby, "The Multi-Faceted Elephant"; Wasby, "Some Horizontal and Vertical Dynamics of Civil Rights Litigation"; Wasby, "The NAACP and the NAACP Legal Defense Fund"; Wasby, "How Planned Is 'Planned Litigation'?" See especially the last cited paper, p. 92, dealing specifically with the pre-*Brown* litigation and quoting one attorney as saying that there was a "lot of improvization, a lot of impromptu." Compare Olson, *Clients and Lawyers*, contrasting the asserted simplicity of the NAACP's litigation with the complexity of recent public interest litigation.
14. See Zangrando, *The NAACP Crusade against Lynching*.
15. Vose, *Caucasians Only*; Barnes, *Journey from Jim Crow*.
16. Hine, *Black Victory*.
17. Irons, *New Deal Lawyers*, p. 39, notes that the same difficulties prevented from becoming a reality the desire of the head of the National Recovery Administration's litigation section for a "Machiavellian" strategy. Such a strategy, writes Irons, "demanded, to be successful, a coherent and well-plotted battle plan. [The lawyers] moved, instead, from one skirmish to another, hampered by internal conflict with the Justice Department and by determined resistance from a largely hostile federal judiciary."
18. A recent presentation of this point is Zald and McCarthy, "Social Movement Industries." For a discussion of its relevance to the civil rights movement, see Morris, *Origins of the Civil Rights Movement*, pp. 120–28.
19. See Kirby, *Black Americans in the Roosevelt Era*, pp. 155–70 (on National Negro Congress), 181; Moore, *Search for Equality*, pp. 88, 95–101, 142–45 (on conflicts with the NAACP), 205–06; Wilkins and Mathews, *Standing Fast*, pp. 185, 189–90.
20. See Ladd, *Negro Political Leadership*, for a survey of relevant typologies.
21. For additional discussion, see text below accompanying notes 27–34. On some interpretations of the "rule of law," there is some tension between concern for the views of accommodationists and the idea of the rule of law. If, as the Supreme Court eventually held, the legal system could not prop up the

southern system of race relations, the accommodationist position deserved no recognition as a matter of law. To the extent that this point differs from the concern that interests be presented even if they ought not ultimately prevail, it rests on a theory of law that must treat "the law of race relations" as something that somehow was well defined even before the Supreme Court decided what the law of race relations was.

22. A good short introduction to the ethical issues raised by public interest law is Hegland, "Beyond Enthusiasm and Commitment."

23. The classic sources on incentive structures are Clark and Wilson, "Incentive Systems," and Olson, *Logic of Collective Action.*

24. A recent discussion of litigation as a process of political education is O'Neill, *"Bakke" and the Politics of Inequality.*

25. For a useful though abstract catalogue, see French and Raven, "The Bases of Social Power."

26. Marshall was a handsome man with a commanding presence. In a sexist society these are attributes that confer some degree of power. Though evidence on the point may be impossible to come by, it may not be irrelevant that an important component in establishing his credentials as one whose judgment should be respected was his work in salary equalization cases where the class of black teachers and its leadership were predominantly female. Though the question is complex, the earlier discussion of plaintiffs' ideological commitments suggests, however, that these matters were not an important source of Marshall's power. For a recent discussion of the issue of male sexual power and female political subordination of the sort here suggested, see Bartky, "Feminine Masochism and the Politics of Personal Transformation."

27. See Eisenberg, "James Weldon Johnson," pp. 40–42; Autrey, "The NAACP in Alabama," pp. 32–35. This is not to say that the NAACP as an organization ignored the interests of the much larger working-class black community. See chapter 1 above; Eisenberg, "Only for the Bourgeois?"

28. The cases are: *Freeman* v. *County School Board of Chesterfield County,* 82 F. Supp. 167 (E.D. Va. 1948) (Hill and Robinson for plaintiffs; successful); *Pitts* v. *Board of Trustees,* 84 F. Supp. 975 (E.D. Ark. 1949) (W. Harold Flowers for plaintiffs; successful); *Butler* v. *Wilemon,* 86 F. Supp. 397 (N.D. Tex. 1949) (U. Simpson Tate for plaintiffs; successful); *Corbin* v. *County School Board,* 177 F. 2d 924 (4th Cir. 1949) (Hill and Robinson for plaintiffs; partially successful); *Carr* v. *Corning,* 182 F. 2d 14 (D.C. Cir. 1950) (Leon A. Ransom and Tate for plaintiffs; unsuccessful); *Carter* v. *School Board of Arlington County,* 182 F. 2d 531 (4th Cir. 1950) (Robinson for plaintiffs; successful); *Brown* v. *Ramsey,* 185 F. 2d 225 (8th Cir. 1950) (J. Robert Booker and Tate for plaintiffs; unsuccessful as to high school); *Blue* v. *Durham Public School District,* 95 F. Supp. 441 (M.D.N.C. 1951) (Hill and Robinson for plaintiffs; successful); *Moses* v. *Corning,* 104 F. Supp. 651 (D.D.C. 1952)

(unsuccessful); *Winborne* v. *Taylor,* 195 F. 2d 649 (4th Cir. 1952) (unsuccessful); *State ex. rel. Hobby* v. *Disman,* 250 S.W. 2d 137 (Mo. 1952) (unsuccessful).

29. In addition to the cases in Lumberton, Hearne, and South Park discussed earlier in this chapter, see also *McSwain* v. *County Board of Education,* 104 F. Supp. 861 (E.D. Tenn. 1952).

30. See generally Burns, "North Carolina and the Negro Dilemma."

31. The relationship of Ransom and Robinson to the legal staff has been discussed above. Tate was Southwest Regional Counsel for the NAACP in 1948–49. See, e.g., Tate to Marshall, Apr. 28, 1949, NAACP Papers, Series II-B, Schools—Texas file. Flowers was a member of the National Legal Committee.

32. For another example of group activity within a community (a state prison, where one might not have expected to find such activity), see Tyranauer and Stasny, *Who Rules the Joint?,* pp. 151–88.

33. Houston spent some time tracking down rumors that Gaines had been killed or paid off to go to Mexico. See White to Sidney Redmond, Jan. 23, 1940, NAACP Papers, Box I-D-95; Redmond to Wilkins, Jan. 15, 1940, ibid. Had Gaines been closely linked to community groups it is unlikely that the NAACP would have been unable to find out what had happened to him.

34. Marshall to Grace Hamilton, Dec. 19, 1944, NAACP Papers, Series II-B, Schools—Atlanta file; Marshall to Joshua Maxwell, Oct. 10, 1945, ibid., Schools—Baltimore file. For additional support for the hypothesis that community backing was essential, see Cohen, "The Urban League and School Integration." Cohen (pp. 3–5) describes efforts to integrate that were aborted when the NAACP branch in Gary failed to support integration with sufficient force.

35. Recent discussions of public interest law have tended to be highly ideological. Statements about the ethics of public interest lawyers and the adequacy of procedures in their cases often rest in the end on views of the substantive merits of the goals the lawyers sought to advance. See Eisenberg and Yeazell, "The Ordinary and the Extraordinary." For an exchange on a procedural issue that reveals the point, see Brilmayer, "The Jurisprudence of Article III"; Tushnet, "The Sociology of Article III"; Brilmayer, "A Reply." For example, Bell's widely cited article, "Serving Two Masters," raises questions about the extent to which NAACP lawyers have represented the interests of the black community in recent years. Bell criticizes the lawyers for seeking to distribute white and black children more equally in schools in such heavily black cities as Detroit and Atlanta, instead of attempting to secure remedies that would directly improve the educational opportunities for black children. As a matter of political judgment, this may be entirely correct. But it is hard to see any true ethical problems in these instances. The NAACP lawyers had real clients and the views of those who sought different forms of relief were presented to, and

in Atlanta adopted by, the courts. It is misleading to mask an essentially political disagreement with supposed ethical concerns.

With a few exceptions, such as O'Connor, *Women's Organizations' Use of the Courts,* and Cook, *Nuclear Power and Legal Advocacy,* most recent discussions of the ethics and politics of public interest law have relied on anecdotes. See, e.g., Brill, "The Uses and Abuses of Legal Assistance." The reason is clear. Concern about the confidentiality of communications between lawyers and clients has made it difficult to obtain information about their relations. Public records such as the transcripts of trials and hearings rarely disclose enough about the relevant issues. Contemporaneous statements to the public are bound to be self-serving, couched so as to influence ongoing efforts in and out of court. Retrospective interviews may be inadequate not only because confidentiality must still be preserved, but also because the participants are likely to impose coherence on episodes, now closed, that were either a jumble of events when they occurred or seemed ordered then by some principle other than the one offered now. The NAACP's papers provide detailed information about how a certain group of lawyers behaved. (For a brief discussion of some limits on the utility of those papers, see the Note on Manuscript Sources in the Bibliography.) But, as discussed in the text, in the absence of similarly detailed information about how other lawyers behave, there is as yet no reason to reject the "null hypothesis" described there.

36. An overview appears in Kritzer, "The Dimensions of Lawyer-Client Relations." For discussions of particular forms of lawyer-client relations, see Evans, "The Model Rules"; Bartlett, *The Law Business,* pp. 61–65; Brooks, *Games Players,* pp. 274–76; Taylor, "Ethics and the Law," pp. 31–33, 46–52; Note, "Government Litigation in the Supreme Court"; Belli, *My Life on Trial,* pp. 209–23.

37. For a comprehensive discussion of the political and formal solutions to the ethical problems discussed here, see Rhode, "Class Conflicts in Class Actions."

38. Closer analysis would show, I believe, that the formal and procedural solutions are also political, in the sense that they transfer the issue from the affected community to a broader one, in which those who perceive problems with what has emerged from the affected community have more power to impose their own views.

39. Lindblom, *Politics and Markets.*

40. But see Weisbrod, Handler, and Komesar, *Public Interest Law.*

41. See Garfinkel, *When Negroes March.*

42. See Bell, "*Brown v. Board of Education* and the Interest-Convergence Dilemma."

43. This is the argument of Weiss, *Farewell to the Party of Lincoln.*

44. The "cost of living" defense to salary disparities is a cousin to this argument. The NAACP's lawyers were concerned that courts would accept that defense, but no court appears to have taken it seriously.

45. Perrow, *Complex Organizations,* pp. 200–247, provides a useful overview of the process of interaction between an organization and its environment. I find it striking that he concludes by discussing the "new direction" that he calls "historical analysis" (p. 244). A historical analysis of the interaction between internal and external elements is plainly valuable, if not terribly illuminating, if it is meant to suggest that everything is loosely connected to everything else. But it is likely to be misleading if it suggests connections stronger than those that create a general atmosphere of thought and sentiment. (This seems to be the conclusion of the literature that Perrow discusses.) The general atmosphere sets rather broad bounds on what happens; within those bounds people choose in light of what they believe to be their options. My emphasis on internal elements attempts to highlight what the NAACP's lawyers and clients saw as the courses open to them.

I believe that, for all its manifest virtues, Kluger, *Simple Justice,* is flawed by the dramatic unity that its style gives to the story. The novelist's talents suggest that each small item in the story contributed in an important way to the larger outcome, and the journalist's talents simplify a complex reality to make it easier to understand. I have tried to suggest in contrast that the parts of the story were related to each other in a less systematic way. On one level, Marshall and his colleagues were a group of lawyers doing the jobs they had chosen, and on a day-to-day basis the job-related dimensions of their work probably dwarfed their sense that they were also making history.

46. See Tushnet, "A Public Interest Lawyer," a review of McNeil, *Groundwork.*
47. For a general discussion of strategy formation in organizations like the NAACP, see Mintzberg and McHugh, "Strategy Formation."
48. It may be significant in this connection to note that the NAACP national staff instituted only one lawsuit during this period against a segregated undergraduate institution, and did so only after the state college for blacks lost its accreditation. *Parker* v. *University of Delaware,* 75 A. 2d 225 (Del. Ch. 1950). Black colleges were of course central institutions in the cultural life of the black community. For an overview of the contemporary situation, see Yearwood, *Black Organizations.*
49. Quoted in Kluger, *Simple Justice,* p. 730.
50. See generally Kennedy, "Form and Substance." See also Judkins, "The Black Lung Movement."
51. *Brown* v. *Board of Education,* 347 U.S. 483, 495 and 495–96 n. 13 (1954).
52. Undated notes, NAACP Papers, Series III, Box C-10 (preparation of reargument on remedy). Marshall probably had in mind *McCready* v. *Byrd,* 195 Md. 131, 73 A. 2d 8 (Md. 1950), in which Maryland was forced to abandon its out-of-state scholarship program for nursing education and to desegregate its own. Marshall's co-counsel in this case was Donald Murray.

Bibliography

A Note on Manuscript Sources

As indicated in chapter 8, this study was written from the perspective of the national office of the NAACP. Ninety percent or more of the material used was available in the NAACP Papers at the Manuscript Division of the Library of Congress. The NAACP Papers are divided into three groups. Series I, covering the period to 1939, is fully catalogued; documents from this group are cited by box numbers: for example, Box I-D-96. When the present study was conducted, the papers from 1940 on were in the process of being catalogued as Series II. One group of papers deals with general organizational matters (Series II-A). The other, more important group for this study involves the legal work of the NAACP from 1940 to 1955 (Series II-B). At the time the manuscript was prepared for publication, the legal papers were in the process of being rearranged. Thus, box numbers for these papers were not available. When they are finally catalogued, the papers will be organized under such headings as "University Cases" or "Teachers' Salary Cases," followed by a state and, sometimes, a city name. I have cited these papers as NAACP Papers, Series II-B, followed by the file name in which the cited document can be found. (Only if the document is located in some file other than the "Correspondence" or "General" file for the state or city have I given any further indication of a file name.) However, the rearrangement of the legal papers may lead to some shifting of documents from one file to a different one; the citations may therefore be insufficient for the location of some documents when the cataloguing is completed.

The 1955 termination date for the legal papers in Series II-B is somewhat misleading. The NAACP Legal Defense and Educational Fund was incorporated in 1939 and shared office space with the NAACP until 1952. In that year separate offices were established, and the NAACP Papers contain very little post-1950 legal material. That material is currently largely uncatalogued in the Library of Congress. When the post-1950 legal materials were housed in the offices of the Legal Defense Fund, I rummaged through them for relevant material. References are to the Legal Defense Fund (LDF) Papers, to be catalogued as NAACP Papers, Series III(C). I am sure that some documents dealing with the direct attack decision remain to be discovered in the Legal Defense Fund Papers.

The NAACP staff was small enough such that many decisions could be made in face-to-face discussions. The organization's papers include enough information, contained, for example, in letters to friends and colleagues throughout the country, to allow one to identify with some specificity the substance of the discussions. They even give some insight into the personal relations among the staff, although of course not every aspect of such personal matters is reflected in the papers. (I should note here some problems that arise from Kluger's reliance on interviews with Thurgood Marshall. Marshall is a great raconteur, and his reconstructions of what happened thirty or forty years before must be accepted with a skepticism born of the knowledge that he is at least as much concerned with telling a good story as with telling the true one. Sometimes, of course, the true story is a good story, too.)

The James Weldon Johnson Papers at the Beinecke Rare Books Library of Yale University and the American Fund for Public Service Papers in the Manuscript Section of the New York Public Library provided additional information on the Garland Fund. I consulted the papers deposited by Richard Kluger in the *Brown v. Board of Education* Collection at the Sterling Memorial Library of Yale University. These papers consist of notes made of interviews and of documents collected during Kluger's research for *Simple Justice*. They were useful primarily as a check on my research in the manuscript collections. I have learned to appreciate the reasons for notes like the following one: The Karl Llewellyn Papers at the Law Library of the University of Chicago throw no light on Llewellyn's decision not to accept the position as NAACP Special Counsel.

Manuscript Collections

Cambridge, Mass.
  Harvard Law School Library
    William Henry Hastie Papers
New Haven, Conn.
  Yale University
    James Weldon Johnson Papers
New York, N.Y.
  New York Public Library
    American Fund for Public Service Papers
Washington, D.C.
  Library of Congress
    NAACP Papers
    Arthur B. Spingarn Papers

Books and Articles

Allison, Graham. *Essence of Decision.* Boston: Little, Brown & Co., 1971.

Autrey, Dorothy A. "The National Association for the Advancement of Colored People in Alabama, 1913–1952." Ph.D. dissertation, University of Notre Dame, 1985.

Baker, Oscar. "Trend of United States Supreme Court Decisions as Affecting Negroes' Rights." *National Bar Journal* 1 (July 1941): 30–37.

Baldwin, Roger N. "The Challenge to Social Work of the Changing Control in Industry." In *Proceedings of the National Conference of Social Work*, pp. 373–79. Chicago: University of Chicago Press, 1924.

Barnes, Catherine A. *Journey from Jim Crow: The Desegregation of Southern Transit.* New York: Columbia University Press, 1983.

Bartky, Sandra Lee. "Feminine Masochism and the Politics of Personal Transformation." *Women's Studies International Forum* 7 (1984): 323–34.

Bartlett, Joseph W. *The Law Business: A Tired Monopoly.* Littleton, Colo.: Fred. B. Rothman & Co., 1982.

Bell, Derrick. "*Brown v. Board of Education* and the Interest-Convergence Dilemma." *Harvard Law Review* 93 (Jan. 1980): 518–33.

———. "Serving Two Masters: Integration Ideals and Client Interests in School Desegregation Litigation." *Yale Law Journal* 85 (Mar. 1976): 470–516.

Belli, Melvin. *My Life on Trial.* New York: William Morrow, 1976.

Bluford, Lucile. "The Lloyd Gaines Story." *Journal of Educational Sociology* 32 (Feb. 1959): 242–46.

———. "Missouri 'Shows' the Supreme Court." *The Crisis* 46 (Aug. 1939): 231.

Boardman, Helen, and Gruening, Martha. *The Crawford Case: A Reply to the "N.A.A.C.P."* New York: Academy Press, 1935.

———. "Is the NAACP Retreating?" *The Nation* 138 (June 27, 1934): 730–32.

Bond, Horace Mann. "The Negro Common School in Oklahoma." *The Crisis* 35 (Apr. 1928): 113, and (July 1928): 228.

Boykin, Leander. "The Status and Trends of Differentials between White and Negro Teachers' Salaries in the Southern States, 1900–1946." *Journal of Negro Education* 18 (Winter 1949): 40–47.

Brill, Harry. "The Uses and Abuses of Legal Assistance." *The Public Interest* 31 (Spring 1973): 38–55.

Brilmayer, Lea. "The Jurisprudence of Article III." *Harvard Law Review* 93 (Dec. 1979): 297–321.

———. "A Reply." *Harvard Law Review* 93 (June 1980): 1727–33.

Brooks, John. *The Games Players: Tales of Men and Money.* New York: Times Books, 1980.

Bunche, Ralph J. "A Critical Analysis of the Tactics and Programs of Minority Groups." *Journal of Negro Education* 4 (July 1935): 308–20.

Buni, Andrew. *The Negro in Virginia Politics, 1902 –1965.* Charlottesville: University Press of Virginia, 1967.

Burns, Augustus S. "North Carolina and the Negro Dilemma, 1930–1950." Ph.D. dissertation, University of North Carolina, 1968.

Carter, Dan T. *Scottsboro.* Baton Rouge: Louisiana State University Press, 1969.

Chayes, Abram. "The Role of the Judge in Public Law Litigation." *Harvard Law Review* 89 (May 1976): 1281–1316.

Choper, Jesse. "Consequences of Supreme Court Decisions Upholding Individual Constitutional Rights." *Michigan Law Review* 83 (Oct. 1984): 1–212.

Clark, Peter, and Wilson, James. "Incentive Systems: A Theory of Organizations," *Administrative Science Quarterly* 6 (Sept. 1961): 129–66.

Clark, Tom, and Perlman, Phillip. *Prejudice and Property.* Washington, D.C.: Public Affairs Press, 1948.

Cohen, Ronald. "The Urban League and School Integration in Gary, Indiana, 1945–1960." Paper presented at the 1983 Annual Meeting of the Organization of American Historians, Chicago, Illinois.

Cook, Constance Ewing. *Nuclear Power and Legal Advocacy.* Lexington, Mass.: Lexington Books, 1980.

Council for Public Interest Law. "Balancing the Scales of Justice: Financing Public Interest Law in America." Prepublication draft. Washington, D.C., 1976.

Cross, George Lynn. *Blacks in White Colleges.* Norman: University of Oklahoma Press, 1975.

Curti, Merle. "Subsidizing Radicalism: The American Fund for Public Service, 1921–41." *Social Service Review* 33 (Sept. 1959): 274–95.

Dalfiume, Richard. "The 'Forgotten Years' of the Negro Revolution." *Journal of American History* 55 (June 1968): 90–106.

Daniel, Cletus. *The ACLU and the Wagner Act.* Ithaca, N.Y.: New York State School of Industrial and Labor Relations, 1980.

Dewing, Roland L. "Teacher Organizations and Desegregation, 1954–1964." Ph.D. dissertation, Ball State University, 1967.

Dreyfuss, Joel, and Lawrence, Charles, III. *The Bakke Case.* New York: Harcourt Brace Jovanovich, 1979.

Du Bois, W. E. B. "The Board of Directors on Segregation." *The Crisis* 41 (May 1934): 149.

———. "The Crawford Case." *The Crisis* 41 (May 1934): 149.

———. "Does the Negro Need Separate Schools?" *Journal of Negro Education* 4 (July 1935): 328–35.

———. "Dr. Du Bois Resigns: The Full Text of His Letter and the Resolution of the N.A.A.C.P. Board Accepting His Resignation," *The Crisis* 41 (Aug. 1934): 245–46.

———. "A Free Forum." *The Crisis* 41 (Feb. 1934): 52–53.

———. "Nation Wide Defense Fund a Success." *The Crisis* 31 (Feb. 1926): 187.

————. "The Right to Work." *The Crisis* 40 (Apr. 1933): 93–94.

————. "Segregation." *The Crisis* 41 (Jan. 1934): 20.

————. "Segregation in the North." *The Crisis* 41 (Apr. 1934): 115–16.

————. "Separation and Self-Respect." *The Crisis* 41 (Mar. 1934): 85.

Dudziak, Mary. "The Limits of Good Faith: Desegregation in Topeka, Kansas, 1950–1957." Paper presented to Law and Society Association, June 1986, Chicago, Illinois.

Eisenberg, Bernard. "James Weldon Johnson and the National Association for the Advancement of Colored People, 1916–1934." Ph.D. dissertation, Columbia University, 1968.

————. "Only for the Bourgeois?: James Weldon Johnson and the NAACP, 1916–1930." *Phylon* 43 (June 1982): 110–24.

Eisenberg, Theodore, and Yeazell, Stephen. "The Ordinary and the Extraordinary in Institutional Litigation." *Harvard Law Review* 93 (Jan. 1980): 465–517.

Entin, Jonathan L. "*Sweatt v. Painter,* The End of Segregation, and the Transformation of Education Law." *Review of Litigation* 5 (Winter 1986): 3–71.

Evans, Donald. "The Model Rules: The Organization as Client." *American Bar Association Journal* 68 (July 1982): 814–15.

Felstiner, William; Abel, Richard; and Sarat, Austin. "The Emergence and Transformation of Disputes: Naming, Blaming, Claiming . . ." *Law & Society Review* 15 (1980–81): 631–54.

Fenton, John. *Politics in the Border States.* New Orleans: Hauser Press, 1957.

Fiss, Owen. *The Civil Rights Injunction.* Bloomington: Indiana University Press, 1978.

Flynn, James J. *Negroes of Achievement in Modern America.* New York: Dodd, Mead & Co., 1970.

French, John R., and Raven, Bertram. "The Bases of Social Power." In *Studies in Social Power,* edited by Dorwin Cartwright, pp. 150–67. Ann Arbor: Institute for Social Research, 1959.

Garfinkel, Herbert. *When Negroes March.* New York: Atheneum Press, 1969.

"Government Litigation in the Supreme Court: The Roles of the Solicitor General." *Yale Law Journal* 78 (July 1969): 1442–81.

Greenberg, Jack. *Litigation for Social Change: Methods, Limits, and Role in Democracy.* New York: Association of the Bar of the City of New York, 1974.

————. "Racial Integration of Teachers—A Growing Problem." *Journal of Negro Education* 20 (Fall 1951) : 584–87.

Grothaus, Larry. " 'The Inevitable Mr. Gaines': The Long Struggle to Desegregate the University of Missouri, 1936–1950." *Arizona and the West* 26 (Spring 1984): 21–42.

Gruening, Martha. "The Truth about the Crawford Case." *New Masses* 14 (Jan. 8, 1935): 915.

Hadley, Worth T. "Roscoe Dunjee on Education: The Improvement of Black Education in Oklahoma, 1930–1955." Ed.D. dissertation, University of Oklahoma, 1981.

~ Harris, John B. "The Fourteenth Amendment." *Georgia Bar Journal* 10 (Feb. 1948): 346–54.

Hart, Henry, and Wechsler, Herbert. *The Federal Courts and the Federal System.* Mineola, N.Y.: Foundation Press, 1953.

Hastie, William. "Charles Hamilton Houston, 1895–1950." *Journal of Negro History* 35 (Oct. 1950): 355–58.

Hegland, Kenney. "Beyond Enthusiasm and Commitment." *Arizona Law Review* 13 (1971): 805–17.

Hine, Darlene Clark. *Black Victory: The Rise and Fall of the White Primary in Texas.* Millwood, N.Y.: KTO Press, 1979.

Hoffman, Erwin. "The Genesis of the Modern Movement for Equal Rights in South Carolina, 1930–1939." *Journal of Negro History* 44 (Oct. 1959): 346–69.

Houston, Charles. "Cracking Closed University Doors." *The Crisis* 42 (Dec. 1935): 364.

———. "Don't Shout Too Soon." *The Crisis* 43 (Mar. 1936): 79.

———. "Educational Inequalities Must Go!" *The Crisis* 42 (Oct. 1935): 300.

———. "Enrollment in Negro Colleges and Universities." *School and Society* 50 (July 29, 1939): 141.

———. "How to Fight for Better Schools." *The Crisis* 43 (Feb. 1936): 52.

———. "The Negro's Educational Advantages under Scrutiny." *School and Society* 57 (Jan. 16, 1943): 69.

Hubbard, Maceo, and Alexander, Raymond Pace. "Types of Potentially Favorable Court Cases Relative to the Separate School." *Journal of Negro Education* 4 (July 1935): 375–405.

Hubbell, John. "The Desegregation of the University of Oklahoma, 1946–1950." *Journal of Negro History* 57 (Oct. 1972): 370–84.

Hudson, James B., III. "The History of Louisville Municipal College." Ed.D. dissertation, University of Kentucky, 1981.

⟵ Hutchinson, Dennis. "Unanimity and Desegregation: Decision-making in the Supreme Court, 1948–1958." *Georgetown Law Journal* 68 (Oct. 1979): 1–96.

Irons, Peter. *The New Deal Lawyers.* Princeton: Princeton University Press, 1982.

Jenkins, J. Craig. *The Politics of Insurgency: The Farm Worker Movement and the Politics of the 1960s.* New York: Columbia University Press, 1985.

Johnson, Charles. S. *The Negro College Graduate.* Chapel Hill: University of North Carolina Press, 1938.

Judkins, Bennett. "The Black Lung Movement: Social Movements and Social Structure." In *Conflicts and Change,* Research in Social Movements, vol. 2, pp. 105–29. Greenwich, Conn.: JAI Press, 1979.

Kellogg, Charles. *NAACP*. Baltimore: Johns Hopkins University Press, 1967.

Kellogg, Peter. "Civil Rights Consciousness in the 1940s." *The Historian* 42 (Nov. 1979): 18–41.

Kennedy, Duncan. "Form and Substance in Common Law Adjudication." *Harvard Law Review* 89 (June 1976): 1685–1778.

Key, V. O. *Southern Politics in State and Nation*. New York: Alfred A. Knopf, 1949.

Killian, Lewis. "Organization, Rationality and Spontaneity in the Civil Rights Movement." *American Sociological Review* 49 (Dec. 1984): 770–83.

Kirby, John B. *Black Americans in the Roosevelt Era*. Knoxville: University of Tennessee press, 1980.

Kluger, Richard. *Simple Justice*. New York: Alfred A. Knopf, 1975.

Kousser, J. Morgan. "Separate but Not Equal: The Supreme Court's First Decision on Racial Discrimination in Schools." *Journal of Southern History* 46 (Feb. 1980): 17–44.

Kritzer, Herbert. "The Dimensions of Lawyer-Client Relations: Notes toward a Theory and a Field Study." *American Bar Foundation Research Journal* 1984 (Spring): 409–25.

Ladd, Everett C. *Negro Political Leadership in the South*. Ithaca: Cornell University Press, 1966.

Lamson, Peggy. *Roger Baldwin: Founder of the American Civil Liberties Union*. Boston: Houghton Mifflin, 1976.

Leflar, Robert A. *One Life in the Law*. Fayetteville: University of Arkansas Press, 1985.

Levy, Leonard. *The Law of the Commonwealth and Chief Justice Shaw*. Cambridge: Harvard University Press, 1957.

Lewis, David Levering. "Parallels and Divergences: Assimilationist Strategies of Afro-American and Jewish Elites from 1910 to the Early 1930s." *Journal of American History* 71 (Dec. 1984): 543–64.

Lindblom, Charles. *Politics and Markets*. New York: Basic Books, 1977.

Macaulay, Stewart. "Lawyers and Consumer Protection Laws." *Law & Society Reivew* 14 (Fall 1979): 115–71.

McAdam, Doug. *Political Process and the Development of Black Insurgency, 1930–1970*. Chicago: University of Chicago Press, 1982.

McMurry, Linda. *George Washington Carver: Scientist and Symbol*. New York: Oxford University Press, 1981.

McNeil, Genna Rae. "Community Initiative in the Desegregation of District of Columbia Schools, 1947–1954." *Howard Law Journal* 23 (1980): 25–41.

———. *Groundwork: Charles Hamilton Houston and the Struggle for Civil Rights*. Philadelphia: University of Pennsylvania Press, 1983.

———. "To Meet the Group Needs: The Transformation of Howard University School of Law, 1920–35." In *New Perspectives on Black Educational History*, edited by Vincent P. Franklin and James D. Anderson, pp. 149–71. Boston: G. K. Hall & Co., 1978.

Marshall, Thurgood. "The Supreme Court as Protector of Civil Rights: Equal Protection of the Laws." *Annals of the American Academy* 275 (May 1951): 101–10.

Martin, Charles H. "The International Labor Defense and Black America." *Labor History* 26 (Spring 1985): 163–94.

Meier, August. *Negro Thought in America, 1880–1915.* Ann Arbor: University of Michigan Press, 1963.

Meier, August, and Rudwick, Elliott. *Along the Color Line.* Urbana: University of Illinois Press, 1976.

Menchan, William. "Florida Public Schools." *The Crisis* 31 (Apr. 1926): 291.

Metcalf, George. *From Little Rock to Boston: The History of School Desegregation.* Westport, Conn.: Greenwood Press, 1983.

Mintzberg, Henry, and McHugh, Alexandra. "Strategy Formation in an Adhocracy." *Administrative Science Quarterly* 30 (June 1985): 160–97.

Monahan, Thomas, and Monahan, Elizabeth. "Some Characteristics of American Negro Leaders." *American Sociological Review* 21 (Oct. 1956): 589–96.

Moore, Jesse Thomas. *A Search for Equality: The National Urban League, 1910–1961.* University Park: Pennsylvania State University Press, 1981.

Morris, Aldon. *The Origins of the Civil Rights Movement: Black Communities Organizing for Change.* New York: Free Press, 1984.

Murphy, Paul. "Communities in Conflict." In *The Pulse of Freedom: American Liberties, 1920–1970s,* edited by Alan Reitman, pp. 23–64. New York: W. W. Norton Co., 1975.

NAACP Legal Defense Fund. *Thirty Years of Building American Justice.* New York, 1970.

Nabrit, James, Jr. "Resort to the Courts as a Means of Eliminating 'Legalized' Segregation." *Journal of Negro Education* 20 (Summer 1951): 460–74.

O'Connor, Karen. *Women's Organizations' Use of the Courts.* Lexington, Mass.: Lexington Books, 1980.

O'Neill, Timothy. *"Bakke" and the Politics of Inequality.* Middletown, Conn.: Wesleyan University Press, 1984.

Olson, Mancur. *The Logic of Collective Action.* Cambridge: Harvard University Press, 1965.

Olson, Susan. *Clients and Lawyers: Securing the Rights of Disabled Persons.* Westport, Conn.: Greenwood Press, 1984.

Parrish, Michael. *Felix Frankfurter and His Times.* New York: Free Press, 1982.

Perrow, Charles. *Complex Organizations: A Critical Essay.* 2d ed. Glenview, Ill.: Scott, Foresman & Co., 1979.

President's Committee on Civil Rights. *To Secure These Rights.* Washington, D.C.: Government Printing Office, 1947.

Purcell, Edward A. *The Crisis of Democratic Theory.* Lexington: University Press of Kentucky, 1973.

Rabin, Robert. "Lawyers for Social Change: Perspective on Public Interest Law." *Stanford Law Review* 28 (Jan. 1970): 207–61.

Ransmeier, Joseph S. "The Fourteenth Amendment and the 'Separate but Equal' Doctrine." *Michigan Law Review* 50 (Dec. 1951): 203–60.

Rebell, Michael, and Block, Arthur. *Educational Policy-Making and the Courts.* Chicago: University of Chicago Press, 1982.

Rhode, Deborah. "Class Conflicts in Class Actions." *Stanford Law Review* 34 (July 1982): 1183–1262.

Ross, B. Joyce. *J. E. Spingarn and the Rise of the NAACP, 1911–1939.* New York: Atheneum, 1972.

Rudwick, Elliott M. *W. E. B. Du Bois: A Study in Minority Group Leadership.* Philadelphia: University of Pennsylvania Press, 1960.

Rumble, Wilfred E. *American Legal Realism.* Ithaca: Cornell University Press, 1968.

San Miguel, Guadalupe, Jr. "The Struggle against Separate and Unequal Schools: Middle Class Mexican Americans and the Desegregation Campaign in Texas, 1929–1957." *History of Education Quarterly* 23 (Fall 1983): 343–59.

Sawyer, Robert. "The Gaines Case: Its Background and Influence on the University of Missouri and Lincoln University, 1936–1950." Ph.D. dissertation, University of Missouri, 1966.

Schlegel, John Henry. "American Legal Realism and Empirical Social Science: From the Yale Experience." *Buffalo Law Review* 28 (Summer 1979): 459–586.

Schmidt, Benno C., Jr. "Principle and Prejudice: The Supreme Court and Race in the Progressive Era. Part I: The Heyday of Jim Crow." *Columbia Law Review* 82 (Apr. 1982): 444–524.

Schwartz, Bernard. "The Negro and the Law in the United States." *Modern Law Review* 14 (Oct. 1951): 446–61.

Segal, Geraldine. *Blacks in the Law.* Philadelphia: University of Pennsylvania Press, 1983.

Smallwood, James. "Texas." In *The Black Press in the South, 1865–1979,* edited by Henry Lewis Suggs, pp. 357–77. Westport, Conn.: Greenwood Press, 1983.

Stern, Robert, and Gressman, Eugene. *Supreme Court Practice.* 5th ed. Washington, D.C.: Bureau of National Affairs, 1978.

Suggs, H. Lewis. "Black Strategy and Ideology in the Segregation Era: P. B. Young and the Norfolk *Journal and Guide,* 1910–1954." *Virginia Magazine of History and Biography* 91 (Apr. 1983): 161–90.

Taylor, Stuart, Jr. "Ethics and the Law: A Case History." *New York Times Magazine,* Jan. 9, 1983, pp. 31–33, 46–52.

Thompson, Charles. "Court Action the Only Reasonable Alternative to Remedy

Immediate Abuses of the Negro Separate School." *Journal of Negro Education* 4 (July 1935): 417–35.

———. "Editorial Comment: Negro Teachers and the Elimination of Segregated Schools." *Journal of Negro Education* 20 (Spring 1951): 135–39.

Tushnet, Mark. "A Public Interest Lawyer in the 1930s." *Reviews in American History* 12 (Mar. 1984): 65–69.

———. "The Sociology of Article III." *Harvard Law Review* 93 (June 1980): 1698–1726.

Tyranauer, Gabrielle, and Stasny, Charles. *Who Rules the Joint?* Lexington, Mass.: Lexington Books, 1982.

Vose, Clement. *Caucasians Only.* Berkeley: University of California Press, 1959.

Walsh, R., and Fox, W. L., eds. *Maryland: A History, 1632–1974.* Baltimore: Maryland Historical Society, 1974.

Ware, Gilbert. "*Hocutt:* Genesis of *Brown.*" *Journal of Negro Education* 52 (Summer 1983): 227–33.

———. *William Hastie: Grace under Pressure.* New York: Oxford University Press, 1984.

Wasby, Stephen. "How Planned Is 'Planned Litigation'?" *American Bar Foundation Research Journal* 1984 (Winter): 83–138.

———. "Interest Groups in Court: Race Relations Litigation." In *Interest Group Politics,* edited by Allan Cigler and Burdett Loomis, pp. 251–74. Washington, D.C.: Congressional Quarterly Press, 1983.

———. "The Multi-Faceted Elephant: Litigator Perspectives on Planned Litigation for Social Change." Paper presented to Law and Society Association, June 1983, Denver, Colorado.

———. "The NAACP and the NAACP Legal Defense Fund: Preliminary Observations on Conflict between Allies." Paper presented to Midwest Political Science Association, April 1984, Chicago, Ilinois.

———. "Some Horizontal and Vertical Dynamics of Civil Rights Litigation: Litigators' Perspectives." Paper presented to Southern Political Science Association, November 1983, Birmingham, Alabama.

Weaver, Bill, and Page, Oscar C. "The Black Press and the Drive for Integrated Graduate and Professional Schools." *Phylon* 43 (Mar. 1982): 15–28.

Weisbrod, Burton; Handler, Joel; and Komesar, Neil. *Public Interest Law: An Economic and Institutional Analysis.* Berkeley: University of California Press, 1978.

Weiss, Nancy J. *Farewell to the Party of Lincoln.* Princeton: Princeton University Press, 1983.

———. *The National Urban League, 1910–1940.* New York: Oxford University Press, 1974.

Wesley, Charles H. "Graduate Education for Negroes in Southern Universities." *Harvard Educational Review* 10 (Jan. 1940): 82–94.

White, Walter. "The George Crawford Case—A Statement by the N.A.A.C.P., Part I." *The Crisis* 42 (Apr. 1935): 104.

———. "The George Crawford Case—A Statement by the N.A.A.C.P., Part II." *The Crisis* 42 (May 1935): 143.

———. "George Crawford—Symbol." *The Crisis* 41 (Jan. 1934): 15.

———. *A Man Called White.* New York: Viking Press, 1948.

Wilkins, Roy, and Mathews, Tom. *Standing Fast.* New York: Viking Press, 1982.

Wilkinson, J. Harvie, III. *From Brown to Bakke.* New York: Oxford University Press, 1979.

Wollenberg, Charles. *All Deliberate Speed: Segregation and Exclusion in California Schools, 1855–1975.* Berkeley: University of California Press, 1976.

Wolters, Raymond. *Negroes and the Great Depression.* Westport, Conn.: Greenwood Press, 1970.

Woodson, Carter. *The Negro Professional Man and the Community.* Washington, D.C.: Association for the Study of Negro Life and History, 1934.

Woodward, C. Vann. "The Case of the Louisiana Traveler." In *Quarrels That Have Shaped the Constitution,* edited by John Garraty, pp. 145–58. New York: Harper & Row, 1962.

———. *The Strange Career of Jim Crow.* New York: Oxford University Press, 1955.

Worthy, Barbara Ann. "The Travail and Triumph of a Southern Black Civil Rights Lawyer: The Legal Career of Alexander Pierre Tureaud, 1899–1972." Ph.D. dissertation, Tulane University, 1984.

Yearwood, Lennox S., ed. *Black Organizations: Issues on Survival Techniques.* Washington, D.C.: University Press of America, 1980.

Zald, Meyer, and McCarthy, John. "Social Movement Industries: Competition and Cooperation among Movement Organizations." In *Conflicts and Change,* Research in Social Movements, vol. 3, pp. 1–20. Greenwich, Conn.: JAI Press, 1980.

Zangrando, Robert. *The NAACP Crusade against Lynching, 1909–1950.* Philadelphia: Temple University Press, 1980.

Index

216

Michelson, Clarina, 13
Missouri: *Gaines* case, 70–77;
　Bluford cases, 83–86
Montgomery County (Maryland)
　teachers' salary case, 59–60, 68
Motley, Constance Baker (NAACP
　staff attorney), 111, 190 (n. 11)
Moton, R. R., 39
Murphy, Carl (publisher), 45, 56,
　58, 65, 114
Murray, Donald (plaintiff), 56, 58,
　201 (n. 52)
Murray case (*Pearson* v. *Murray*), 72
Myrdal, Gunnar, 119, 129

NAACP: founding, xi, 1; legal activi-
　ties in general, 1–2; challenges to
　elections in South, 7; concern with
　economic issues, 8, 10; contro-
　versy with Du Bois, 10; relations
　with Garland Fund, 16–18, 19–
　20; Legal Committee, 29, 31–32,
　55; antilynching campaign, 37,
　44, 145, 158; interests in litiga-
　tion, 37–38; relations with Com-
　munist party, 38, 42; educational
　efforts, 80–81; growth of, 135;
　role of legal staff, 157–58
NAACP Legal Defense Fund, creation
　of, 100
Nabrit, James L. (attorney), 141
Nashville, Tennessee, teachers' salary
　case, 89
National Civil Liberties Bureau, 3
National Negro Congress, 147
National Teacher Examinations, 92–
　93
National Urban League, 8, 147, 170
　(n. 19)
Nearing, Scott, 2, 13
New Orleans, Louisiana, teachers'

salary case, 97–99
Nice, Harry (Maryland governor),
　59, 61
North Carolina: university cases,
　52–53, 82, 147, 153–54; teachers'
　salary cases, 58

Ocala, Florida, teachers' salary case,
　96
Oklahoma university cases (*Sipuel*
　and *McLaurin*), 116, 120–24
Orange County (California) elemen-
　tary and secondary school deseg-
　regation case, 119–20

Painter, Theophilus (president, Uni-
　versity of Texas), 126
Palm Beach, Florida, teachers' salary
　case, 96
Pearson, Conrad (attorney), 52, 53,
　58
Perkins, J. E. (NAACP activist), 97
Perlman, Philip (solicitor-general),
　130
Perry, Marian Wynn (NAACP staff at-
　torney), 106, 111, 116
Perry, Victor (teacher), 90
Peterson, Willie, 39
Pettigen, Enolia (teacher, NAACP ac-
　tivist), 59, 62
Pickens, William (NAACP staff), 41
Pittsylvania, Virginia, elementary
　and secondary school desegrega-
　tion case, 68
Plessy v. *Ferguson*, xi, 21–22, 71,
　121, 131
Prince Edward County (Virginia) ele-
　mentary and secondary school de-
　segregation case, 140
Prince Georges County (Maryland)
　teachers' salary case, 61–62